Thinking Musically

Thinking Musically

∞

EXPERIENCING MUSIC,
EXPRESSING CULTURE

∞

SECOND EDITION

BONNIE C. WADE

New York   Oxford
OXFORD UNIVERSITY PRESS
2009

Oxford University Press

Oxford   New York
Auckland   Bangkok   Buenos Aires   Cape Town   Chennai
Dar es Salaam   Delhi   Hong Kong   Istanbul   Karachi   Kolkata
Kuala Lumpur   Madrid   Melbourne   Mexico City   Mumbai
Nairobi   São Paulo   Shanghai   Taipei   Tokyo   Toronto

Library of Congress Cataloging-in-Publication Data
Wade, Bonnie C.
    Thinking musically : experiencing music, expressing culture / Bonnie Wade. -- 2nd ed.
        p. cm.—(Global music series)
    Includes bibliographical references and index.
    ISBN 978-0-19-534191-1 (pbk.)
  1. Ethnomusicology. I. Title.
    ML3798.W33   2008
    780.9—dc22

                                                                    2008036485

Printing number: 9 8 7 6 5 4

Printed in the United States of America
on acid-free paper

GLOBAL MUSIC SERIES

General Editors: Bonnie C. Wade and Patricia Shehan Campbell

Contents

Foreword

⚮

In the past three decades interest in music around the world has surged, as evidenced in the proliferation of courses at the college level, the burgeoning "world music" market in the recording business, and the extent to which musical performance is evoked as a lure in the international tourist industry. This heightened interest has encouraged an explosion in ethnomusicological research and publication, including the production of reference works and textbooks. The original model for the "world music" course—if this is Tuesday, this must be Japan—has grown old, as has the format of textbooks for it, either a series of articles in single multiauthored volumes that subscribe to the idea of "a survey" and have created a canon of cultures for study, or single-authored studies purporting to cover world musics or ethnomusicology. The time has come for a change.

This Global Music Series offers a new paradigm. Teachers can now design their own courses; choosing from a set of case study volumes, they can decide which and how many musics they will cover. The series also does something else; rather than uniformly taking a large region and giving superficial examples from several different countries within it, in some case studies authors have focused on a specific culture or a few countries within a larger region. Its length and approach permits each volume greater depth than the usual survey. Themes significant in each volume guide the choice of music that is discussed. The contemporary musical situation is the point of departure in all the volumes, with historical information and traditions covered as they elucidate the present. In addition, a set of unifying topics such as gender, globalization, and authenticity occur throughout the series. These are addressed in the framing volume, *Thinking Musically*, which sets the stage for the case studies by introducing ways to think about how people make music meaningful and useful in their lives and presenting basic musical concepts as they are practiced in musical systems around the world. A second framing volume, *Teaching Music Globally,* guides teachers in the use of *Thinking Musically* and the case studies.

The series subtitle, "Experiencing Music, Expressing Culture," also puts in the forefront the people who make music or in some other way experience it and also through it express shared culture. This resonance with global history studies, with their focus on processes and themes that permit cross-study, occasions the title of this Global Music Series.

Bonnie C. Wade
Patricia Shehan Campbell
General Editors

Preface

∝∽

This book is written to frame and complement a series of case study volumes in the Global Music Series. Whereas each case study focuses on a specific culture or one designated part of the world, this text offers a basis for the contrast and comparison of diverse musics. Whereas each case study is conceived around themes that are significant in its one area, this book speaks to a set of unifying topics that recur in multiple case studies. Whereas authors of the case studies naturally present their material from ethnomusicological perspectives, this volume addresses the field of ethnomusicology more explicitly.

Comparing is not an intellectual exercise I have cared much for, but as a teacher I know that it is inevitable when diverse materials are presented in a course. My task, then, was to find a way to lay the foundation for careful comparison without actually doing it much myself. In deciding how to lay that foundation in this book, there was another major consideration. As co-general editor of the series, I established a guideline for authors that they were not to spend precious pages introducing basic elements of music; their aim was to provide depth in their particular subject. Yet basic elements need to be explained; therefore, while laying a foundation for comparison, I also took on that task.

How was I to do it? Organization by genre (as in Japanese music study), by historical periods (as in study of the European tradition), or by issues (the purview of the case studies in the series) would not make much sense. Turning to my experience of studying North Indian music, I remembered that my teachers initially focused on *rāga* (melody), and one of the first things I had to do was learn how to play the drone ("harmony") and simultaneously sing melody. Then came a focus on *tāla* ("rhythm"), and I was taught to sing in a *rāga* according to a certain formal structure. That experience resonated with the established order of presentation of Western-style music scholarship, and I first drafted the book on that model. Reflecting on my teaching experience in the course of shaping and reshaping the book, I kept returning to the realization that through the years most nonspecialist students actually relate much more easily to rhythm than to discussions of melody and harmony. A reader of the manuscript for Oxford University Press affirmed this and thus liberated me; I decided to break the mold. Each of the basic ingredients of music is indeed discussed in turn, but rhythm comes first. In chapters 3 and 4 I examine the organization of time and then of pitch (both melodically and harmonically), exploring ways they have been conceived and used in the creative musical imaginations of music makers around the globe. This is not a study of repertoire; it is a study of ideas and practices. Likewise, in chapter 5 I examine the structuring of musical selections. Most examples, but not all, are coordinated with the case studies. While the variety of music in the examples may seem bewildering at first, many of them are considered several times in this volume so that they become very familiar.

Topics that unify the case studies are interwoven throughout the book. Consideration of the teaching and learning of music comes in chapter 1. In chapter 2 I present numerous ways of thinking about musical instruments and in chapter 6 speak to issues that are lively in the field of ethnomusicology and that recur in multiple case studies.

With music, the focus that is the most significant in ethnomusicology is people. People make music what it is, and *people make music meaningful and useful in their lives.* That last statement encapsulates much of what ethnomusicologists are interested in, and I offer it as a framing perspective throughout the book for ways of thinking about music. The most distinctive method of ethnomusicological research—learning about music from people—is the subject of chapter 7, a practical guide to students for doing field research on their own.

I must offer a few caveats. In this volume I have scarcely used three terms with which scholars are grappling: "culture," and its extensions, "a culture," and "a music culture" (see chapter 6). The concept of "culture" resulted when modern European nation-states were emerging, bounded and distinctive. The struggle for recognition by a nation-state causes a rhetoric to develop that defines cultural and historical substance or attributes upon which national existence can be said to rest. Thus the idea of "a culture" emerges—something "authentic" that exists only with "a nation." Recently, however, studies of modernization, with its attendant Westernization, and of globalization, with its flow of people, ideas, and goods around the earth, have problematized that bounded concept of "a culture." More generically, social scientists have used the word "culture" to refer to ideas (values, worldview, concepts) and beliefs of individuals and groups of people as well as practices that emerge from those ideas and beliefs. That sense of "culture" is complemented by the term "society," that is, the systems (kinship, political, economic, etc.) that people construct to manage relationships among themselves. Conflating those different senses, common vernacular usage of "a culture" is likely to refer to the society—that is, the social group or social system—with which the cultural set of ideas, beliefs, and practices are associated. In the few instances where I cautiously use the contested term "music culture," I mean the ways in which people make music meaningful and useful in their lives—the ideas, beliefs, practices, and also the systems in evidence in the sphere of music.

Another extension of the idea of "culture" is the "culture area." Beyond the nation-state, large geographical areas of the world, such as Southeast Asia, have been clustered for political reasons, mostly, and scholars, including ethnomusicologists, have also thought in terms of region. In this book I refer to musical areas carefully and seldom. As we learn more about musics on the planet we are less inclined to feel comfortable with the level of generalization they imply.

A final caveat concerns the rubric of "Western music." It is problematic on several counts. The term "Western music" is all too often invoked when reference is intended to refer specifically to music of or derived from European classical musical practices. The term "Western music" is also problematic when viewed from the perspectives of modernization, colonization, and globalization. Resulting from serious enculturation for more than a century, many peoples around the world consume and create music that is still referred to as "Western music" although it is now arguably just as much theirs as "the West's." "The West" is, on the one hand, a concept and, on the other, a geographical location. In this book I use the term "Western music" carefully, preferring a greater degree of specificity.

In the following pages I speak to a number of musical ideas and practices from around the world. In addition to helping you enjoy many kinds of music, I hope that this book will help you to think musically.

ACKNOWLEDGMENTS

This Global Music Series began as a partnership with myself, Patricia Campbell, and then-Oxford University Press music editor Maribeth Payne. I want to acknowledge here the years of stewardship and support by Payne to help the project come to fruition. I thank Campbell as well for being such a good colleague in this large and complex endeavor and for her volume, *Teaching Music Globally*.

This book, *Thinking Musically*, is the most difficult project I have ever undertaken. I could not have written it without the help of many people, too numerous to mention here. Several of them are noted in the figure and CD credits. I want particularly to acknowledge the teamwork and help of my companion authors in the Global Music Series: Matthew Allen and the late T. Viswanathan (South India), Greg Barz (East Africa), Benjamin Brinner (Java), Shannon Dudley (Trinidad), Lisa Gold (Bali), Scott Marcus (Middle East), Adelaida Reyes (United States), Timothy Rice (Bulgaria), George Ruckert (North India), Stanley Scott and Dorothea Hast (Ireland), Daniel Sheehy (Mexico/Mexican-American), Ruth Stone (West Africa), Frederick Lau (China), John Murphy (Brazil), Beverley Diamond (Native North American), and Tom Turino (The Andes). Dave Brubeck's personal attention to my remarks about his music and Fred Lerdahl's response to the chapter on time are greatly appreciated. Special thanks also to colleagues Jocelyne Guilbault, for her helpful suggestions on chapter 6, to Karen Rozenak for her encouragement of such a volume and her thoughtful reading of an early draft, Benjamin Brinner and Eliot Bates for their help with the CD. Cathy Carapella of Diamond Time was most helpful in sorting out the byzantine details of the permission process. And I appreciate the help of Department of Music staff member James Coates with the numerous details involved in those permissions. I also thank the anonymous readers of this manuscript in its various incarnations for their insightful comments and helpful suggestions. And special thanks also go to Jan Beatty, Lisa Grzan, and Cory Schneider at Oxford University Press.

Last, but not least, I thank the students in my freshman seminar *Thinking Musically* (spring 2001) at the University of California, Berkeley, for their critical reading of a very early draft, their considered suggestions, assistance with compiling the CD, and other creative efforts, some of which are credited individually in the text. Responses from students in classes since then had much to do with the preparation of this second edition.

CD Track List

∞

Disc 1

1-1   Second *sura* of the *Qur'ān, al-Baqara* (Islamic recitation). Ceremony of the Qadiriya Sufi brotherhood, Mevlevi Sufi, Turkey. *Archives internationales de musique populaire* (*Musée d'ethnographie*, Geneva, 1988).

1-2.   Demonstration of different parts in arrangement of "Back Line," recorded by Phase II on Phase II Pan Groove, © 1986. Performed by students and faculty at the University of Washington. Used by permission.

1-3.   "Zhonghua liuban" ("Moderate Tempo Six Beats"). *Jiangnan sizhu*, excerpt. Field recording collected by Frederick Lau in Shanghai. Reproduced with permission.

1-4.   "Tar Road to Sligo" and "Paddy Clancy's Mug of Brown Ale" (Irish jigs). Becky Tracy, fiddle; Stan Scott, mandolin; Dora Hast, whistle. From *Jig Medley* cassette. Courtesy of Becky Tracy, Stan Scott, and Dora Hast.

1-5.   *Atsiagbeko* (Ghanaian narrative dance). West Africa drum ensemble. Recording and notes by Richard Hill, n.d. Courtesy of Lyrichord Discs.

1-6   "The Ballad of César Chávez" (*corrido*). Pablo and Juanita Saludado. From *Las Voces de los Campesinos*, n.d. Courtesy of the Center for the Study of Comparative Folklore and Mythology, UCLA.

1-7.   P. D. "El son del perro." Mariachi "El Capiro de Jalisco," Audio Archive of the National Council for the Traditional Arts (NCTA), *Raices Musicales* tour, Stanford University, Palo Alto, California, November 9, 1990. Bruce Loughry, recording engineer.

1-8   Joe Heaney, "The Rocks of Bawn" from *Say a Song: Joe Heaney in the Pacific Northwest*. Northwest Folklife and the University of Washington Ethnomusicology Archives, 1996. Permission given from Northwest

Folklife and the Joe Heaney Collection of the University of Washington Ethnomusicology Archives. Special thanks to Laurel Sercombe.

1-9 "Ketawang Subakastawa Pathet Sléndro Sanga," Hardo Budoyo, directed by Midiyanto, 2000. Used by permission of Ben Brinner and Midiyanto.

1-10 "Corn-grinding song" from the recording titled *Navajo Songs*, SF40403, provided courtesy of Smithsonian Folkways Recordings. © 1992. Used by permission.

1-11 "We Shall Overcome" by C. A. Tindley. Sung in a 1964 mass meeting, Hattiesburg, Mississippi. From the recording titled *Voices of the Civil Rights Movement: Black American Freedom Songs, 1960–1966*, SF 40084, provided courtesy of Smithsonian Folkways Recordings. © 1997. Used by permission.

1-12. "Ṛgveda—Vikṛit recitation" by R.K. Subrahmanya Sastri and K. Balasubrahmaniam, from the recording titled *Four Vedas*, Folkways 01426, provided courtesy of Smithsonian Folkways Recordings. © 1968. Used by permission.

1-13 "Liushui" ("Flowing Water"). *Guqin* solo, excerpt. From *Favorite Qin Pieces of Guan Ping-hu*. Guan Ping-hu (*guqin*). ROI: RB-951005-2C. 1995. Courtesy of Frederick Lau.

1-14 *Ālāp-jor-jhālā* excerpts from "Raga Jog," Ravi Shankar, *sitār*. First issued on World Pacific Records WPS 21438, © 1956. Reproduced from *Ravi Shankar: Flowers of India*, reissue by él in association with Cherry Red Records. ACMEM117CD. Used by permission from St. Rose Music Publishing Co.

1-15 *Gat* excerpt from ibid.

1-16 "Tuta kashua," Peruvian courting song self-accompanied on *charango*. Field recording used by permission of Tom Turino.

1-17 "First Wine Offering: A-ak" (Chinese Confucian music in Korea). Confucian ritual ensemble. Orchestra of the National Music Institute, Seoul, Korea, Kim Ki-su, director. Recorded by John Levy. Lyrichord Discs, 1969.

1-18 "Rak Badjalarr" (Lambudju's *wangga*), sung by Bobby Lambudju Lane and Tommy Barrtjap with Nicky Jorrock (*didjeridu*). Recorded in 1986. For *didjeridu*, clapsticks and voice. By permission of the Aboriginal Research Institute.

1-19 *"Riachao"* (Brazilian *capoeira*). São Bento Pequeno de Angola e São Bento Grande de Compasso. From *Capoeira: A Saga do Urucungo* (Luzes: Silvio Acaraje, n.d.)

1-20 "Conch call" (Tibetan Buddhist ritual). Conch. From *Musique rituelle tibetaine* (Ocora Records OCR 49, [1970]).

1-21 "Hifumi no Shirabe Hachigaeshi" (Zen Buddhist music). Goro Yamaguchi, *shakuhachi*. Japan Victor, n.d.

1-22 "Unnai Nambinen" (South Indian *Ādi tāla*). *Rāga Kirawāni* (21st *mela*). T. Vishwanathan, singer; David Nelson, *mṛdaṅgam*; Anantha Krishnan, *tāmbūra*. Music by T. M. Swami Pillay, Text by Muttuttandavar. Courtesy of Matthew Allen, T. Vishwanathan, David Nelson, Anantha Krishnan.

1-23 "Festival Music" (offstage [*geza*] ensemble). From *Music from the Kabuki*. Nonesuch H-72012, [1970].

1-24 Korean *Komungo Sanjo: Chinyango, Chungmori, Onmori*. Han Kapdeuk, *komungo*; Hwang Deuk-ju, *chang-gu*. Recording offered by the National Center for Korean Traditional Performing Arts, Seoul.

1-25 *Kotekan "norot"* (Balinese *gangsas*). Recorded by Lisa Gold. Used by permission.

1-26 Mary MacNamara (concertina), "The Ash Plant/The Dog Among the Bushes" (reels), recorded by Stan Scott and Dorothea Hast at the MacNamara home. Permission given by Mary MacNamara.

1-27 "Travelling in Soochow" (Chinese folk instrumental music). Chinese *di-tze* (flute). China Records, n.d.

1-28 Analysis of sound of *shakuhachi/syakuhati*. Provided by David Wessel.

1-29 "Kiembara xylophone orchestra," Famankaha, Sous-Prefecture of Korhogo, Ivory Coast, West Africa. From *The Music of the Senufo*. Bärenreiter, UNESCO Collection. *Anthology of African Music*, vol. 8, n.d.

1-30 Cantonese opera (Chinese vocal, Cantonese style). Fung Hang Record Ltd. (Hong Kong, n.d.).

1-31 Georges Bizet, "L'amour est un oiseau rebelle" (Habanera) from *Carmen*. Robert Shaw Chorale and Children's Chorus from l'Elysée Francaise. Robert Shaw, Conductor. Fritz Reiner conducting the RCA Victor Orchestra. Carmen: Rise Stevens; Don José: Jan Peerce; Micaëla: Licia Albanese; Zuniga: Osie Hawkins; Moralès: Hugh Thompson. English translation of the libretto by Alice Berezowsky. RCA Victor Records, © 1951.

1-32 Sargam (North Indian vocal solfège). From Bonnie C. Wade, *Khyāl: Creativity within North India's Classical Musical Tradition* (Cambridge: Cambridge University Press, 1984). Cassette tape master in the collection of the author.

1-33 Andean panpipes: three *cortes* (sizes). An example of the Peruvian "Toril" genre, in *conima* style. Performed by Patricia Hinostroza, Jesus Jaramillo (*chili* melody); Vanessa Luyo, Jose Carlos Pomari (*sanja* melody); Illich Ivan Montes, Hubert Yauri (*malta* melody). Followed by a traditional *sikuris* ensemble, including panpipes recorded in the Andean highlands, city of Puno, during the festival La Candelaria, in 1991. Courtesy of Raul Romero Cavallo, Centro de Etnomusicologia, Pontificia Universidad Católica del Perú, Lima.

1-34 "Ma Ram" "Dancing Horse" (Thai *pî phât* ensemble). From *Traditional Music of Thailand*, 1968. Institute of Ethnomusicology, UCLA Stereo ier-7502. Courtesy of the UCLA Ethnomusicology Archives (David Morton Collection).

1-35 *Ketawang* colotomic pattern (without gender). Provided by Midiyanto, Berkeley, California, 2008.

1-36 *Ketawang* colotomic pattern (with gender). Provided by Midiyanto, Berkeley, California, 2008.

1-37 Paul Desmond "Take Five" (jazz). The Dave Brubeck Quartet (Dave Brubeck, Paul Desmond, Joe Morello, Gene Wright). Copyright © 1960, renewed 1988, Desmond Music Company (USA) Derry Music Company (world except USA); used with permission; all rights reserved.

Disc 2

2-1 "*Aruh li Min*" in *maqām rāst*. Egyptian instrumental ensemble with vocal, © 1958. Umm Kulthum, singer. "*Aruh li min*," composer: Riyad al-Sinbati; poet: `Abd al-Mun 'im al Saba'i. Used by permission of Sono Cairo.

2-2 "Hyōjō Netori" (Japanese *gagaku* ensemble). Gagaku Music Society of Tenri University, n.d. Courtesy of Koji Sato, Director, Gagaku Music Society of Tenri University.

2-3 "Te Kuki Airani nui Maruarua" (Polynesian homogenous choral song/chant from the Cook Islands, in the joyous old style called *ute*). Singers from the Cook Islands National Arts Theatre. From *Festival of Traditional Music: World of the South Pacific* (New York: Musical Heritage Society, © 1974).

2-4 Witold Lutosławski, "Mini Overture" (1982). Meridian Arts Ensemble: Jon Nelson, Richard Kelley (trumpet), Daniel Grabois (horn), Benjamin Herrington (trombone), Raymond Stewart (tuba). Courtesy of Music Sales Corporation and Channel Classics CCS2191, © 1991.

2-5   Gamelan Gong Kebyar. "Jaya Semara" (Sanggar Çudamani). Recorded by Lisa Gold. Courtesy of Lisa Gold.

2-6   "Mi bajo y yo" (*salsa*). Oscar d'Leon, bandleader. From *Exitos y Algo mas* Company, n.d.

2-7   "West End Blues" (New Orleans jazz). Louis Armstrong, trumpet, et al. Courtesy of MCA Universal.

2-8   "Marieke." Words and Music by Eric Blau, Jacques Brel, Gerard Jouannest. Recording and text translation courtesy of Suzanne Lake. Recorded by Suzanne Lake, *The Soul of Chanson*, CD. Copyright © 1968 Universal-MCA Music Publishing, a division of Universal Studios, Inc. (ASCAP) International Copyright Secured. All rights reserved.

2-9   Frédéric Chopin, *Waltz in C-sharp Minor*. Performance by Jean Gray Hargrove. Recording courtesy of Jean Gray Hargrove.

2-10   Bruce Springsteen, "Born in the USA." Columbia CK 38653.

2-11   Dave Brubeck, "Three to Get Ready and Four to Go" (jazz). The Dave Brubeck Quartet (Dave Brubeck, Paul Desmond, Joe Morello, Gene Wright). Copyright © 1960, renewed 1988, Derry Music Company; used with permission; all rights reserved.

2-12   "Forró em Monteiro" by Arlindo dos Oito Baixos. Arlindo dos Oito Baixos (*sanfona de oito baixos*), Raminho (*zabumba*), Adilson (bass). Field recording by John Murphy, 2001. Used by permission.

2-13   "Makedonsko horo" (Bulgarian *tambura*). Recorded by Tsvetanka Varimezova, 29 December 2001. Courtesy of Tsvetanka Varimezova and Timothy Rice.

2-14   North Indian *tāla* patterns (*thekas*): *chautāl, ektāl, tīntāl, tilwādā*. Recited by George Ruckert.

2-15   Three traditional Egyptian eight-beat rhythms, each recited and played four times: *maqsūm, maṣmūdī; ṣaghīr*, and *ṣa'īdī*. Recited and played by Hany El Sawaf. Courtesy of Scott Marcus.

2-16   Exercise in *Tisra Triputa Tāḷa*: the pattern "ta ki ta" in three speeds. Recited by Matthew Allen.

2-17   Numerical patterns (1-9, articulated with mnemonics) used for rhythmic variety in India's music. Recited by George Ruckert.

2-18   Richard Strauss, *Also Sprach Zarathustra*, excerpt. Columbia MK 35888, 1980.

2-19 Harmonic and inharmonic sounds, demonstrated by David Wessel.

2-20 "Seki no To" (Japanese *shamisen* and vocal). Example of *Tokiwazu*, a section from the *Kabuki* play *Tsumoru koi yuki no Seki no to*, music by Tobaya Richoo I, text by Takarada Jurai. 1784. From *1,000 Years of Japanese Classical Music*, vol. 7, *Tokiwazu, Tomimoto, Kiyomoto, Shinnai*. Nihon koten ongaku taikei. (Tokyo: Kodansha, 1980–82).

2-21 Balinese *jublag*. Recorded by Lisa Gold.

2-22 Western orchestra tuning process. University of California, Berkeley, Orchestra.

2-23 "Frère Jacques" ("Are you sleeping?"). Recorded by Viet Nguyen and Jane Chiu.

2-24 Western major (diatonic) scale. Recorded by Viet Nguyen and Jane Chiu.

2-25 "Oriental" scale. Excerpt, *Cante Flamenco Agujetas en Paris* (Ocora, 1991).

2-26 The notes of the major scale and of *maqâm rāst* played on the *qānūn.*" Played by James R. Gripppo. Courtesy of Scott Marcus.

2-27 *Maqām rāst*, with a lower tetrachord of *rāst* on C (C-D-E^b-F) and an upper tetrachord of *rāst* on G (G –A-B^b-c). Played by James R. Grippo. Courtesy of Scott Marcus.

2-28 *Maqām rāst*'s three upper tetrachords: *rāst* on G (G-A-B^b-c)[this flat is half-flat], *nahāwand* on G (G-A –B^b-c), and *hijāz* on G (G-A^b-B-c). Played by James R. Grippo. Courtesy of Scott Marcus.

2-29 Western vertical intervals.

2-30 Three-part Shop singing from the village of Vrazhdebna, Bulgaria. Timothy Rice, 1972. Courtesy of Timothy Rice.

2-31 Progression of pitches (roots of chords).

2-32 Excerpt from "il-Kalām Da Kabīr." Sung by Hakim. Lyrics composed by 'Abd al-Mun'im Taha; music composed by Aḥmad Shahīn; music arranged by Ḥamīd ish-Sha'rī.

2-33 "Sumer is icumen in" (medieval European *rota*). Courtesy of the Chamber Chorus of the University of California, Berkeley, Paul Flight, director, 2001.

2-34 Episode from *woi-meni-pele* (Kpelle epic performance). Liberian *Womi* epic pourer. Courtesy of Ruth Stone.

2-35 *"Yaegoromo"* (Japanese *sankyoku* ensemble). Jiuta Yonin no Kai Ensemble (Tokyo: Ocora, n.d.).

2-36 Scottish bagpipe drone. Recording by John Pedersen. Courtesy of Lucia Comnes.

2-37 Rāga "Miyāṅ ki Toḍi" (North Indian vocal). Dagar Brothers, CD 4137.

2-38 Ludwig van Beethoven, *Symphony No. 5*, excerpt. London Symphony Orchestra, Wyn Morris, conductor. MCA Classics, n.d.

2-39 "The Great Ambush." Tsun-yuen Lui, Chinese *pipa*. Courtesy of Tsun-yuen Lui and the UCLA Archives of Ethnomusicology.

2-40 "Kumbaya." Kenyan. Courtesy of Greg Barz.

2-41 Kpelle Children's counting song. Totota, 1976. Recorded by Ruth M. and Verlon L. Stone. Courtesy of Ruth Stone.

2-42 Angsel in "Topeng Keras." Balinese music and dance to accompany a strong character in the *topeng* dance form. Courtesy of Lisa Gold.

2-43 North Indian cadential *tihāī* pattern 1. Recited by George Ruckert. Courtesy of George Ruckert.

2-44 North Indian cadential *tihāī* pattern 2. Recited by George Ruckert. Courtesy of George Ruckert.

2-45 Inuit juggling game song. Unidentified singers. Field recording by Beverley Diamond. Courtesy of Beverley Diamond.

A Note to Readers

∞

Dear Readers,

Please permit me to introduce myself, as I would on the first day of a new course. I am a professor in the field of ethnomusicology, with which you will gradually become acquainted through this book. My special interests in teaching and research lie in the musics of Japan and India. My students always ask how I got there, so here's the story in a nutshell. I grew up as many people in my generation did—studying piano, singing in a church choir, loving to dance, and generally enjoying music. First, I dreamed of becoming a concert pianist. Then I wanted to be a professor of music history; although I didn't realize it at the time, that meant being a professor of the history of European art music only. Then, one day, I experienced an epiphany—a life-changing experience. Friends treated me to a trip to Latin America when I was between my junior and senior years in college. I was too poor to go otherwise, and besides, Latin America was nowhere in my imagination. On that "one day," I was standing at the edge of an Andean mountain precipice near Cuzco, Peru, when up from the chasm below floated music like none I had ever heard before—a flute melody that didn't fit my musical expectations. But it was beautiful! What struck me most that day was that no one in my years of music study had ever mentioned *other* music to me; granted, recordings were relatively few in those days, but really! Not acceptable, I decided. That turned me to ethnomusicology.

As a person, I guess I was just always willing to be open to difference—although I am definitely attracted to some differences more than to others. As an ethnomusicologist, I am quite accustomed to listening to music of any and every sort. As a teacher, I recognize that students' ways of thinking musically range from a clam closed tightly to a giant squid ready to consume anything and everything that comes along. You fit somewhere along that continuum. I hope that, through this book that is about difference—about the infinitely creative imagination of humankind—you will experience something that intrigues you, or moves you, but in any case causes you to think more deeply about music.

I wrote this book with the aim of engaging with you and therefore, I ask certain things of you. If I pose a question that you think is too simple to take seriously, hang in there because you might discover that simple questions don't always have simple answers. When I suggest that you do something (see the Activities through the book), do it, because, in the doing, you will be taking more from the book than if you just read words passively. That is to say, you will experience and internalize the ideas under discussion rather than just receiving them in an abstract way. I suggest that you keep a journal in a notebook or computer file that records what you do in response to the Activities, for purposes of a record and for review. Be prepared to *listen* constantly to the musical examples; the CD icon in the margin signals you to listen, even when I don't direct you to do so in words. The musical examples vary in length, depending on what it takes to demonstrate a point or—in some cases—depending on the availability of rights to the material. Whether long or short, the musical examples are deeply integrated with the prose, and I return to many of them multiple times. Finally, I ask you to enjoy yourself, as you learn more about ways to think musically.

Most sincerely,

Bonnie Wade

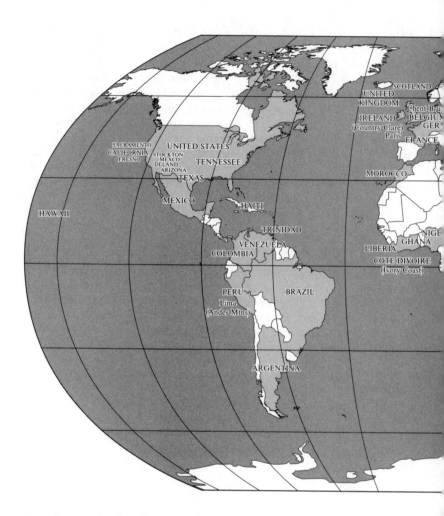

Locations mentioned in this text are highlighted.

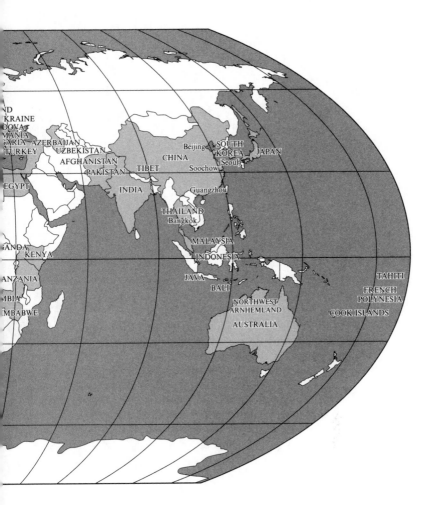

ND
KRAINE
DOVA
MANIA
ARIA AZERBAIJAN
TURKEY   UZBEKISTAN
       AFGHANISTAN   CHINA
       PAKISTAN   TIBET
EGYPT
            INDIA
                        THAILAND
                        Bangkok
ANDA
   KENYA   MALAYSIA
                            INDONESIA
ANZANIA   JAVA
                          BALI
MBIA
MBABWE   NORTHWEST
                          ARNHEMLAND
                          AUSTRALIA

Beijing   SOUTH
          KOREA   JAPAN
          (Seoul)
Soochow
Guangzhou

                                    TAHITI
                                    FRENCH
                                    POLYNESIA
                                    COOK ISLANDS

xxvii

CHAPTER 1

Thinking about Music

∞

If you can speak you can sing; if you can walk you can dance.
(Zimbabwean Shona proverb)

People make music meaningful and useful in their lives. That statement
encapsulates much of what ethnomusicologists are interested in and
offers a framing perspective for many ways of thinking both about people and about music all over the world. In this chapter I shall explore
each word in the statement with two purposes in mind: to suggest new
ways you might think about music that you regularly hear, and to begin
to expand your musical horizon. Because this is a teaching book, I shall
also begin by speaking briefly about the dissemination of music, the
ways it is taught and learned.

PEOPLE

Music Makers.   Who makes music in our familiar world? Music makers are individuals and groups, adults and children, female and male,
amateurs and professionals. They are people who make music only for
themselves, such as shower singers or secretly-sing-along-with-the-
radio types, and they are performers, people who make music purposefully for others. They are people who make music because they are
required to and people who do so simply from desire. Some music makers study seriously, while others are content to make music however
they can, without special effort.

    To think about music makers globally, you might ask whether music
makers are regarded in any particular way in a particular place. At one
end of a spectrum, some societies expect people who make music to be
specialists, born into the role or endowed with a special capacity. At the

1

other end of that spectrum, in some societies it is assumed that the practice of music is a human capacity and that all people will express themselves musically as a normal part of life. Both ends of the spectrum can be found in African societies, for example. In East Africa, many communities collectively choose a single individual or group of individuals to act as ritual or musical specialists. Once chosen, the individual often develops particular skills and is empowered by the community to assume authority to lead its important rituals or musical celebrations. For that reason, Gregory Barz (2004), author of the East Africa volume in this series, digs deeper into the roles and practices of particular musical individuals. In West Africa, where a basic concept prevails that performing is like speaking one's native language, everyone is expected to be able to sing and dance to a certain level of competence. Beyond that, talented young men and women are selected for special training. In other cases, families of musicians train children born into the lineage to carry on their parents' occupation (Stone 2005).

Local terminology is a clue to the ideas held about music makers.

Shortly after arriving in Sofia in 1969, I took a bus to a nearby village on Mount Vitosha in the Shop (rhymes with "hope") region, home to a subgroup of Bulgarians with a distinct linguistic dialect and musical culture. My goal was to meet some village musicians. Using my dictionary and limited Bulgarian, I asked people in the village square if they could introduce me to some *muzikanti* ("musicians"). One woman helpfully pointed me in the direction of the home of a man who played trumpet and then asked if I would be interested in hearing a women's vocal group that she belonged to. Her response surprised me for two reasons. First, she seemed to understand the word "musician" as referring to someone who played a Western musical instrument, not a traditional one, like the *gaida*. Second, she didn't seem to understand that if I was interested in "musicians," then I would also be interested in "singers."

My first attempt at fieldwork was teaching me what ethnomusicologists know generally, namely, that different cultures have different ways of thinking about and categorizing music and musical behaviors. (Timothy Rice, in his book in this series on Bulgaria (2004: 29).

When you hear or use the word "musician," to what sort of music maker are you referring? Most students in my courses respond to that question with an impression that is clearly derived from the sphere of Western classical music. In this volume, however, I use the word **musician** more generically, to cover all people who experience music as a practice (figure 1.1).

Many questions about musicians embed them in their musical context. Who makes music with whom? Who learns music from whom? Who is permitted to be a teacher? Who can perform where? Who can perform for whom? Is anyone prohibited from making some particular type of music, and if so, why? Who plays which instrument, and why? Do musicians have high cultural status (i.e., is their music making highly valued by a group)? Do musicians have high social status (i.e., a high ranking in the society)?

ACTIVITY 1.1 *Make an inventory of music makers in your individual context, including friends and family members. Don't forget to include yourself, if you make music. Then, for each person, consider whether or not you would categorize him or her as "a musician" and why or why not. Also, use your list to consider the questions posed in the previous paragraph that particularly interest you.*

Listeners.   When I speak about people making music meaningful and useful in their lives, I include people who "just" listen. They are, after all, most of the world's musically involved population. Listeners, like musicians, are consumers of music. They are the audience to which performers cater—patrons who are willing to pay to hear performances and buy recordings.

Answers to questions about listeners reveal a great deal about the musical context in which they live. Do they prefer to listen alone, or is listening a social activity? Is it more expensive to listen to one kind of music than another, and if so, what does that mean for the listener? Are certain types of listeners associated with certain types of music? Is a listening audience restricted by gender or religious belief or membership? Does a listening context foster immediate interaction between performer and listener?

ACTIVITY 1.2 *Agree or disagree with this statement: listening to music is different from hearing music. Be prepared to give reasons for your opinion.*

FIGURE 1.1 *1.1a: Benedict Tchinburur playing* kenbi [didjeridu] *at Wadeye (Australia). (Photograph by Allan Marett. 7 November 1998.)*

1.1b: Sakar Khan Manganiyar playing kamaicha. *Hamira village, Rajasthan, India. (Photo by Shalini Ayyagari)*

1.1c: *Marika Kuzma, Director of Choruses, University of California, Berkeley.* (Photo by Peg Skorpinski)

1.1d: *Two members of a Chinese music troupe in Bangkok, Thailand. The writing on the drum stand says "Disciples of Lǔang Pù Sêng, Kalayaan Temple, Thonburi." The stand displays a photo of and offering to their teacher, who is a monk. They are performing at a blessing ceremony for the opening of a new music store, called Dr. Sax, owned by music professor Dr. Sugree Charoensoek. 1989.* (Courtesy of Deborah Wong)

1.1e: *Irish session:* seisun *in Ocean View, Miltown Malbay Co. Clare. Michael Falsey (pipes), Mary Anne Sexton (accordeon), Gabi Wolff (flute).* (© Peter Laban, Miltown Malbay Co. Clare)

MUSIC

In Terms of Sound. I am standing at the edge of a body of water, the ripples sounding alternately like gentle lapping and heavy crashing waves. Nearby, hammers and electric saws are punctuating the air. Above me, soaring and dipping and singing a variety of songs are goldfinches and mockingbirds and cooing doves. The wind whistles across the land. Car horns toot in the distance. In this wonderful soundscape there is melody and rhythm. Can any of that be called *music?*

ACTIVITY 1.3 *To begin thinking musically, think about sound. Conduct some field research: taking pen and paper with you, listen for thirty minutes to the soundscape around you and keep a record. Any sound—a motorcycle roaring by, a cluster of people laughing, sounds of nature, the whirring of an elevator's approach, the selection on the radio of a passing motorist, the music you choose to play. Some of the sounds you hear must be what you would automatically call "music." Articulate how you distinguish between what is and what is not music.*

In fact, what is music? The ethnomusicologist John Blacking defined it as "humanly organized sound" (1977), but I suggest that we take that statement one step farther. "Music" is not only a thing—a category of organized sound, or compositions—but also a process. Every known group of people in the world exercises their creative imaginations to organize sound in *some way* that is different from the way they organize sound for speech.

Calling Something "Music." Having a word for a particular aesthetic category of organized sound that I as an individual think of as "music" is by no means universal. In Bali, as in many places, the concept of "music" is context specific. Rather than a single category called "music," types of instrumental ensembles, **repertoires** (groups of pieces that are linked in some way), and vocal practices are each named and associated with the specific functions that it fulfills (Gold 2005: 2). In India, the word for "music," *saṅgīta,* is used to encompass dance as well as vocal and instrumental music, but in other places, a word for "music" refers only to instrumental music. In the Islamic worldview, the mellifluous recitation of the sacred **Qur'ān** (CD track 1-1), which many non-Muslim listeners have called "music," is not considered *musiqa*; **musiqa** is a category encompassing **genres** (that is, types of music) that may elicit negative associations of secular musical practice. Furthermore, the imperative of avoiding inappropriate juxtapositions of the human and the divine has led to a conceptual categorization in Muslim societies that distinguishes between music, on the one hand, and forms of melodic religious expression, on the other hand. Thus, the melodic recitation of the Qur'ān is not considered to be music (Marcus 2007:94). Clearly, just because something sounds like music to me, I have no right to insist that it is "music" to someone else. It is the local or even personal idea that counts.

Significantly, music does not have to be thought of as a kind of "thing." For example, none of the hundreds of First Nation Native American groups has a word for "music." In these groups' opinion, the word "music" as a noun creates a category apart from other things; it fails to convey the processes of social action, for example, or of the integration of traditional knowledge and modern knowledge and the relationships that singing and drumming embody in many Native American contexts (Diamond 2008). Likewise, sociologist Christopher Small has taken the position that music is not a thing at all but an activity, something that people do. Ethnomusicologists generally concur. He calls doing music "musicking": "to music is to take part, in any capacity, in a musical performance, whether by performing, by listening, by rehearsing or practicing, by providing material for performance (what is called composing), or by dancing" (1998: 9). He sometimes—and I always would—extends musicking to all the activities about which I wrote above under "People."

Aesthetic Values in Music. If I, in my American culture, use the expression "that's music to my ears," you will know that I have heard something I want to hear, or in terms of sound, something beautiful. Ideas about beauty are one aspect of a set of artistic values referred to as **aesthetics**—in this case, music aesthetics. Those ideas are not necessarily shared, even within one society. A letter to an editor about Trinidadian **steelband** encapsulates the obvious fact that a beautiful sound to one person is abominable to another (CD track 1-2, figure 1.2):

> Can beating is pan beating in any language and in any form. It does nobody any good, and when it is indulged in all day all night, day in and day out, it is abominable. . . . If it must continue and if by virtue of its alleged inherent beauty and charm it will someday bring

FIGURE 1.2   *Barry Nanton of Desperadoes steelband, Trinidad.* (Photo courtesy of Shannon Dudley)

popularity and fame to the island and a fortune to the beaters, then by all means let it go on—but in the forests and other desolate places. (C. W. Clarke, *Trinidad Guardian*, 6 June 1946)

While individual ethnomusicologists have personal ideas about musical beauty in terms of the quality of the sound (**timbre**) that is cultivated, it is a tenet of our field that we will keep our ears and minds open and respect the fact that many timbres are considered beautiful.

Aesthetic ideals are also manifested in the ideas about the relationship between the musical selection and the way a performer is expected to treat it. For many types of music, the ideal is that a composition will be reproduced intact. That is the case with many genres of European art music, for instance, wherein a composition is expected to be performed with a high level of technical proficiency, coupled with artistic expressivity that does not change the musical material. In contrast, the aesthetic process involved in most popular music not only permits, but expects, artists to render pieces in distinctive ways.

The aesthetic ideal of some kind of change in performance is found in untold numbers of musics. In an ensemble rendition of a familiar

FIGURE 1.3 Salsa *drummers. From left to right: on congas, Shannon Dudley; on timbal, Greg Campbell; on bongo, Marisol Berrios.* *(Courtesy of Marisol Berrios)*

tune in many amateur music traditions in China, each performer may "add flowers" by embellishing and varying the melody, thus shaping a collecting "sound" that is inclusive of personal styles and voices (CD track 1-3). In a similar manner, Irish musicians practice and discuss the aesthetic of never playing a tune the same way twice, keeping its melodic identity intact, but playing subtle variations each time around. They embellish their playing with ornaments and small melodic or rhythmic variations that make each repetition of a tune slightly different (CD track 1-4).

If, as in Christopher Small's terms, musicking articulates ideals of human relationships, then the aesthetic preference for the content of both music and dance of the West African Kpelle peoples provides a wonderful example (Stone 2005). Short segments (facets) that interlock are highly valued; Kpelle dance movements consist of short, quick, tightly orchestrated steps, for instance. In much African drumming, short rhythmic patterns are repeated in close coordination with other short rhythmic patterns, as an example from CD track 1-5 demonstrates. It is the process of interlocking the short segments that creates "the music"; the musical experience is a social experience.

> **ACTIVITY 1.4** *By this time you have been directed by the CD icon in the margins to listen to multiple musical examples. In my introductory note, I told you that you would find the musical examples deeply integrated with the prose and that I would return to many of them several times. Information about them and your understanding of them will accumulate gradually. It's time now for you to start a written record of each occurrence of each track; half a page in a notebook allotted to each track or—at this point—a list of tracks in a computer file should suffice. Make a heading of track number and identifying title for each selection and add information under it each time I refer you to the track. For instance, I have just made a point about an aesthetic preference that is expressed by the content of Ghanaian dance drumming (CD track 1-5). To record it, under the track number and title, enter the page number and the point made. I refer to this track again on pp. 94 and 96 to make different points.*

For many people, the highest value of music is placed on affect, that is, its expressive capacity. The first time I consciously thought about the tremendous power of music for affecting emotion was years ago when I watched the classic movie *Ben-Hur*. The chariot race between Ben-Hur and his adversary was nearing its climax. With whips cracking, horses' hooves pounding, chariot wheels clashing, crowds and the orchestra roaring, we in the theater could hardly stand the tension. Suddenly, the sound system failed. Without the furor of the music egging us and the action on, the race looked silly, for the emotional impact of the scene was expressed by the music. Contrasting utterly with that were the feelings that welled up in me as I heard "Taps" and the American national anthem as I stood with other countrymen in the military cemetery in Manila, the Philippines, where I was just after President Kennedy was assassinated in 1963. As one of my students put it, "It is music that makes me want to dance, or feel. It not only reminds me of times I have felt emotions, but it prompts me to feel emotions" (Lyndsey Brown, 2001). Yes, music has the power to move our hearts, minds, and bodies.

∽

Student Lucia Comnes: "I feel that the youth in my community are drawn to this music [reggae] and culture because it is liberating. We are about to inherit this monster that is our society—including the government, the educational system, the work force, the media, the capitalist philosophy, the technology, the developed civilization, the destruction of the earth, the inequality, the separating illusions of racism, sexism, ageism, homophobia, etc. and the list goes on—I often find this overwhelming, confusing, and terrifying. When the communities at home and at school are not strong or secure, we yearn for another place that speaks to us deeply, a place that brings us to a higher consciousness. Reggae culture provides this for many—a place where people are brought together through music, music coming from the heart, speaking to the power of the people, music that is alive and encouraging, fulfilling and in the spirit of celebration" (2001).

Student Aron: "There is another subject to be very critically thought about, reflecting on the upper-middle-class white audience, joining or co-opting a poor black protest. This is not really talked about and there is so much to be addressed. As a white middle-class kid myself who listens to a lot of dance hall and reggae, I am constantly checking in with the fact that I can't call it mine. So reggae causes me to think. When you're in clubs and there are white and black audiences grooving to reggae, it is a lot more apparent and you are confronted with this" (2001).

∽

MEANING

Having briefly spoken of ways of thinking about people and music in the main premise of this chapter that *"People make music meaningful and useful in their lives,"* I now turn to meaning and use. That music is meaningful, no one doubts. However, great debates have ensued over whether the meaning resides in musical materials themselves or is ascribed to musical materials by someone for some particular reason. Is there something really martial about the music played by a brass band as an army marches by, or is that an association we have learned? Does a lullaby really put a child to sleep, or is it something else such as loving attention that lulls the child into secure rest? With most ethnomusicologists, I think the latter: people make music meaningful, whether that meaning is individual or communally agreed upon.

Music and Textual Meaning. Melody set to words constitutes much of the world's musical repertoire. Perhaps it is because just about everyone can sing, with or without an instrument. Perhaps it is because of the capacity of music to heighten the expressivity of a text. In the Baroque period (c. 1600–1750 C.E.) of European music, composers used what was called "word painting" to heighten expressivity in quite literal ways— a falling melody on the word *morire* (to die), for instance. Blues singers in America improvise expressively to elicit even more meaning from already meaningful texts.

Another reason for singing texts is the license it gives musicians to say something not permitted in ordinary speech. A great deal of covert and overt political protest has been delivered in song. In "Calypso Freedom," Sweet Honey in the Rock reminds listeners of the necessity of the civil rights movement of the 1960s while renewing the protest in 1989 with new text set to an old song.

ACTIVITY 1.5 *Find songs of political protest. You can easily find "Calypso Freedom" on the Internet, and that's a good place to start. Look for others as well. For one, transcribe the lyrics and then listen to the musical setting. Do the musicians use the music in any purposeful way to deliver the message of the text?*

Through the ages narrators have told their tales musically. The Texas-Mexican *corrido* is a genre that has proved to be an effective avenue for

El Corrido de César Chávez	*The Ballad of César Chávez*
En un día siete de marzo	*On the seventh day of March*
Jueves santo en la mañana,	*Good Thursday in the morning*
salió César de Delano	*César left Delano*
componiendo una campaña.	*Organizing a campaign.*
Compañeros campesinos	*Companion farmers*
este va a ser un ejemplo	*This is going to be an example*
esta marcha la llevamos	*This (protest) march we'll take*
hasta mero Sacramento.	*To Sacramento itself.*
Cuando llegamos a Fresno	*When we arrived in Fresno*
Toda la gente gritaba	*All the people chanted*
y que viva César Chávez	*Long live César Chávez*
y la gente que llevaba.	*And the people that accompany him.*
Nos despedimos de Fresno	*We bid good-bye to Fresno*
nos despedimos con fe	*We bid good-bye with faith*
para llegar muy contentos	*So we would arrive contented*
hasta el pueblo de Merced.	*To the town of Merced.*

FIGURE 1.4   *Song text: "The Ballad of César Chávez." Texas-Mexican* corrido.
(From Las Voces de los Campesinos: Francisco García and Pablo and Juanita Saludado Sing Corridos about the Farm Workers and Their Union. Reproduced with permission from the Center for the Study of Comparative Folklore and Mythology, UCLA, FMSC-1.)

protest, as well as a narrative. "The Ballad of César Chávez" (figure 1.4, CD track 1-6) relates an important event in American history: the march of that famed Mexican American leader in the struggle for rights for migrant farmworkers. In spring 1965 the first major strike against grape growers took the form of a march from Delano, California, to the state's capital, Sacramento, to meet with then-Governor Edmund "Pat" Brown. Because of the religious orientation of Mexican culture, the march became a nexus of the religious tradition of pilgrimage and the contemporary form of demonstration. You can follow the route of the demonstrators on a map of California and on CD track 1-7 hear **mariachi**s, the sort of musicians who greeted them in Stockton. References to the lady of Guadalupe allude to the Virgin Mary, as she is enshrined at a major shrine in Mexico, the Basilica of the Lady of Guadalupe.

In song text, then, we can feel the personal experience of oppressed people even in history. Irish ballads are another good example, accounting as many of them do, the results of English determination to control Ireland beginning in 1532 with Henry VIII. The Catholic presence in Irish life was regulated over the next three hundred years by a

Ya vamos llegando a Stockton	We are almost in Stockton
ya mero la luz se fue	Sunlight is almost gone
pero mi gente gritaba	But the people shouted
sigan con bastante fe.	Keep on with lots of faith.
Cuando llegamos a Stockton	When we arrived at Stockton
los mariachis nos cantaban	The mariachis were singing
que viva César Chávez	Long live César Chávez
y la Virgen que llevaba.	And the Virgin of Guadalupe.

(The selection on CD track 1-6 ends here; following is the remainder of the corrido.)

Contratistas y esquiroles	Contractors and scabs
ésta va a ser una historia	This is going to be your story
ustedes van al infierno	You will all go to hell
y nosotros a la gloria.	And we will go to heaven.
Ese Señor César Chávez	That Mr. César Chávez
él es un hombre cabal	Is a very strong man
quería verse cara a cara	He wanted to speak face to face
con el gobernador Brown.	With Governor Brown.
Oiga, Señor César Chávez,	Listen, Mr. César Chávez,
su nombre que se pronuncia	Your name is well known
en su pecho usted merece	On your chest you well deserve
la Virgen de Guadalupe.	The Virgin of Guadalupe.

FIGURE 1.4 *Continued.*

series of laws that formally excluded Catholics from participation in public life, voting, and ownership of land. In the seventeenth century, displaced landowners were sent to infertile, rocky land in the province of Connaught. On CD track 1-8, the eminent Joe Heaney (1919–1984) sings "The Rocks of Bawn," a traditional **ballad** that he associated with the banishment to Connaught. Sweeney, a laborer who can't plow the fields because the land is too rocky, speaks in verse one, while his wife or sweetheart seems to speak in verse two. Verse three assumes the voice of the bailiff or agent of the absentee landlord who accuses Sweeney of being lazy. In verse four, we again hear from Sweeney, who feels trapped by his poverty and inability to till the rocky land. In the last verse, Sweeney ironically decides his only hope is to enlist in the army of his oppressors.

THE ROCKS OF BAWN

Come all you loyal heroes, wherever you may be;
Don't hire with any master 'till you know what your work will be
For you must rise up early, from clear daylight 'till dawn;
I'm afraid you'll ne'er be able to plow the rocks of Bawn.

Oh rise up lovely Sweeney, and give your horse some hay
And give him a good feed of oats before you go away.
Don't feed him on soft turnip, put him out on your green lawn;
For I'm afraid he'll ne'er be able to plow the rocks of Bawn.

My curse attend you Sweeney, you have me nearly robbed;
You're sitting by the fireside with your dudeen in your gob,
You're sitting by the fireside from clear daylight 'till dawn;
But I'm afraid you'll ne'er be able to plow the rocks of Bawn.

My shoes they are well-worn now, my stockings they are thin;
My heart is always trembling, I'm afraid I might give in,
My heart is always trembling from clear daylight 'till dawn;
I'm afraid I'll ne'er be able to plow the rocks of Bawn.

I wish the Queen of England would send for me in time
And place me in some regiment, all in my youth and prime.
I would fight for Ireland's glory from clear daylight 'till dawn;
But I never will return again to plow the rocks o'Bawn.
(cited in Scott and Hast 2004: 28–9)

Among the narrative genres that link music to text for the expression and heightening of meaning, musical drama is perhaps the single best example. In Balinese theater the nexus between music and the narrative both in terms of mood and action is so close and so familiar to audiences that the dramatic meaning is automatically remembered when the same musical material occurs without words in a nontheatrical context.

We might assume that a sung text is meant to be understood. Not necessarily so! Even when a Central Javanese **gamelan** (ensemble) includes vocalists, the text they sing may not be immediately intelligible. Not only do their voices blend into the greater ensemble sound, but the poems are usually in old Javanese language that few listeners know (CD track 1-9; figure 1.5). For the few who can understand, the meaning lies both in the text itself and in the singing of it; for the less

FIGURE 1.5   *Central Javanese* gamelan *playing for* wayang kulit *(leather puppet play).*   *(Photo by Kathleen Karn)*

knowledgeable, the meaning lies in the recognition that an old text is
being sung, in the assurance that tradition continues.

Sometimes melody is sung to text that is not linguistically meaningful—
syllables such as "fa la la" in English carols. You might hear people use
the phrase "meaningless syllables" for such text, but ethnomusicologists no longer do so. Syllables assumed to be meaningless have been
found upon further investigation to be archaic language, or mystically
meaningful. Instead, ethnomusicologists refer to the syllables as **vocables,** suggesting their function in the music. The text of CD track 1-10,
a Navajo corn-grinding song recorded in 1940 with the lead singer Joe
Lee, in Lukachukai, Arizona, consists completely of vocable phrases.

Aghei ha yana ghei aghei	*Aghei ha yana ghei aghei*
Aghei yolei yolei hanei-hana	*Aghei yolei yolei hanei-hana*
O—weya hena a nana	*O—weya hena a nana ghei aghei*
Aghei ha yana ghei aghei	*Aghei ha yana ghei aghei.*

Vocables are practical in the texts of powwow songs, in which participants may speak dozens of different Native American languages.

Sometimes there are lexically meaningful words known by the singers who nevertheless may choose to sing the song with vocables (Diamond 2008).

The opposite of texted song without linguistic meaning is **program music**—instrumental music without a text that is treated as if it had one. With its many narrative genres and operatic styles, Chinese music, even instrumental music, is very text-oriented. A title such as "Plum Blossoms" is subject to interpretation, but each instrumentalist may express it differently. The "text" is not in the musical sound but in the musicians' and listeners' meaningful interpretations of the title.

Music as Text. In a subtle pairing of melody and text, the singer of the Alha epic in North India might deliver the bravado words of a warrior to the familiar melody of a woman's song genre. The bravado words are a text certainly, but so is the musical commentary on his womanly personality. Such subtlety requires a knowledgeable audience to be understood.

As that example illustrates, music can acquire meaning from the situation in which it is made or heard and then become a kind of text in itself. Its meaning is then "situated." My favorite theory about the reason that we continue to hate or love (if not get stuck in) the popular music of our teenage years is that it is situated: we absorbed that music when we were experiencing love and other emotions intensely as adolescents. It is not only the style of the music that stays with us, but also the embedded memory of the meaning it had at that crucial time in our lives.

I can think of another important instance of situated music as text. "We Shall Overcome" has a text, but even the melody alone came to be so closely associated with demonstrations that we do not have to hear any text to understand its meaning. That song also provides an illustration of how one song can assume new meanings, assume new functions, and mark different identities. In her book, *Music in America* in this series, Adelaida Reyes tracks this (2005: 55–6). "We Shall Overcome" was originally a Christian church hymn; C. A. Tindley, who became America's first important African American gospel songwriter, had written it for his congregation. In the 1960s, it was adopted by the civil rights movement and became an anthem associated in the minds of the nation with the African American struggle for equality and freedom from discrimination. CD track 1-11 was sung in 1964 at a Hattiesburg mass meeting in Mississippi.

Reyes recounts her experience of an American Thanksgiving Day celebration in Oxford (United Kingdom) in 1996 to illustrate further how the symbolism of even such a clearly situated song as "We Shall Overcome" may undergo transformation—with shifting senses of "community" and meaning to individuals as well as for a community.

In the presence of other Americans and guests from the local and international community (mostly Europeans and Africans), one Anglo-American after another stood up to describe their connection to the Pilgrims. Then an African American began to sing "We Shall Overcome." Immediately, the other guests who knew the song joined in. In no time, the one voice had become a rousing chorus.

I hazard to guess that when he began, the singer had intended the song to call attention to his difference from the earlier speakers and to the fact that, though American, he, as an African American, had no connection to the Pilgrims. As the other Americans joined in, the song assumed new meaning. The emphasis shifted from the difference that the African American singer was signaling to the shared meanings that "We Shall Overcome" has for all Americans. Finally, as the non-American guests added their voices, the scope of the song's meaning expanded beyond the boundaries of one national ideology. The non-Americans may just have been joining in on a party activity. But they may also have been expressing solidarity with the African American individual who initiated the singing in the narrow context of that Thanksgiving celebration. Alternatively, they may have been expressing solidarity with what he stood for in the wider context of racism and universal human rights (Reyes 2005: 56).

While the meaning of "We Shall Overcome" was initially expressed through the text of the song, music entirely without text can be equally meaningful to those who know how to "read" it. In his book on music in Bulgaria, Tim Rice writes on the politics of wedding music, which, in the Communist era, had become significant musically and economically (2004: 68–73). Besides the brilliance of the instrumentalists, he recounts, people's increasing dissatisfaction with the communist government also contributed to the enormous popularity of wedding music. The government had created problems for itself in the 1980s by instituting draconian measures against the Turks and **Roma** (previously known as gypsies), Bulgaria's Muslim minorities. Apparently fearing that these minorities had grown so large in number that they might begin to demand cultural autonomy, the government decided to solve the problem by symbolically erasing them and their culture from the national consciousness. This included banning all forms of "oriental" public cultural display, including the playing of Rom forms of music and dance, such as *kyuchek*, with its elaborate nonmetrical improvisations. (I'll explain the musical terms later.)

Bulgarian cultural officials began to claim that all these practices, including much of what was popular about wedding music, were "aggressively antistate." At one level, wedding music was antistate simply because it operated in an economic sphere largely beyond state control. But in the highly charged political environment in Bulgaria in the late 1980s, the musical form of wedding music also became an icon of people's hopes for freedom and a more democratic form of government. (An icon is a symbolic form that possesses some of the properties of the thing it represents.)

Wedding music's emphasis on improvisation by individual instrumentalists, especially forms of improvisation that broke the bounds of traditional practice, could be interpreted as an iconic representation of the individual freedom Bulgarians increasingly sought in the political arena. It also provided a new "structure of feeling" that allowed people to experience some release and relief within an otherwise repressive and restrictive society (citing Williams 1977: 128–35)

Furthermore, if folk music, including all its features (highly arranged, emphasis on traditional instruments, narrow-range diatonic melodies, lack of real improvisation), was, by its association with governmental institutions, an obvious symbol of the state, then wedding music, with all its contrasting features, could be interpreted as a symbol of antistate sentiments. Those features included a flexible structure that was responsive to the audience, rather than completely prearranged; an emphasis on modern instruments; wide-ranging, chromatic melodies; and a preference for amplified over acoustic sound. While these features by themselves cannot be said to be iconic of anything, let along antitotalitarian feelings, in this particular context, where they existed in striking contrast to the music patronized by the state, such features can be interpreted as expressions of the yearning for political freedom (Rice 2001 and 2004: 72–3).

ACTIVITY 1.6 *It is not always easy to figure out the value to you of a kind of music or a performance. Perhaps its situated meaning has something to do with it. Try to sort out why you value one piece of music that you really love and write a paragraph about it.*

Conde Nast Traveler (CNT), interviewing artist Yo Yo Ma:

CNT: You said that your trip to the Kalahari [Desert in South Africa] in 1993 changed your life. What does a Bushman have to say to a virtuoso Chinese cellist, and vice versa?

Ma: I participated in their transcendent practices, dancing for hours in a circle around the fire. I listened to the old-style music, with people playing for the hunt, for prayer, and for art. That experience was more powerful than almost anything I've done. I asked a woman, "Why do you do this?" She said, "It gives us meaning." How cool is that? That's as good a reason as any to do something.

CNT: How did it affect you?

Ma: It changed my perception of art. It was no longer about high art, low art, medium art. I realized that doesn't matter.

(*Conde Nast Traveler*, May 2007: 42)

USE

Although the meaning and the use of music are inseparable, thinking specifically about use permits us to focus on people's intentions. People make music useful in so many ways that one can think of—socially, as a mode of interaction or to create a romantic mood; politically, to control or unite; spiritually, for sacred expression and worship; economically, to make a living; medically, for soothing or healing; and so many more ways.

I have asked many people about the place of music in their lives. Many have replied: "Oh, I'm not interested in music at all." Then they admit regularly listening to music in their cars, occasionally going to a performance, dancing on a date, exercising with an iPod, or otherwise putting music into their lives. This they may categorize as enjoyment, as entertainment rather than musical activity. However they regard it, they are making music useful.

Untold numbers of people make a living from music—from paid performers to students who work in music libraries and record shops. Students in one of my courses had these comments to make: "Involvement in music looks good on a college application; that's a status function, a statement of self-worth." "Music helps me understand other people and their actions, to place myself in another person's shoes." "It's a stress reliever." "It quiets my anger and otherwise improves my mood." "Music helps me focus while doing repetitive tasks." "I remember things through song." "I use music to escape from chaos!"

One of the most significant uses to which people put music is to express an identity. Performers do this to establish an individual identity as a musician, of course, but music can also be emblematic of a group—a college, as in a school song; a heritage group, as in the Polish polka or the blues; a nationality, as in a national anthem. The meaning of such music is highly situated and useful for purposes ranging from contestation to solidarity. My favorite example is "We Are Family," which was adopted by the 1979 Pittsburgh Pirates baseball team for the purpose of uniting fans in song. In a contrasting use, it is entertainingly employed for irony in the feature film *The Birdcage*, when the conservative senator character and his family, unrecognizable in drag, are generously escorted out incognito through a gay nightclub, past the hovering press, as patrons dance obliviously and joyfully. And one day as I waited on campus for a ride home, I heard "We Are Family" blasting forth from the open patio of the UC Berkeley Haas School of Business, where it was being used to send a meaningful message at an alumni fund-raising event.

In the United States, the assertion of black ethnicity and African roots through music has been extremely effective sociopolitically. So effective, in fact, that some Americans of Asian descent have modeled their political musical activity on that of African Americans. Without a shared musical heritage, Japanese American and Chinese American musicians joined the world of jazz performance in the 1970s, thereby lifting that powerful African American musical voice in the assertion of their Asian American identity and rights. Influenced in the 1970s by the black power movement in the United States and Rastafarianism in Jamaica, black ethnicity became a major sociopolitical issue in Brazil. Music groups endorsed the ideology of the 1940s and 1950s that is still called "negritude;" their songs evoked their African ancestry and the "black is beautiful" theme, but also raised quite vehemently the questions of racism and its resulting socioeconomic injustices (Gerard Behague, personal communication, 2001).

ACTIVITY 1.7 *Think about the music that you choose to have in your life. How do you use it? You might do a mini-fieldwork project and return to the list of music makers you made for Activity 1.1; ask them how they use music.*

In the real world and now in the virtual world, however, music can be heard in vastly different places and at any time. It can easily be experienced as utterly decontextualized—divorced from its time and place, cut off from its original makers, meanings, and uses as musicians collect sounds from all over the world to create, as the singer Marc Anthony put it, "world music in a Long Island basement" (Buia 2001: 10). We can no longer assume that ethnic musical materials will serve as markers of particular ethnic identities, for example. Such globally shared music is constantly recontextualized by those who listen to it, given new meanings, and made to perform new as well as the same old functions—a process that some ethnomusicologists call glocalization (global localization). Other musical boundaries are being superseded as well. Senses of musical ownership are routinely challenged by sampling and online filesharing. Boundaries between musical genres such as jazz, rock, and classical are routinely breached. The creative process continues as music and music making become what people want them to be.

TRANSMISSION

Three words prevail to name the process by which musical knowledge is passed among people: "dissemination" and "circulation" have increasingly been used since the burgeoning of popular music studies in the 1980s, while "transmission" is a well-worn word that has mostly been used for one of the most crucial factors for music anywhere—the process by which musical knowledge is taught and learned. The means by which music is transmitted are tactile, oral, and visual (usually referred to as written). In this section, I shall briefly address these processes, returning to dissemination and circulation later in the book.

If you have ever taken partner-dance lessons, you know that **tactile** communication of the movements is important. In her book on music in Bali in this series, Lisa Gold describes how, in coaching the remarkably young dancer of the *legong* style (always female), the teacher stands behind and manipulates the student's arms and body while singing the sequence of movements, indicating the melody and drum pattern, and counting out the steps (figure 1.6). In this way, the student learns the entire sequence by feel while integrating it with the music. Tactile transmission can also help in learning to play an instrument; I remember my piano teacher putting his hand over mine on the keys to demonstrate how I should shift my hand to play in another register.

With regard to **oral** means by which music is transmitted, in ethnomusicology we have become increasingly careful to distinguish between oral and aural transmission: oral transmission takes the perspective of the teacher and implies interaction between the teacher and the learner,

FIGURE 1.6 *Tactile transmission of* legong *dance. Master teacher I Nyoman Cerita with student Ni Made Ayu Septhan. A strong energy is often conveyed as the teacher firmly holds the arms and hands of the student, puts a knee into the arch of the back, holds the head, smacks an elbow up to convey the dynamic power and element of surprise that is so essential to Balinese dance. When the teacher holds or touches the student, it is about technique but also a transmission of energy; for the student it is about learning how your teacher feels something. (Photo and comment by Emiko Saraswati Susilo)*

while aural transmission takes the perspective of the learner, who hears the music through some aural source.

"Written" is the remaining mode of transmission that is usually acknowledged, implying the use of music notation. That is but one mode of **visual transmission**, however. Another is observation; how many have learned to play an instrument by watching musicians! Also, a great deal can be taught and learned from paintings, photographs, video, and film, as well as observation and notation. I will return to this point at the end of the chapter.

Important to be understood from the outset of this section, however, is that there are different views about whether or not musical knowledge should be shared and, if so, under what conditions. In her book on First Nations peoples, Beverley Diamond informs us that there are currently different views about whether Indigenous beliefs, songs, and customs (including those that constitute "musical knowledge") should be shared with outsiders—both members of other tribes or nations and non-Native Americans. In a few cases, people feel the pain of being misrepresented by outsiders over and over again, and, as a result, some believe that nothing should be shared, that Native American knowledge should be accessible only to the Native American community from which it came. In Diamond's experience, that was not the majority view, although she considers it to be an understandable one. It's not that knowledge is secret, but rather that those who are entrusted with knowledge must know how it should be used. My teachers of North India's music, on the other hand, related to me instances of other teachers who would transmit certain knowledge only to students from their families.

Oral and Aural Transmission. Most music is learned aurally—both by intentional listening and by osmosis, that is, by absorbing what we hear around us. This was already the case before the early twentieth century, when radio and recordings expanded the potential material that was available for learning. The mass media are without doubt the single greatest teaching force, playing an enormously significant role in the transmission of musical knowledge.

Where music is taught primarily by oral transmission, the teacher plays a significant role, as a repository of knowledge and technique, the individual responsible for musical quality, and often a guide in life (as the Indian *guru* is). The availability of recordings can change the degree of dependence of a pupil on a teacher, as well as the degree of control a teacher has over musical knowledge, but personal instruction provides a qualitatively different learning experience. Student-teacher relationships vary greatly. Particularly where music is being transmitted orally, but within a written tradition as well, a teacher might or might not be willing to make verbal explanations, preferring instead that the student listen, watch, and do.

A student of mine, Nontapat Nimityongskul, told me in 1999, "There are two main ways we can keep music. One is to write it down. The other is to know it in your heart." Nontapat raises an issue concerning oral and aural versus written transmission. Will music learned aurally be remembered and preserved? Quite possibly it will fade from memory, unless one or all of three conditions exist. The first and most necessary condition is that one intends to remember the music precisely as learned. This is a matter of personal or group motivation. The motivation would exist, for example, when there is a fear that incorrect rendering will cause some disaster.

The second condition is a system for learning the music so thoroughly that it is not likely to be forgotten. The most evidently successful such system was devised for the chanting of religious texts that have survived in Hindu Indian culture since the Vedic period (roughly 1500–500 B.C.E.). Without any reference to written materials, the chants have been transmitted from Brahmin priests to young Brahmin boys through untold numbers of generations. The teaching priest has his pupils repeat the sentences of the sacred text, using a well worked out memorization technique: using patterns that arrange the words of sentences in different order, the text is repeated endlessly until truly absorbed. Among the several patterns, the *krama* pattern is a simple one: *ab, bc, cd, de,* and so on. Each letter (*a, b, c,* etc.) indicates a word (Activity 1.8). Thus the sentence "Why am I doing this?" would be chanted as follows: "Why am / am I / I doing / doing this?" With innumerable repetitions, you will remember the sentence well.

ACTIVITY 1.8 *Listen to CD track 1-12, the teaching of Vedic recitation, until you can follow these patterns. The line of text is: "Devīṃ vacam ajanayanta devās tām vísvarūpāh paśavo vadanti / sā . . . ." ("The gods gave birth to the goddess of speech, spoken by animals in all forms. . . ."). First the priest reads the line as a normal sentence, announcing "padam." Then he announces each pattern and recites the line in that pattern. The first pattern he chants is mālā. (Endings of some words change, by the Sanskrit rules of connecting words, depending on ending and beginning vowels and consonants.)*

mālā *pattern:*   ab / ba / ab / bc / cb / bc / cd / dc / . . .

jaṭā *pattern:*   abbaab / bccbbc / cddccd / deedde / . . .

Once you understand this technique, make up your own short sentence and subject it to the patterns. Memorized in this manner, it is no doubt a sentence you will remember for a long time.

The third condition is a system of reinforcement: a system that assures that memory of the music will be periodically renewed. "Oldies" radio broadcasts perform this function; recurring music in a religious calendrical cycle does as well, such as carols sung at Christmas or prayers chanted at Passover. In some situations, the responsibility for reinforcing memories is taken by institutions. In Java (Indonesia), musicians at the royal courts hold rehearsals expressly to maintain musical compositions and choreographies that are transmitted mainly through oral tradition. Referring to something written is another way to renew the memory periodically.

The best way to maintain musical memory is to have a sound recording available, for so much is excluded from even the most comprehensive system of notation—sensual vocal production that is characteristic of a style, for instance. Preservation was an unintended achievement of the recording industry when it began to record all kinds of musics in the early twentieth century as a way to sell the new phonograph machines. Using that technology, ethnomusicologists, folklorists, and some anthropologists have been motivated to preserve the world's musical treasures, and there are now numerous sound archives around the globe. Touching stories circulate about groups whose traditional music no longer exists for some reason—radical change from international influence or memory loss where no system of reinforcement was in place—but recovery and revival is possible through recordings that someone deposited in an archive.

Visual Transmission. The nature of a notation system depends on the purpose people intend it to serve, and numerous types are in use around the world. If any musician wants to write a brief reminder of music already held in memory, a minimalist notation will suffice, recording only the musician's choice of crucial information. If the minimalist information that is recorded gives a performer instructions on *how* to play the music—what to do on an instrument to sound out the music—it is called **prescriptive notation**. For a xylophone player, for instance, if the notation tells him or her which key to hit, that is prescriptive notation. If a composer or other musician wants to record in detail *what* a performer is to play or sing, it is called **descriptive notation**. That is the intention of Western staff notation.

Prescriptive notation for stringed and some historic keyboard instruments (often called **tablature**) gives technical instruction to players—where to place their fingers on a stringed instrument and perhaps more. Whereas there are any number of such systems that could illustrate this notation, I chose the historic notation for the **qin** (pronounced "chin," figure 1.7), a Chinese zither-type instrument (CD track 1-13). Like other **tablature**-type notations, it is intended to transmit performing instructions. Reproduced in figure 1.8 is the beginning of a piece, "Flowing Water." To read Chinese-language texts, start at the right side of the page and follow the characters in each column, from top to bottom. In figure 1.8, the title of the piece, "Flowing Water," is written at the top of the far right column, and the label for section one is given in the next column toward the left. The musical notation begins at the top of the third column, toward the middle of the page. Basically, the notation specifies left- and right-hand playing techniques and the strings on which they are to be executed. Figure 1.9 shows the Chinese numbers used to indicate the six strings of the instrument. Figure 1.10 shows the right-hand techniques specified in the first column of notation of the piece. Figure 1.11 shows you how indications of playing techniques and string numbers are combined in the first three characters of the piece.

ACTIVITY 1.9 *Your first task is to locate the string numbers in the characters. Fig. 1.9 gives you those numbers. Try copying those numbers to give you a visual feel for them.*

In Fig. 1.8, count to column 5 (from right to left). To get you started, I'll give you the string numbers in the first five characters of column 5, from the top down: 3 & 4, 2, 3, 4, 3. Now try to identify the string numbers for the whole of column 3 from the right, that is, from the beginning of the piece.

As you can see, the numbers are embedded within the characters, surrounded by indications of playing techniques. Using Figure 1.10 and 1.11 as a guide for those in column 3, you can see how the player is instructed to play each pitch.

Once you understand what the notation is giving you, try copying the first column of melody to experience the flow of it.

*Most important, think about what this notation does and does not tell you. Each time this notation would be used, the player would render it according to his own **dapu**, a process of realizing the notation in sound. This notation is prescriptive, rather than descriptive.*

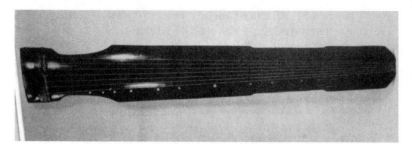

FIGURE 1.7 *Chinese qin.* *(Courtesy of UCLA Ethnomusicology Archives)*

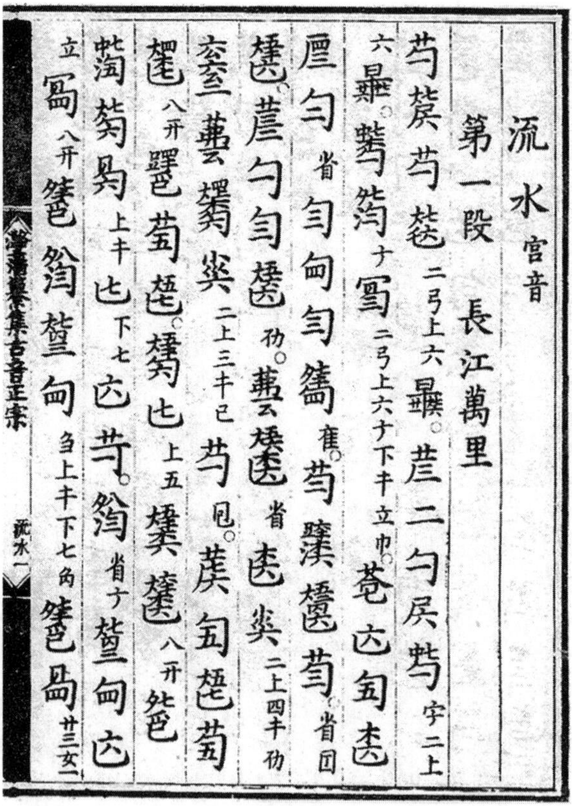

FIGURE 1.8 *Qin notation of "Liushui" ("Flowing Water") (Courtesy of Frederick Lau)*

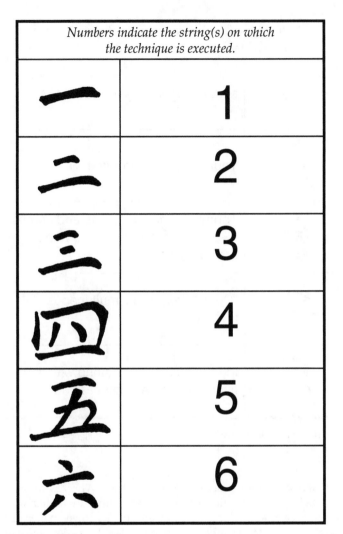

Numbers indicate the string(s) on which the technique is executed.	
一	1
二	2
三	3
四	4
五	5
六	6

FIGURE 1.9   *Chinese numbers.*   *(Chart by Jane Chiu, Viet Nguyen, and Pamela Han)*

At the beginning of the piece (column 3 from the right), these right hand techniques are required.	
勹	Middle finger pulls the string.
尸	Thumb pulls string with nail.
乇	Thumb pushes the string and comes to rest against the next string without sounding it.
早	"Chord" from two simultaneous techniques
厂	Index finger pushes string with tip of fingernail, twice in succession.

FIGURE 1.10   Right hand qin techniques (Chart by John Groschwitz)

Notation is a kind of access to information. Whereas in an orally transmitted musical tradition the teacher controls whether or not a pupil may learn something, writing the music down makes it more accessible to greater numbers of people. Unlike in Western music, where all voices and instruments use staff notation (though a few instruments, notably guitar and hip-hop turntable, use specialized tablatures) in Japan each traditional instrument has its own system of notation. Standardized notation assumes that the music is to be shared among the general music-reading public, whereas the Japanese system is tailored to in-group exclusivity.

勹	Middle finger pulls string 1.
 戻	Thumb pulls string 6 with nails.
 毡	Thumb pushes string 6.

FIGURE 1.11   *Techniques and string numbers combined in qin notation (Chart by John Groschwitz)*

The five-line **staff notation** system is so detailed that it requires a literacy that is specifically musical. With colonialism, however, its use was disseminated so widely in the world that it now constitutes a kind of international musical language. Because learning some of its basic principles can be of great help as a tool for musical communication, I give a brief guide here. An explanatory list of a few basic elements is given in figure 1.12, and others are added in figure 1.13, a sample of Western notation featuring a portion of the song "Aloha Oe," composed by Queen Liliuokalani of Hawaii (1838–1917).

An adage often voiced by one of my former teachers, Mantle Hood, is one I endorse: "A written tradition is only as strong as the oral tradition that supports it." If you have tried to read any notation system without some further verbal explanation and hearing what is notated, you can recognize that to be true. In the end, an interplay between the oral/aural and written transmission of music is the reality for many musicians.

In this chapter I have introduced briefly the interests of ethnomusicologists in exploring how people all over the globe make music meaningful and useful in their lives. Instruments through which people make music are the subject of chapter 2.

Before going there, however, I want you to think about one more basic question. At the beginning of this chapter, concepts of "music"

1. The basic unit is a staff of five lines (▤); staves meant to be read simultaneously are joined by a vertical line at the left margin.
2. Individual musical sounds are represented by notes. ♩ ♩
3. Pitch is indicated by placing notes both on staff lines and in spaces between staff lines. ▤♩♩♩♩♩♩♩
4. Melodic contour is visible: Even if pitches cannot be identified, the rising and falling of the pitches can be followed.
5. When multiple musical parts are intended to be sounded together, they are aligned vertically.
6. Rhythm is shown by altering the appearance of notes. "Black" notes (with filled-in noteheads) are of shorter duration than "white" notes. A flag on the stem (♪) attached to a note shortens the duration. Additional time on the pitch is indicated by a dot after the note. For example:

   ♩ = 1 count

   ♪ = ½ count (half-counts are often linked by a beam ♫)

   ♩. = 1.5 counts

   𝅗𝅥 = 2 counts

   𝅗𝅥. = 3 counts
7. Meter (grouping of counts) is shown by vertical lines called bar lines. The space between two bar lines is called a measure. (In "Aloha Oe" each measure consists of four counts.) See chapter 3.

FIGURE 1.12 *Basic Guideline to Western Staff Notation*

in general were explored. But what about "the music" or, as is frequently said, "the music itself"—TMI? What constitutes "the music itself—the ubiquitous TMI?" asked my brilliant young colleague who made a guest presentation in my class recently. Nicholas Mathew was speaking to the assumption of many of his students that the notated piece or the single recording (think MP3 file) is TMI. "But is it?" he queried and wrote across the board: Composer, performer, audience. Demonstrating the importance of the question, he showed us a clip from the 1947 feature film *Song of Love*. In the scene, the flambuoyant and fabulously famous nineteenth-century performer-composer, Franz Liszt, was playing his transcription for piano of composer Robert Schumann's romantic "Widmung" ("Dedication") that he had written for his beloved wife Clara, who sat listening in the inti-

FIGURE 1.13 *Western notation through "Aloha Oe."* *(with the assistance of Joseph Dales)*

mate salon gathering. The select, elite audience applauded Liszt's bombastically virtuosic version of the piece with the sort of admiring adulation that Liszt hoped to receive from the transcriptions he made of other composers' compositions; the audience valued virtuosity, and he gave them just that. As other guests wandered off, Clara sat at the piano and played the piece as her husband had intended it to be—a quiet, lyrically tender love song. Before we in the class could see Liszt's reaction in the film, Mathew brought the showing to an end. It was up to the students to think about what "the music" was in that instance. The conclusion: the composers, the performers, and the audience all contributed to what "the music" was. It certainly wasn't any one thing!

CHAPTER 2

Thinking about Instruments

∞

The countless and varied musical instruments that have existed through time are evidence of how people make music meaningful and useful in their lives. Because people have taken them wherever they have gone— for signals in war, for entertainment on expeditions, as items for trade, as gifts for foreign potentates—instruments also provide evidence of cultural diffusion. A notice posted by Craig McCrae on the Society for Ethnomusicology internet list offers an excellent example of this, with the accordion as example:

> One vital but little-known accordion tradition is found in the Khorezm region of Uzbekistan, in recent centuries seat of the Khiva khanate and an important center of high civilization since ancient times. The most typical Khorezmian ensembles combine the diatonic accordion with vocals, *doyra* (frame drum) and the Azerbaijani *tar* (a plucked, fretted lute with sympathetic strings, a bit smaller than the Iranian *tar*). . . . Russian colonists brought the accordion to the region in the late nineteenth century and the locals quickly adopted it for their own use. A high point in Khorezmian accordion history was in the 1930s when Soviets organized women's ensembles with forty or fifty accordions. (27 July 2000; cited with permission)

When people design and craft instruments, they both express cultural values and create musical practices through them. One basic question is whether instruments should be standardized. "Definitely!" say music makers and instrument makers wherever mass production and ensemble practice foster standardization. "Definitely not!" says the player of *sitār* in North India. "Add a string for me" (CD tracks 1-14, 1-15). Most Indian music ensembles are small, and mass production of instruments is still low, so the idea of idiosyncratic instruments flourishes.

FIGURE 2.1 *Principal instruments of a Mexican mariachi ensemble. From left to right:* vihuela, *Armando Quintero;* guitarrón, *Francisco "El Capiro" Castro; violin, Hilario Cervantes; trumpet, Luis "El Loco" Pérez. (Courtesy of Daniel Sheehy)*

"Standardize the pitch of all instruments in this ensemble for me," says a Javanese purchaser to a smithy, "but make its tuning slightly different from the tuning of all other *gamelans*" (CD track 1-9). Where ensemble-specific pitch is an ideal, individuals in Java do not bring their own personal instrument to play in a *gamelan*; instead, they gather to play a set owned by a person, company, or club.

Variations within an instrument type can be found almost everywhere. For example, a huge number of local instruments modeled on the Spanish guitar but in various sizes and with various numbers of strings, and tunings and distinct names exist throughout Latin America. The Mexican **guitarron** (Fig. 2.1, CD track 1-7) is the largest of them, and the **charango** is the smallest (Fig. 2.2, CD 1-16). On a relatively more "local" level, *charangos* used by indigenous musicians in the Andean region vary in shape, size, materials, and numbers of strings, depending on local preferences and the whims of specific makers (Turino, 2007).

Indeed, instruments are items of expressive culture as well as material culture, works of art, symbols, technological inventions, tools for earning a livelihood. In this chapter I examine various ways in which

FIGURE 2.2 Charango *player comes a-courtin' in the Saturday market in Descanso, Canas, Peru. Highly decorated with ribbons and mirrors, the instrument indicates his seriousness of purpose. (Photo courtesy of Tom Turino)*

people have thought about instruments, considering them first as physical objects apart from the music made with them, then as instruments in music, that is, as people use them musically. I include both voices and bodies among musical instruments.

INSTRUMENTS AS OBJECTS

Ideas about Instrument Types. In two of the world's oldest civilizations—China and India—musical instruments have for millenia been considered particularly significant items of culture. While individual instruments had their specific meanings and uses, in China and India people also thought systematically about them to develop **classification** systems for instrument types.

The ancient Chinese classification system resonated with the value that culture placed on nature. Chinese classified their instruments according to the natural material that produced each instrument's sound. The "eight sounds" (*ba yin*) were those of metal, stone, skin, vegetable gourd, bamboo, wood, silk, and earth (i.e., pottery). As shown in figure 2.3, the sounds were associated with cardinal directions and seasons. When musicians performed on specified instruments, the "eight sounds" were incorporated into significant rituals—not to provide musical variety, but to manifest a link with nature (CD track 1-17).

> **ACTIVITY 2.1** *Identify the natural sounds in CD track 1-17, Confucian ritual music. It originated in China but has been preserved in Korea, as a–ak. Figure 2.4 may help you hear the different instruments.*

The *ba yin* classification system has fallen out of use, but the phrase "silk and bamboo" (*sizhu*) is still widely used in Chinese music to designate a string and wind ensemble. The phrase still names natural materials, but the intention now is to suggest a pleasing combination of different timbres (CD track 1-3).

Scholars in ancient India also cultivated an intellectual tradition of systematic thinking. They loved to classify and devised a variety of exhaustive categorizations—from character types in drama (in the *Nātya Sāstra* treatise) to physical positions in lovemaking (in the *Kāma Sūtra*). The classification system for musical instruments, dating from the early centuries of the Common Era and still viable today, identifies four basic types, according to the primary sound-producing medium: the vibrating body of the instrument itself, a vibrating membrane, a vibrating string, and a vibrating column of air.

In the European system of classification, there are four groups of instruments, based on the selection in the largest ensemble, an orches-

Ba yin system of instrument classification from
the Zhou Dynasty (c. 1000–200 BCE)

Type	Direction	Season	Instruments
Metal	West	Autumn	Bell-chimes
Stone	Northwest	Autumn to Winter	Stone-chimes
Skin	North	Winter	Drums
Gourd	Northeast	Winter to Spring	Mouth organ
Bamboo	East	Spring	Flutes, pipes
Wood	Southeast	Spring to Summer	Wooden tiger (scraper)
Silk	South	Summer	Zithers
Earth	Southwest	Summer to Autumn	Ocarinas, vessel flutes

FIGURE 2.3. *The ancient Chinese* ba yin *instrument classification system.*

tra: strings, winds, percussion, and keyboard (figures 2.5 to 2.9). Wind instruments are also referred to in more specific categories, brass and woodwind. This system mixes the criteria for classification: strings and winds name the sound-producing medium; percussion and keyboard refer to the means of playing; and brass and woodwind pertain to the material of construction.

Nineteenth-century Europeans, in the interest of science (but to a large extent as a result of imperialistic colonialism), began to gather instruments from around the world and to deposit them in museum collections, where they were documented as physical objects rather than meaningful items of culture. The task of cataloguing them presented a challenge. While efficient in their own musical context, the basic European criteria were too inconsistent to be useful for scientific classification. In the late nineteenth century, searching for a consistent system, the Belgian curator Victor Mahillon turned to the ancient Indian system with its one consistent criterion: the primary sound-producing medium of the instrument. As adapted, the categorical terms are as follows. An instrument whose body vibrates to produce sound is an **idiophone** (from the Latin *idem*, the thing itself). An instrument on which a vibrating membrane produces sound is a **membranophone**. A vibrating string produces the sound on a **chordophone**, while vibrating air is

FIGURE 2.4 *Instruments of the Korean* a-ak *ensemble. Transverse bamboo flute (ji) played by seated musicians on left; in rear just to their right—wooden barrel-shaped drum (jin'go) and hanging stone lithophone slabs (p'yeon'gyeong); hanging large bronze bell in center (teukjong); set of hanging bronze elliptical bells played by musician on right (p'yeonjong).* (Photo courtesy of Donna Kwon)

the primary sound-producing medium on an **aerophone** (see figure 2.10). Some instruments draw on more than one sound source, but this system designates only the primary one.

Early in the twentieth century, the German scholars Curt Sachs and Erich von Hornbostel espoused and expanded Mahillon's system, which is now used by museums and scholars worldwide. For greater specificity, they devised criteria for distinguishing instruments within each of the four major categories. A complete explanation of the system is found in Baines and Wachsmann (1961); here I provide only a few helpful defini-

FIGURE 2.5 *European instrument classification system: Strings. From left to right: Sophia Hanae Kessinger, Hoon Ku Lee (violin), Judy Minn (cello), Devin Kha Lac Tim (viola).* (Photo by Kathleen Karn)

FIGURE 2.6 *European instrument classification system: Winds (Brass). From left to right: Michael Fraser (tuba), Christy Dana (trumpet), Karen Baccaro (trumpet), Beth Milne (horn), Suzanne Mudge (trombone).* (Photo by Kathleen Karn)

FIGURE 2.7   *European instrument classification system: Winds (Woodwinds). From left to right: Flutes and oboes played by members of the UC Berkeley University Symphony Orchestra.*   (Photo by Kathleen Karn)

FIGURE 2.8   *European instrument classification system: Percussion. From left to right: Chimes, snare drum, cymbal, bass drum, xylophone.*   (Photo by Kathleen Karn)

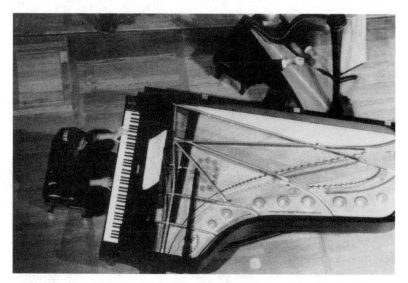

FIGURE 2.9 *European instrument classification system: Keyboard (and string). Nalini Ghuman (piano), Henry Spiller (harp). (Photo by Kathleen Karn)*

tions from that source. Note particularly the numbering system in the list below and the consistency from category to category, to the extent possible. For examples of instruments in the categories, see Figure 2.10.

1. Idiophones are subdivided by playing technique.
   - 11 Struck
   - 12 Plucked
   - 13 Friction
   - 14 Blown

2. Membranophones are subdivided first by playing technique.
   - 21 Struck
   - 22 Plucked
   - 23 Friction
   - 24 Singing membranes

Beyond further subdivision by shape, as shown in Figure 2.10, membranophones are then subdivided by number of heads and playing method.

3. Chordophones are subdivided by construction.
   - 31 A **zither** (simple chordophone) consists solely of a string bearer; the strings are parallel to the sounding body and run almost the entire length of the instrument.

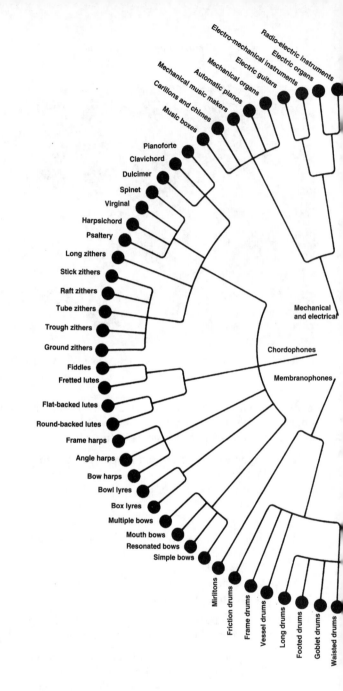

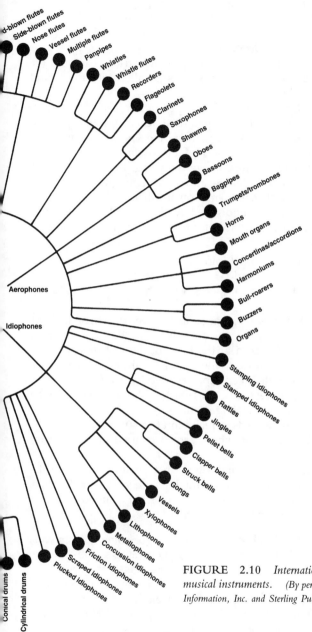

FIGURE 2.10 *International classification of musical instruments.* *(By permission of Diagram Visual Information, Inc. and Sterling Publishing Co.)*

End-blown flutes
Side-blown flutes
Nose flutes
Vessel flutes
Multiple flutes
Panpipes
Whistles
Whistle flutes
Recorders
Flageolets
Clarinets
Saxophones
Shawms
Oboes
Bassoons
Bagpipes
Trumpets/trombones
Horns
Mouth organs
Concertinas/accordions
Harmoniums
Bull-roarers
Buzzers
Organs
Aerophones
Idiophones
Stamping idiophones
Stamped idiophones
Rattles
Jingles
Pellet bells
Clapper bells
Struck bells
Gongs
Vessels
Xylophones
Lithophones
Metallophones
Concussion idiophones
Friction idiophones
Scraped idiophones
Plucked idiophones
Conical drums
Cylindrical drums

32 Composite chordophones

    321 A **lute** has a neck along which strings run, and the plane of the strings runs parallel with the sound table

    321.1 **Lyres,** classified as a type of lute, are important in Africa. The strings are attached to a yoke, which lies in the same plane as the sound table and consists of two arms and a crossbar.

    322 On a **harp** the plane of the strings lies at right angles to the sound table, and a line joining the lower ends of the strings points toward the neck.

All chordophones are further subdivided by playing technique. In ordinary conversation we are likely to refer to those techniques as struck, plucked, and bowed.

  4. Aerophones are subdivided into

    41 Free aerophones and

    42 Wind instruments proper, on which the column of air is confined

        421 On **flutes** a stream of air is directed against an edge.

        422 On **reed pipes** the air stream has, through means of a reed placed at the head of the instrument, intermittent access to the column of air that is to be made to vibrate. Reed pipes are subdivided into:

        422.1 **Double reeds**, on which a double layer of reed vibrates against itself

        422.2 **Single reeds**, which vibrate against a plane

        422.2 **Free reeds**, where a reed secured inside vibrates freely.

        423 **Horn** and **trumpet**-type instruments, on which the air stream passes through the player's vibrating lips, so gaining intermittant access to the air column that is to be made to vibrate

Updating the Sachs-Hornbostel system calls for some adjustments, because it is designed only for acoustically generated sounds. Figure 2.10 includes **mechanical** and **electrical instruments.** A category of **corpophones** is another possibility, to include handclapping, finger snapping, body slapping, and the like into the system. In addition, the idea of membrane as animal skin requires stretching to include fiberglass heads of drums in the category of membranophones. While a number of instruments are hybrids and do not fit neatly into the categories of

the Sachs-Hornbostel system, it continues to be extremely useful for the
study of musical instruments.

ACTIVITY 2.2   *To correlate the numerical listing of the Sachs-
Hornbostel system with Figure 2.10, add the numerals to the
figure.*
  *To understand the subdivisions in the classification system,
investigate these: Among the struck idiophones, what distinguishes
a bell from a gong and then a xylophone, a lithophone, and metallophone from each other? Among the aerophones, what distinguishes a trumpet from a horn, an oboe from a bassoon?*
  *An electronic instrument depends on electricity to produce a
sound; if you unplug it—no sound. If you're feeling really adven-
turous, experiment with devising a classification system for electronophones. Start by listing a few instruments you think belong
in this category and work from there.*

A number of relatively more contemporary ideas about grouping
musical instruments are in use, meant not for worldwide comparative
study but for local purposes. The Kpelle of West Africa, for example,
categorize instruments by playing technique, as either struck (including plucked strings and drums) or blown. This local classification
works because all Kpelle stringed instruments are plucked, rather than
bowed, and the finger in their view strikes the string (Stone 2005: 20).
In Javanese *gamelan* the two major groupings are "loud-playing"
(drums and louder bronze instruments) and "soft-playing" (flute,
strings, and quieter bronze instruments). Those Javanese groupings are
explained by historians as dating to the use of different ensembles for
different performance contexts, but instruments from the two groupings have probably been combined in ensembles for about four hundred years.
  The West African Igbo provide two conjunct systems for categorizing their musical instruments: according to the sounding material or the
technique of sound production (Nzewi 1991: 57). At the same time they
acknowledge musical roles and sociocultural musical importance
informed by variety and popularity, as follows.

1. The most popular and varied are the wooden, metal, and membrane instruments. Without producing definite pitches, these are capable of a wide range of phonic manipulation: to "sing," to "talk," and to play percussion roles in ensembles. Nzewi uses the term *melorhythm instruments* for these.

2. The second in importance are blown instruments, which are melody or phonic-effects-producing instruments.

3. Next are the shaken and pot instruments, which play percussive roles in ensembles.

4. Finally there are plucked (soft-toned) melody instruments, which are played primarily as solo instruments.

ACTIVITY 2.3   *Choose an instrument in each of the four basic categories of the Sachs-Hornbostel classification system that you see pictured in this book. Classify each of them in the other systems discussed on p.47 and above. If classifying in one of the systems doesn't seem to work, articulate the reason or reasons.*

Classification systems facilitate the comparison of instruments of the same basic type as they are found in various places around the world. One need only think of lute-type instruments, which most historians agree originated in the Middle East and spread gradually by the process of diffusion. Middle Eastern plucked lutes traveled different routes across the continent of Asia—east to China, west to Europe and beyond, becoming the Chinese *pipa*, the guitar, and the mariachi *vihuela* and *guitarrón*, respectively, all of which you will see pictured and hear on selections in this volume. A Middle Eastern bowed lute is the origin of the fiddle/violin, which, recycled back to Asia, was adopted into contemporary Middle Eastern and Indian music.

Ideas about Particular Instruments.   Some instruments carry extra-musical associations so clear and strong that the mere sound of them will transmit meaning to anyone in a knowledgeable group. The *didjeridu* (CD track 1-18, figure 1.1a), used as background music in television promotionals, evokes images of the Australian outback, *Crocodile Dundee*, or the lone Aboriginal on walkabout. Because of its historical association with court culture, European classical music imparts high class status in advertisements for expensive automobiles and expensive perfumes. The saxophone connotes "cool": a student, Tamina Spurney, noted, "When I hear it, I think of jazz and sunglasses and nightclubs and sophistication" (2001). Because of international circulation of sound recordings, performances by émigré musicians and the adoption of it for instruction in many American schools, the distinctive sound of the steel band (CD track 1-2) immediately invokes the Caribbean—or specifically Trinidad—for many of us.

ACTIVITY 2.4 *To focus on extra musical associations with instruments, watch for a few in TV ads and other contexts. Then, to think further about this, look for bands on YouTube that include instruments from two or three different cultures. (One example is Bela Flack playing jazz with a Tuvan throat singer and African drummers.) Do you ascribe extra musical associations to them, or do you think the musicians are suggesting some?*

For examples of relatively more local musical knowledges, I draw on three of the case study volumes in the Global Music Series. Brazilians recognize in the distinctive sound of the **berimbau** the spirit of rebellion, resistance, and liberation that the present practitioners of **capoeira** are able to draw from it (CD track 1-19, Fig. 2.11). A common story has it that *capoeira* was a martial art developed by slaves to aid in rebellions and escapes, but that it had to be disguised as a dance to fool the masters, who had forbidden all martial art training to slaves. *Capoeira* players agree that even after the abolition of slavery, a *capoeirista* would never carry a gun or even use one if captured in a fight. It was a matter of pride that one did not need a firearm to emerge victorious. Today this spirit is directed toward socially engaged projects that are intended to improve the lives of Brazilians of African heritage, and the legacy of slavery is remembered in the names of *capoeira* groups (Murphy 2006: 62).

For Native Americans, the vertical bass drum became the horizontal powwow drum. It was "turned"—a concept that is often used to describe how the energy or power of an object may be changed, in this case to change its energy and its related meaning from war to peace. Multiple men sitting around one drum to play in a spirit of peace become "the drum" (Diamond 2007).

FIGURE 2.11 *The* bateria, *or* capoeira *ensemble, at a children's* capoeira *ring in the Grupo de Capoeira Angola Pelourinho. On the left can be seen the* agogô, *the double bell-gong, as well as a child playing a tambourine-like* pandeiro, *and three* berimbaus *(the* gunga *with the largest gourd is the leftmost in the hands of the child leading the singing). Another student plays a* pandeiro, *and on the right end of the bench is the tall* atabaque. *(Photo courtesy of Greg Downey)*

Then there is that small Andean *charango* (Fig. 2.2, CD track 1-16), an instrument so strongly associated with courting that if a married man were seen walking around his village carrying one, people would joke that he was fooling around. For an unmarried boy, simply playing the instrument repeatedly near the girl of his heart on market days communicates his interest without having to say a thing. I'll let author Tom Turino, of this series' book on Peruvian music in the South American Andean region, relate how he discovered this association (and use) of the *charango* during his field research; it provides a good segue to the next section on the association of instruments with gender and sexuality.

I initially traveled to Canas in 1982 because I had heard that the *charango* was an important indigenous instrument in that region, and that *charango* players commonly came into the district capital towns on market days with their instruments. I arrived in Descanso for the Saturday market; catching a truck into the region from the Vilcanota river valley far below was easiest on market days. Like Conima, the town of Descanso was centered around a large plaza. Sitting on the ground around the square, women and girls from local communities and elsewhere were selling potatoes, meat, clothing, and other products. With a feeling that I had hit the mother lode for recording indigenous *charango* music, I also noticed five or six young men standing around in different parts of the plaza holding and sporadically playing their instruments. I especially noticed one extremely well-dressed young man whose instrument was ornately decorated with ribbons and mirrors. I approached him as he was entering the plaza and after some conversation was allowed to record the piece he was strumming—a tune, I was to learn later, known as the **tuta kashua** (night *kashua*, or night dance). I asked him if the tune had words and so he sang for my tape recorder [CD track 1-16]. After a while I approached another young man in another part of the plaza and found that he was strumming the same tune, as were all the others I approached that day. At my request these boys would play one or two other tunes for me, but left to their own devices they returned to strumming the *tuta kashua* as surely as water finds its way down hill. I must admit that I felt let down. I had traveled two days to get to Descanso from Cusco city and these young musicians seemed to only want to play one tune!? So much for recording a rich repertory of indigenous *charango* music, I thought.

True to my quest, I stayed in Canas traveling to other towns for their market days, but encountered the same situation. In the town of Langui I approached a *charango* player who had a particularly forceful manner of playing the *tuta kashua*. Prompted by my questions he told me that he lived in another area but had not had any luck there and so came to the Langui market hoping to do better. "Better at what?" I asked. "There is no one at home who will go with me to the *punchay kashua* (day dance)," he said sadly, clutching his *charango*, "I was hoping I could find a girl here." No luck here either, as it turned out.

Back in Descanso for the following Saturday and the Saturday after that I began to notice that boys playing *charango* were hovering around a particular girl—nonchalantly strumming the *tuta kashua* tune somewhere in her vicinity, decked out in their best, *charangos* decked out too, little eye contact, cool guy. The girls were equally cool, looking down at the ground, off in the distance, or anywhere but (with the occasional slip) in his direction—or if anything, looks of disinterest or boredom. It is not easy being an adolescent boy, or girl for that matter. This is where the *charango* and the *tuta kashua* song come in. With few exceptions, only young unmarried men played the *charango* in Canas" (Turino 2007: 43-7)

Associations of Sexuality and Gender. Referring to the physical body, and specifically biological attributes of male and female, some instruments are accorded sexual associations. Is not B. B. King's guitar named Lucille, and do not instrument teachers sometimes tell pupils to hold the instrument as they would a loved one? The flute of the Hindu god Krishna is playfully suggestive of phallic sexual innuendo, enjoyed by poets and singers and devotees. In Liberia and other places in Africa, drums might be thought of as female. In surprising contradiction to "our" ideas of female and male physicality, in Bali (Indonesia), some sets of instruments have two large gongs: the larger of the pair (lower in pitch) is considered female, while the smaller (higher) is considered the male (Gold 2005: 41).

Ideas about **gender** sometimes dictate who may and may not play an instrument. In Bulgaria traditionally only men played musical instruments, and the playing of an instrument was an enactment of maleness. Women who played were so exceptional that they were the immediate targets of gossip. There are exceptions, of course. Returning to the powwow for a gendered perspective, it is meaningful that women have historically been excluded from sitting around the powwow drum. The explanation for this exclusion, however, sometimes surprises non-Native students, says Beverley Diamond in her book in this series, since it relates, not to any restrictions on women's expressive potential, but to the power of their bodies. Women have the ability to purify their bodies monthly when they menstruate. Men, on the other hand, do not have this power and must drum to acquire the same spiritual strength. In some communities, the prohibition against women touching the drum has been relaxed, but in other places, it is still respected. A role that women do play is to form a circle around the drum, symbolically holding the circle together and participate in the singing (Diamond 2008).

In modern global life, gender restrictions in music are decreasing. In China, for example, modern concert traditions are more egalitarian than older ones, and there are many famous female soloists. The widespread gendered idea that females should, for instance, play the flute and males the percussion and brass is changing, if not disappearing, from American school music programs.

It can be the performing context that contributes to gender associations, rather than the instrument itself. In Japan, male musicians play *shamisen* (**syamisen**, hereinafter, as per Japanese preference) for *kabuki* and the *bunraku* puppet plays when they are staged, whereas women may play those theatrical repertoires only in concert versions. Men and women equally perform nontheatrical musical genres on *syamisen*, however (figure 2-12). In recent decades women have been hired to play professionally in symphony orchestras in Europe and the Americas as well.

Spiritual Associations.   We find throughout the world the idea of an instrument's giving voice to a sacred spirit. In the Poro or Sande secret society of the Kpelle people of West Africa, an official plays pottery flutes to produce the voice of the spirits. In Buddhism, the conch shell produces the voice of Buddha symbolically; the call on CD track 1-20

FIGURE 2.12   *Japanese* sankyoku *ensemble. From left to right: Keiko Nosaka* (koto), *Fukami Satomi* (syamisen/shamisen), *Kozan Sato* (syakuhati/shakuhachi). *(Courtesy of Keiko Nosaka)*

invites monks to assemble at a Tibetan monastery temple at dawn. Not the voice of a sacred spirit, but a spiritual connection with nature and Zen Buddhist meditation, distinguishes the Japanese *shakuhachi* (figure 2.12, CD track 1-21).

Religious associations suggest many other meanings. To some Christian Protestant groups the fiddle is "the Devil's instrument," and the names of fiddle tunes and legends certify it: "Devil's Dream," "Devil in the Kitchen," "Devil Went Down to Georgia." The harp, on the other hand, is the instrument of angels. While conservative elements within Islam have condemned many instruments for distracting the faithful, followers of Sufism, who pursue a more mystical interpretation of Islam, often embrace specific instruments in their ritual practices. The Mevlevi Sufis, for example, place the *ney* (flute) in the center of their rituals and philosophy. In the Hindu pantheon the *mṛdaṅgam* drum CD track 1-22 is associated with Ganesh, the deity of auspicious beginnings, and drummers in South India perform a brief ritual in praise of him to initiate instruction on the instrument. From the offstage instrument room beside the traditional Japanese stage of the *kabuki* theater the deep-sounding strokes of a bell invoke the meditative atmosphere of a Buddhist temple or of impending death (CD track 1-23), while the chipper combo of flute, drums, and lute invokes the fun of a Shinto shrine festival to complement the dramatization that the audience sees on stage (CD track 1-23).

Cultural Status.   Some individual instruments are accorded more prestige than others. Many peoples give primary status to the voice as the best of instruments. In South India vocal music is so dominant that there is no independent instrumental repertoire of compositions; instrumentalists perform songs (CD track 1-22). The reason for this is that the voice is the vehicle for sacred chant (CD track 1-12), from which Indian music evolved, and music remains primarily a treasured mode for the expression of religious devotion.

In Japan as in Western countries, the piano holds a high status. When European music was adopted there in the process of modernizing the nation in the nineteenth- and early twentieth centuries, the piano was a rare item; only relatively wealthy persons could afford one or had the space to house one. By the time it became widely accessible from Japanese manufacturers such as Yamaha and Kawai, the piano had accrued the prestigious socio-economic associations that it still holds. Americans can understand this easily, thinking of grand pianos that sit unplayed in living rooms as a piece of furniture, transmitting visually the aura of high cultural status.

An instrument's status can be transferred to players and makers of that instrument, so that a sociomusical pecking order develops. In the prestigious Korean court music ensemble the zither-type *komungo* is the instrument of highest status (figure 2.13, CD track 1-24); consequently, until a few years ago, when the present, more democratic system was introduced, the musician who played it held the highest personnel rank. Drums in South India are an interesting case: although the skins of dead animals are considered polluting, drums are considered powerful instruments. Whereas makers of drums, who work with the skins, are of lowest status, players who invoke the power of the instrument are Brahmins, with the highest caste status.

FIGURE 2.13 *Korean* komungo *played by Han Kap-deuk. The* komungo *is a very unusual zither-type instrument in that it has both frets and individual bridges. Its six strings are made of twisted silk. Strings 2, 3, and 4 rest on 16 graduated frets, while strings 1, 5, and 6 are supported by moveable bridges shaped like the foot of a crane. Fine tuning of the strings is executed by round wooden pegs at the bottom of the instrument. The strings are struck with a small bamboo rod.* (Courtesy of the National Center for Korean Traditional Performing Arts)

ACTIVITY 2.5 *With a classmate or two, plan a mini-fieldwork project to inquire further among your peers and in the media to discover other examples of the sorts of ideas about instruments that I have pointed out—ideas about particular instruments, associations of sexuality and gender, spiritual associations, and cultural status—and others if you wish. See particularly "Picking a Project" and "Planning the Project" in Chapter 7 for guidance. If this proves interesting to you, you may decide actually to conduct the research.*

Aesthetic Value.   As exhibitions in museums around the world attest, an instrument may be treated as an object of aesthetic value apart from its musical capacity. A drum inlaid with mother-of-pearl, a harpsichord lid embellished with painted flowers and birds, the wooden body of a grand piano gently undulating around a sturdy steel frame—craftsmanship endows these physical objects with artistic beauty.

You can find multiple meanings in the carved case of a bamboo xylophone from *gamelan Jegog* of West Bali (figure 2.14): elaborate embellishment of a valued instrument, yes, but also invocation of Bhoma, son of the forest in the Hindu Balinese pantheon, the fanged protector whose face is often carved over doorways to the inner courtyard in temples and over house doorways to prevent evil from entering.

Item of Technology.   Instruments have always been items of technology. It takes only one experience with trying to make one to appreciate the extent to which that is true. However, it took mass production and the burgeoning popularity of electronic instruments to make most of us think of them in technological terms. An average popular music band carts around and sets up an astounding amount of equipment; "the technology" is a member of the band.

People change instruments technologically on a regular basis. For example, the piano did not have even a marginally successful steel frame until about the 1820s. Only after the frame was universally in place, after the middle of the nineteenth century, could thicker and higher-tension strings increase the tonal power, brilliance, and therefore expressive capacity of the piano. Bluhmel added valves for brass instruments in 1818, and Boehm developed a system of mechanical keys for woodwinds in 1832–39. Various durable materials are being used to replace

FIGURE 2.14   *Bamboo xylophones from* gamelan Jegog *of West Bali. Carved on the center* instrument *is Bhoma, fanged protector against evil.* (*Photo by Lisa Gold*)

animal skins (i.e., membranes) on drums and strings of natural material on chordophones, and tuning mechanisms have been added to many instruments around the world, from drums to zithers.

No matter how technological a process, the manufacturing of an instrument can become imbued with deep meaning and the maker of an instrument be deemed a person of special cultural significance. The making of gongs in Java and Bali is a spiritually charged craft. Forging a large gong (figure 2.15) is a formidable task, requiring special skills and precise coordination among the members of a team of five or more men. From fieldwork observation, Lisa Gold wrote this description of the process.

Watching a gong being forged is almost like witnessing a musical performance: a number of gongsmiths work together so that every movement is coordinated. First copper and tin are melded together to produce molten bronze, which is poured into a mold in the shape of a pancake. When hardened it is placed in a fire and hammered into the three-dimensional, bossed gong shape. One person operates the handheld bellow to fan the fire while another holds the gong with

FIGURE 2.15　*Balinese gong.*　*(Photo by Lisa Gold)*

tongs and turns it to allow two other people to hammer it into shape. The hammers strike consecutively after each turn of the gong, sounding in a rhythm that recalls interlocking parts in *gamelan* music (Gold 2005: 31; CD track 1-25).

The bronze is unpredictable, and even an experienced team will occasionally fail, having to melt down and reforge. But gongsmiths have long believed that it is a spiritually dangerous task as well, requiring the smith and his men to make particular offerings and take on the names of characters from the medieval Panji legends.

Returning to Activity 2.2—the classification of electronic instruments (electronophones)—you can think of all sorts of relatively more recent instruments that are items of technology. For instance, the varieties of electronic keyboards have revolutionized the possibilities for that ilk of instrument, have they not! I count the computer as the ultimate keyboard. And the turntable has morphed into being an instrument in itself, requiring considerable skill to manipulate for musical purposes. In the hands of a vocalist, the microphone can rightfully be considered a musical instrument. In most popular music, it plays an important role in projecting the voice. By manipulating the distance of the microphone from the mouth, a singer can apply subtle control to the dynamics and timbre of the voice.

Electronic instruments are playing an increasingly important role in music making in so many ways. For instance, electronic keyboards and synthesizers, connected to powerful computers and driven by sophisticated software, offer an infinite variety of sonic possibilities, allowing musicians not only to play the notes but actually to design the sounds that their instrument makes. One further example: computers equipped with sensors that capture body gestures are now used as musical instruments. They can offer the same level of intimate control as their acoustic counterparts (Wessel & Wright 2002). In such computer-based musical instruments, software plays an essential role in interpreting the gestures and applying them to the control of processes that generate sound and musical patterns.

Item of Commodity.   Besides the economic side of instruments as items of commodity, there may be interesting effects of such trade on musical practice. The concertina in Ireland is a case in point (CD track 1-26). The **concertina** belongs to the free reed family of instruments (see the Hornbostel classification 422.2), including accordions and melodeons, all of which are popular in Ireland today. The concertina came to Ireland by the late 1800s. Mass produced in Germany and England, the instruments were poorly made but extremely loud and therefore good for accompanying dances. While they were soon supplanted in most places by the even louder accordion, concertinas continued to remain popular in County Clare. Many houses had concertinas that were used for practice and for house dances. A large number of cheap German models flooded the market there from 1900 to 1950. Because of their poor quality, the instruments had to be replaced often; they were your quintessential consumer product in a capitalist economy. Women were able to buy them at local hardware stores, and because of this, the concertina became known as a woman's instrument. That remains the case to the present; a woman plays concertina in Fig. 5.5 of this book at an Irish session. One by-result of the concertina trade in the nineteenth century, on the other hand, was the decline of the distinctive Irish uilleann bagpipe. (See Scott and Hast 2004)

ACTIVITY 2.6 *If you think of the incredibly complex set of instruments, amplifiers, and speakers (and lights, risers, backdrops, and so forth) that adorn the stages of most popular music concerts at present, it is clear that technology reigns in that sphere of musicking. Agree or disagree with this statement and be prepared to say why: in addition to musical values, other aesthetic, economic, and cultural values are being expressed in the degree to which technology is used and displayed on such occasions.*

Timbre and Aesthetics of Sound.   Finally, in this discussion of instruments as objects, there is the matter of **timbre**—the quality of the sound of an instrument or voice. "Reedy," "nasal," "growly," "golden": timbres are difficult to describe precisely in words.

It is remarkable how different instruments whose morphology is similar can be made to sound so different. The sound of a basic bamboo flute is modified on the Chinese *di-tze* by placing a paper membrane near the blow hole; the resulting reedy sound can be contrasted with that of the *shakuhachi* without membrane (*syakuhati* hereinafter, as per Japanese preference), for instance (CD track 1-27, compared with CD track 1-21).

In recent years the analysis and synthesis of the sounds of musical instruments has reached a high level of refinement (Risset & Wessel 1999). These acoustical analysis techniques have helped us better understand the ingredients of musical timbre and the corresponding synthesis methods provide composers with an expanded palette of sounds. An example of the analysis and synthesis of the *syakuhati* is provided on CD track 1-28. First, one hears the full sound of the *syakuhati* with its characteristic noiselike transients. The sound is then decomposed into its constituent frequency components. First, only the fundamental frequency is played. Then harmonics are added one by one to build up the tone. The noisy transients are then played alone, and finally the sound of the *syakuhati* is completely reassembled. The synthesized sound is virtually indistinguishable from the original.

ACTIVITY 2.7 *Pick one instrument type that you like to lis-ten to—flute, plucked lute, double reed, or drum, for example. Using the Internet or another source, find at least three greatly contrasting timbres produced on instruments of this type. Explore the reasons why the sounds are so different.*

Perhaps the most meaningful question about timbre brings us to the matter of aesthetics, in this case, values concerning the qualities of musical sound. In accordance with the sound aesthetics of many African groups, the natural sounds of instruments are likely to be disguised or complemented in some way. In CD track 1-29, a recording of the Kiembara group of the Senofo (Ivory Coast, West Africa), you can hear several examples of this. The ensemble consists of four xylophones and three bowl-shaped drums of different sizes; rattle-type idiophones attached to the xylophone players' wrists add to the sound. On the xylophones, each wooden bar is resonated by a gourd; each gourd has one or two membranes, which cover specially bored holes to alter the timbre of the sound as they vibrate. The membranes are made from the webs with which certain spiders protect their eggs. In addition, jingles made of pieces of tin and metal rings are fitted to both the smaller kettledrums.

For variety of timbre, perhaps no instrument is more flexible than the human voice. While the variety of timbres produced on chordophones, aerophones, idiophones, and membranophones can be significantly different from instrument to instrument, the variety of timbres that are cultivated by singers around the world is perhaps equalled or surpassed only by sounds created technologically on electronophones. Compare, for example, the aesthetic choice for a beautiful sound in Cantonese opera's female vocal style (CD track 1-30) and that of European bel canto opera style (CD track 1-31). Those two examples offer a contrast in the cultivation of nasality as opposed to a clear, open sound. If the aesthetics of vocal timbre particularly interest you, there are plenty of examples on CD tracks 1-1, 1-6, 1-8, 1-32, 2-1, 2-30, and 2-33.

Consensus about desirable quality of vocal sound is behind exclamations such as "Oh, I don't have a good voice" or "Doesn't she have a wonderful voice!" In the context of Western classical music, those statements are likely to have been made with reference to the European bel canto style. That particular kind of sound is best achieved by focusing on only one portion of a possible vocal **range** (pitch span).

The basic ranges from high to low are called **soprano, alto, tenor,** and **bass.** The expectation that every voice has a naturally comfortable range and that each singer will cultivate and probably expand that range only slightly is a culture-specific idea about the use of the voice. I suggest that it goes hand in hand with the popularity of singing in choruses which give people with different natural comfortable **pitch registers** (area within a pitch range), as well as less "beautiful" voices, an opportunity to make music together.

In other musical traditions the expectation for the pitch range of singers is entirely different. In North Indian (Hindustani) classical music the ideal is to sing in three pitch registers (high, middle, and low), resulting in a range that is considerably wider than most people's "natural voice." I suggest that the requirement for such a wide range is embedded within aesthetic ideas about vocal music: while a singer with a "good voice" according to the Hindustani sound aesthetic will be praised for that, vocalists are more likely to be evaluated for their musical knowledge and improvisatory creativity. Not surprisingly, with single singers taking responsibility for such range, classical vocal music throughout the Indian subcontinent is a solo tradition. (CD track 1-32)

ACTIVITY 2.8 *In your recording collection, find examples of singers you consider to have a "good voice." Try to articulate what the qualities are that make it good. Compare your selection with those of your classmates to see if there is a group consensus about vocal aesthetics.*

INSTRUMENTS IN MUSIC

Put a person together with a musical instrument and a world of possibilities opens up. Such different kinds of music can be made on the same instrument! One need only think of the violin in the hands of a Romanian Roma musician, a bluegrass fiddler, a Cajun fiddler, an Irish fiddler, a South Indian classical violinist, and a European classical violinist to realize that it is not so much the instrument as human creativity that determines the music's character.

Instrumental Capacity.   On the other hand, an instrument must have certain capabilities to meet the expectations of the players or the performing context. Instruments with small sounds (low volume) are appropriate for relatively intimate music making circumstances, and adjustments have to be made if they are to be heard in a large concert hall. Amplification techniques have made a considerable difference there, but some instruments have actually been changed—the piano among them, as European keyboard performance moved from the chamber to the concert hall.

Instruments have their own peculiar characteristics that present the players options that are idiomatic to them. One important physical characteristic is the length of the decay once a sound has been initiated. On some instruments the decay will be relatively rapid, and sustaining a sound means developing a specific technique. It is possible to sustain a pitch on a fiddle with repeated bowing across a string. Singers work on their breath control, as do players of aerophones (particularly those whose instruments have no mechanism for storing air, such as the bladder on a bagpipe). On some instruments a sustained sound is not achievable, so the effect of a sustain is created by other means; on a hammered dulcimer, a xylophone, or a drum, repeated striking will do it.

The Peruvian Andean *siku* panpipe provides a good example of achieving a sustained tone both by breath control and cooperative music making (fig. 2–16). In *sikuri* ensemble practice, a melody is played on a pair of instruments, requiring two musicians to interlock their parts (each of the first three segments of CD track 1-33). Within the large circle formation in which *sikuri* ensembles usually play, the paired musicians who interlock parts typically stand next to each other, listening most closely to their partners. Ethnomusicologist Tom Turino has often heard the musical value stated that ensembles should "play as one" or "sound like one instrument" and that there should be no "holes" (rests, silences) in a group's sound. This and other aspects of the panpipe ensemble music appear to him to be strongly guided by the broader ethical system of the community that is characterized by close cooperation and reciprocity that underpin social life more generally (Turino 2008). Each member of the pair usually holds his note, slightly overlapping with his partner's so that there are no gaps of silence in the melody due to decay of sound (Turino 1993: 44).

Conversely, the long decay of the sound of a gong (CD track 1-34) or a bell must be coped with; one possibility is to assign a sparse musical role to those instruments in an ensemble in order to avoid a muddle of sound, while another possibility is to develop damping techniques. Composers for carillon have a special challenge.

FIGURE 2.16 *Peruvian sikuri ensemble in procession.* *(Courtesy of Raul Romero, Center for Andean Ethnomusicology, Catholic University of Peru)*

ACTIVITY 2.9 *The beginning moments of Chinese ensemble music on CD track 1-3 illustrate a sustained pitch played on flute and plucked lute. Once you understand the principle of listening for the different techniques for achieving a sustained pitch, listen to CD track 1-34, played by a Thai* **pî phât** *ensemble (figure 2.17). Try to identify the instrument types. Then listen for the characteristic pattern of decay on each instrument, and how each musician handles the decay in a way that is idiomatic to that instrument.*

Another aspect of the morphology of instruments has been considered by scholars of music cognition: spatial properties, such as the arrangement of slabs or lamellae on an idiophone, relative to the move-

FIGURE 2.17   *Thai pî phât ensemble from the Fine Arts Department in Bangkok, Thailand, performing a ritual to honor teachers, 1986. On* ranât êk, *Natthaphong Sowat, on* pî nai, *Pip Khonglai Thong. These are some of the best musicians in Central Thailand. From left to right:* taphôn, ranât êk, pî nai, ching, ranât thun.
(Courtesy of Deborah Wong)

ments that occur in the process of playing that instrument. Several scholars have focused on this spatiality for African musics (von Hornbostel 1928, Blacking 1955, Berliner 1978, Kubik 1979), as have Baily for Afghani (1985) and Brinner for Javanese (1995) musics. Analyzing tunes played on the Nsenga *kalimba* (thumb piano) and considering the layout of the lamellae relative to the motions of playing, for example, Blacking concluded that "the most significant common factors of the kalimba tunes are not their melodic structures, but the recurring patterns of 'fingering' which, combined with different patterns of polyrhythms between the two thumbs, produce a variety of melodies . . . the tunes are variations on a theme, but the theme is physical and not purely musical" (1961: 6–7). Musical style, then, can be partially a result of the idiomatic morphology of an instrument, and "creativity in music may often consist of deliberately finding new ways to move on an instrument" (Baily 1985: 257).

Ideas about Ensemble. When musicians play together, the possibilities are infinite. Many factors can obtain, depending on the situation—whether they are jamming or performing formally, or the extent to which they expect to improvise music on the spot as opposed to playing what a composer or arranger provides, or whether a sociomusical hierarchy among the music makers gives one player authority. There is a great deal to listen to and think about with ensemble music making.

A good way to begin listening to music made by a group is to identify the instruments (remembering to include the voice as an instrument). In some performances or compositions or even musical styles the **instrumentation** is clear. As performed by the Dave Brubeck Quartet, for instance, the instrumentation in "Take Five" is clear (CD track 1-37). Each instrument can be tracked as it enters the performance. The drummer starts the piece, then the pianist comes in. They are joined by the string bass player and finally the sax, in prominent position. The instrumentation of the jazz quartet is nicely balanced, including all of the major categories of instrument types. The drum set incorporates membranophones and an idiophone (high hat cymbal); two chordophones and an aerophone round out the ensemble.

Heterogeneous and Homogeneous Sound Ideals. This performance of "Take Five" demonstrates both the principles of heterogeneous and homogeneous sound ideals played out in one ensemble. It would be completely heterogeneous (instruments producing clearly different timbres), were it not for the string bass's sounding so similar to the low keys on the piano. Those two sounds are homogeneous.

The **heterogeneous sound ideal**, the love of timbral variety, is widespread. Prominent examples can be found in African music (CD track 1-29) and in African musics in diaspora—of which jazz is one, of course (Wilson 1992). It is also enjoyed in eastern Arab music; the Egyptian ensemble on CD track 2-1 includes violin, flute, *qanun* (struck board zither) and vocalist. Figure 2.17 explains why the Thai ensemble in CD track 1-34 presents a heterogeneous sound ideal; some of the instruments are very different from each other.

A second reason why the instrumental parts are clear in "Take Five" is that each instrument enters separately, therefore noticeably. The heterogenous sound ideal and the same principle of bringing in instruments in clear succession occurs in other ensemble music—in the ancient Japanese court music, *gagaku*, for instance (CD track 2-2; figure 2.18). In the brief prelude in CD track 2-2, the instruments enter in almost

FIGURE 2.18 *Japanese* Gagaku *ensemble. From left to right: Front row, shōko, taiko, kakko; middle, kotos, ryūteki, hichiriki, biwas; rear, ryūtekis, hichirikis, shōs. Members of the Tenri University Gagaku Ensemble.* *(Courtesy of Koji Sato)*

ritualized order; this has become standardized in the approximately thirteen hundred years of the music's existence.

> **ACTIVITY 2.10** *Listen to the* gagaku *selection (*netori*) on CD track 2-2. Identify each type of instrument as you hear it enter; here I give you the instrumentarium, but not the order of entry: Stringed (*koto *and* biwa*), flute (*ryūteki*), organlike free reed (*shō*), sharp-sounding drum (*kakko*), and double-reed (*hichiriki*).*

Conversely, the idea of a timbral blend—a **homogeneous sound ideal**—occurs in countless ensembles around the globe, in groups as different as a Polynesian chorus from the Cook Islands (CD track 2-3) and a brass quintet (CD track 2-4, figure 2.6). Sometimes, *seeing* the ensemble playing is the only way to *hear* the instruments individually. You might hear Central Javanese *gamelan* music in that way (CD track 1-9, Figure 1.5); the homogeneous sound on primarily bronze **metallophone**s (pitched metal percussion instrument) and the style of the music create a kind of floating, calm sound. Santosa (2001) writes eloquently about the quality in *gamelan* music desired by villagers with whom he did field research. Listening mostly to radio broadcasts, they sought an atmosphere that evokes the contemplative state: "I want to cite an example in which a middle-aged man claimed that the atmosphere of gamelan performance is similar to that [atmosphere] people want to get when meditating. . . . When conducting meditations he felt *nganyut-nyut*, the state of mind that brought him close to God." It is music meant to hold desire in check. Above all, Santosa found that the *gamelan* tradition is an activity that conserves relations not only among patrons and musicians but also among members of the community; it is a communal practice in which no one individual stands out. Thus the homogeneous sound of the *gamelan* expresses Javanese culture.

The idea of the homogeneous sound ideal is stretched somewhat when an ensemble consists of instruments whose sounds are basically similar but are distinguished by difference in the pitch range—the brass instruments in CD track 2-4, for instance, and the European bowed lutes from high to low—violin, viola, cello (figure 2.5), and bass.

Dividing a large pitch range among several instruments of the same type occurs in much larger ensembles as well. An instance of this is the Peruvian *sikuri* ensemble, which consists of three (sometimes five) sizes (*cortes*) of the *siku* panpipe (figure 2.16) plus drum, usually the wooden double-headed *bombo* drum. Playing the same melody in multiple pitch registers simultaneously greatly enriches the sound of the ensemble (CD track 1-33). The first thirty seconds of CD track 1-33 features the *cortes* called *chili* or *suli* playing a melody of the "Toril" genre, at the highest pitch register of the three sizes of the panpipe demonstrated here. The next thirty seconds gives the same melody played on the middle-register *corte* called *malta*; musicians identify the *malta* as the principal melody carrier of the sizes of *siku* panpipe. The unmistakably lower-register *sanja* is played in a third segment of thirty seconds. For the final portion of CD track 1-33, all three are featured, entering one by one. For this recorded example an ensemble of twenty to twenty-four performers is pared down to six, two playing interlocking parts on each size of panpipe. A large ensemble might even include two more sizes of the instrument (Turino 1993: 41–47).

The practice of dividing a large pitch range among several instruments of the same type ooccurs in a number of ensembles in Southeast Asia, as well. In figure 1.5 you can see two of the three sizes of **saron** in the Central Javanese *gamelan*; the lowest-pitched in the third row has bigger, thicker slabs than the middle-pitched in the center. (The highest-pitched is not visible.) Their musical parts are quite different: the higher the register of the instrument, the faster the musical part moves. The performance practice, then, is different from that of the Peruvian *sikuri* ensembles.

One final example brings into play all three ideas I have presented thus far about ensemble: timbral mix, multiple sizes of similar instruments, and highlighting of selected instruments. The sound of the mariachi ensemble combines both homogeneity and heterogeneity (CD track 1-7). Homogeneity is there instrumentally with the two plucked lutes: the *vihuela* and *guitarrón* that are special to the mariachi ensemble. They were created in Mexico, and although they were based on earlier instruments brought from Spain, they are unique in origin and to western Mexico and are easily recognizable by their shape and sound (figure 2.1, CD track 1-7). When combined with the violin, as was often the case before the 1940s, the ensemble sound was still relatively homogeneous. Dynamic heterogeneity is assured by the trumpet that was added to the string ensemble in the latter half of the twentieth century, as well as by the voices in contrast with instruments and the one voice contrasting with the vocal duo.

ACTIVITY 2.11 *Pick three of your favorite musical performing groups and think about the instrumentation. Do the instruments contribute to a homogeneous or heterogeneous sound ideal, or a bit of both?*

Musical Roles. An additional way to think about ensembles is to consider the nature of the musical roles assigned to the instruments. In an ensemble making North Indian classical music, three musical roles will be filled: the playing or singing of a melody, maintenance on an instrument of a basic pitch reference (a drone), and rhythmic accompaniment on a percussion instrument (CD track 1-15, 1-32). In large steelband ensembles, in which there are multiple sizes of pans and complex arrangements, the musical roles are likewise delineated: the high-pitched tenor pans play melody, the lowest-pitched bass pans play a bass line, and midrange pans "strum" as if they were the plucked lute (*quatro*) of Trinidadian calypso. CD track 1-2 permits you to hear parts separately for "Back Line," a composition for steelband by arranger Len "Boogsie" Sharpe (Activity 2.12); you can hear the full ensemble, Phase

II Pan Groove, playing "Back Line" on the CD of Shannon Dudley's book on Trinidad in this series.

ACTIVITY 2.12. *CD track 1-2, separate steelband parts of "Back Line," is played by a small group of six people instead of twenty-five, students at the University of Washington, Seattle, and friends of Shannon Dudley. A full ensemble would include more instruments—including a whole battery of other percussion referred to as "the engine room." This recording starts with only a pair of conga drums to give the steady underlying beat. Follow this guide as you listen.*

0:15   1. Bass pans playing bass line.
0:34   2. Bass + double second pans strumming chords. (Notice that the seconds' strum is constantly off-beat, contrasting with the on-beat pulse of the bass.)
0:54   3. Bass + double seconds + tenor pan playing melody
1:14   4. Adding double tenor to double the melody at the octave. The double tenor is a pan that is similar to the seconds that adds depth and power to the melody by playing it in a lower register.
1:34   5. Adds triple cellos strumming chords (played twice). Cellos enrich the harmony and play a strum that contrasts somewhat with the seconds; you can hear the low-pitched cellos strum best in the second half of the section.

Although melody is often the easiest part to identify, all the parts together greatly influence how one hears and feels music.

The words **solo** and **accompaniment** delineate musical roles. "Soloist" is a somewhat confusing word, since on the one hand it means someone who makes music totally alone and on the other refers to a person in an ensemble whose music is meant to stand out most prominently—like the opera singer on CD track 1-31 and the North Indian singer on CD track 1-32. We are likely to assume that a musical hierarchy is at work, with the "soloist" more important than the "accompanist(s)." Beware of that, however! In musical styles like jazz (CD track 1-37 "Take Five") and North Indian instrumental genres the "soloist" role might pass from music maker to music maker, so the role of "accompanist" shifts too (CD track 1-15).

The words "conductor" and "leader" and "master" also name musical roles. In some performance traditions, a leader is visually obvious: the conductor of a Western orchestra, for example. In both the Central Javanese *gamelan* (CD track 1-9) and some Chinese ensembles, however, a drummer leads the timing of the performance; he sends musical signals by drumming patterns that are embedded in the fabric of the music. There are, then, both highly visible and clearly audible types of "conductor." The master drummer in an African musical ensemble is both visible and audible; he is the one musician who is free to improvise, and he signals through drumming when the other musicians should change their musical parts (figure 2.19, CD track 1-5).

FIGURE 2.19 *West African Music Ensemble. C.K. Ladzekpo, master drummer, teaching a class at the University of California, Berkeley. Left to right:* gangokui *(bell); C. K. Ladzekpo, standing (playing* atsimevu *[lead drum]); George Glikman, standing (playing* gangokui*); Tsz Hin Ng, sitting (playing* sogo*); Katherine Bones, sitting (playing* kidi *[2]); Kevelyn Hare, sitting (playing* kagan*). (Photo by Kathleen Karn)*

Musical roles in ensembles may be taken by persons other than performers. In Trinidadian steelbands (CD track 1-2), an arranger makes musical decisions, assuming a leadership role that in earlier days was accorded to those who were able to make the instruments—the tuners—because it was not possible to buy them from someone else. They work with section leaders of subgroups in the ensemble who are appointed for their playing skills.

Aesthetics of Ensembles. Perhaps the most important ideal for an ensemble is the way the musicians interact during performance, the way they contribute to enhancing the overall sound of the group but also the silence. Balinese *gamelan* music exploits sudden starts and stops, requiring split-second coordination as silence as well as sound is used to dramatic effect (CD track 2-5).

Musicians in the ensemble coordinate their movements so well that they seem to move as one musician with a single spirit. For an individual Balinese musician, the ultimate goal is to contribute to a sense of oneness with a group of musicians, whether the group is a duo or a forty-five-member ensemble. This oneness results from years of training and practicing together, working toward the ultimate aesthetic of tight precision, called **kompak** ("compact") or *sip* ("tight"). Balinese music is a deeply communal practice. The aesthetic of tight ensemble coordination can be found in a number of musical practices. The Venezuelan artist Cheo Navarro articulated the aesthetic of *salsa* as "the rhythmic feel" resulting from the well-performed interlocking rhythmic patterns of the timbal, conga, and bongo drums (Berrios-Miranda 1999; figure 1.3, CD track 2-6).

In this chapter I have considered several ways of thinking about instruments. As objects they have been classified in different ways in different cultures, have accrued extra-musical associations, and expressed aesthetic values both visually and in terms of sound quality. Interrelationships among musicians, their instruments, and the music they make were explored through ideas about ensemble. In the next chapter I turn my attention to the organization of musical time, focusing first on rhythm, then on speed.

CHAPTER 3

Thinking about Time

∞

In this chapter I explore the ways in which musicians organize time in music. Except when there is a constant drone, there is always **rhythm** in musical sound, created by successions of durations. In a context filled with sound, the absence of sound (i.e., silence) becomes significant as well. A consistent set of terms is used in talking about time in music, including "rhythm," "pulse," "beat," "count," "feel," "groove," "rhythmic mode," "meter," and others.

> **ACTIVITY 3.1** *Conduct this mini-fieldwork project with at least five of your friends. (1) Before you read further, write definitions of these terms: "pulse," "beat," "count," "feel," "groove," "rhythm," "meter." (2) Ask your friends to define the terms. (3) Play for each friend a musical piece of your choice and ask each separately to talk about it using those words. Where is there consenus, where difference, among the definitions? If they use other words to describe time in the music, keep track of them. You will emerge with a sense of your and their perceptions about the flow of musical sound.*
>
> *One of my students, William Cho, made an interesting observation after doing this activity: "One friend did notice the same thing I did—that most of these terms are used for distinct categories. For example, you would not say that "Für Elise" has a nice groove . . . a nice rhythm perhaps" (2007). Did you find the same thing?*

In coordinating the definitions of terms as authors are using them in the case studies in this Global Music Series, I found the greatest differences in the way we understand the practices encompassed by terms pertinent to the organization of time. That is because concepts of musical time differ greatly in different traditions. Our teachers have explained the ideas in their own ways, and we ethnomusicologists assume the task of translating them. In so doing, we draw on a vocabulary that is small because relatively little attention has been paid to time in European art music—the source of most musical terminology in English-language writing. This has caused single words to have multiple meanings; the term "meter," for instance, is applied to qualitatively different concepts about the organization of musical time. The implications of the words "rhythm" as opposed to "meter" and "pulse" as opposed to "beat" are particularly confusing.

RHYTHM

It is useful to distinguish between **rhythm** in general and "a rhythm." By "rhythm" I mean the aspect of music having to do with the duration of sonic events in time—any succession of durations. "A rhythm," in contrast, is a specific succession of durations.

Pulse. More often than not, musicians organize rhythm in some purposeful fashion. Rhythm in dance music, for example, or in rap, is very purposefully organized. Whether you call the steady, equal-length durations that organize rap "pulse" or "beat" or something else, it is clear that organizing time is a defining characteristic of the rap style. Enunciating steady, equal-lengthed durations is a basic unit in music with organized time. I call this **pulse,** comparing it to the heartbeat; calling it **beat** is common too.

A good way to focus on the organization of time in music is to try to feel a pulse—steady, equal-length durations that are somehow enunciated musically. It helps to move with the music—nod your head, pat your foot, clap your hands, tap a finger discreetly, get up and dance. Move! In giving this direction to move, I acknowledge that growing up dancing or embodying a sense of rhythm in some other way is not in everyone's experience. In some cultures young people are taught to move their bodies as little as possible; whatever the reason—gender, class, religious belief—that can affect their perception and practice of rhythm. So I recommend strongly that you do a lot of beat-keeping to music when you listen, even if it is a mental rather than physical exercise.

ACTIVITY 3.2 *Play some of your favorite music and, as you listen, express the pulse you feel. Do not try to count anything; just feel the pulse. For variety, you might try feeling regular durations in some of the music on this book's CDs.*

This is a good time to review all the musical selections I have referred you to thus far and to be sure that your accumulative record of each track is complete. As you double-check, relisten to them all for the purpose of feeling a pulse—or not.

Without Pulse. On the other hand, as you will have discovered by doing Activity 3.2, musicians sometimes purposefully leave rhythm unorganized, that is, with little or no sense of predictability about the organization of time. Scholars speak of the resulting music in various ways: as being in free rhythm or **nonmetrical**, as (*parlando*) **rubato** or pulseless free flow in time. Such a rhythmic style occurs in many musical practices around the world, and any number of reasons could account for the practice. A specialist in Balkan music, Tim Rice, suggests a sociocultural value when he writes of how Bulgarians perform nonmetrical melodies primarily when people get together to socialize while sitting around a table—as at a wedding. Sitting around a long table on which the hosts place food and drink is a configuration that in Bulgaria nurtures good conversation and good company and, Rice suggests, symbolically represents and performs the unity of the gathering. The playing of slow, nonmetrical melodies or the singing of slow, nonmetrical songs that the community knows helps this performance of unity because such songs link the event to events that people have experienced in the past (2004:13).

In some instances, music without pulse is a structural principle, an expected way of beginning a musical selection. On CD track 2-5 Balinese *gamelan music*, the rhythm of the entire first section of the composition (through 2:30) is tightly organized, but not by pulse; it is nonmetrical.

The whole of CD track 1-14 is free rhythmically; that is, the musician was free to do whatever he liked rhythmically, as long as it was not constrained by a meter (see p. 86). Indian musical selections are likely to begin in free rhythm.

On CD track 1-34, an entire Thai *pî phât* ensemble plays nonmetrical rhythm (not organized in regular units) to initiate a piece. Louis

Armstrong chose to begin "West End Blues" (CD track 2-7) with a trumpet solo in free rhythm.

Extending this principle, in much Japanese *syakuhati* music the rhythm of an entire selection (beyond an excerpt such as that on CD track 1-21) is nonmetrical, sustaining a meditative mood. The music is precomposed to be that way, as is the nonmetrical beginning of CD track 2-1, Egyptian ensemble music. The selection on CD track 2-1 is the instrumental introduction (**muqaddima**) and beginning of a song performed by the legendary Umm Kulthum. Scott Marcus refers to this initial ensemble section as "the *rubato* section," in *parlando rubato* (2007).

Coordinating through "breathing rhythm," the members of the conductorless Japanese *gagaku* ensemble introduce the melodic mode of the selection they are about to play with an introductory prelude-like **netori**. Trying to find regular durations through CD track 2-2 is fruitless; breathing with it is a more appropriate idea.

> **ACTIVITY 3.3** *Pick up whatever object you have at hand to use as a percussion instrument and play with creating rhythm that is first regular, then free, then regular, then free. This will help you embody these two different senses of rhythm in time.*

Rhythm for the Text Alone.　In some music the rhythm is the servant of the text. **Recitative** in Western opera is one example of this. As its name implies, recitative is singing that imitates and emphasizes in both rhythm and pitch the natural flow of speech. Although the melody has been precomposed, an opera singer can have fun with the rhythm as Carmen does in her four-line response to the soldiers who are anxious for her attention: "When will I love you? Really, I don't know. Perhaps never, perhaps tomorrow. But not today. That's certain!" (CD track 1-31, from 0:32 to 1:01).

Traditions of religious chant exist for the purpose of rendering sacred texts, so the rhythmic setting of the text is of particular concern. On CD track 1-1, moments of recitation of the second chapter (*sura*) of the Qur'ān express these words: "In the Name of God, the Merciful, the Compassionate." Not only these devotees of the Qadiriya Sufi brotherhood in Turkey but all Muslims everywhere adhere to rules for the rhythm that were established to elucidate the text when reciting the sacred text revealed to the Prophet Muhammad.

ORGANIZING TIME INTO UNITS

In most of the world's music, musicians organize time into units longer than one pulse/beat/count. Terms for the different sorts of units are "meter," "rhythmic mode," "clave," and others. In the rest of this chapter, I provide examples of different sorts of units—meters of several varieties, rhythmic modes, polyrhythm, and such. I lay them out for you with two perspectives—quantitative, and qualitative.

The quantitative perspective is numerical, giving us, for instance, the basic defining feature of units of musical time: some total number of beats. The quantity can be anything—from a two-beat *samba* meter to a South Indian *tāla* cycle of 128 counts. In every case, the unit functions to mark off musical flow through time. The qualitative perspective takes into consideration, for instance, how the unit may be articulated—performed so that you feel it (or not) in musical practice.

One more general point for you to think about. In the case of the first types of meter I present—duple and triple, simple and compound, assymetrical and then South Indian *tāla*—performers and composers can choose whatever qualitative way they wish to make listeners aware of the metric structure—melody, harmony, instrumentation, drum pattern, dance pattern, hand clapping, or something else. In the systems I get to beyond those, the means of articulating the meter is "given" in some way.

Duple and Triple Meters.   Quantitatively, the simplest meters have two or three counts; the former is called "duple," the latter is called "triple." Each unit of two or three counts constitutes a **measure** or **bar**, terminology from Western music notation, which puts vertical bars (measure bars) between units (see figure 1.12).

Meters with multiples of two counts are considered to be duple meters—units of four counts, for instance: **1** 2 3 4 | **1** 2 3 4 |. It is common for a four-count unit to feel like it comprises subunits (2 + 2), owing to stress being put on count 3 in addition to the expected strong stress placed on count 1 (the **downbeat**): | 𝅘𝅥 • 𝅘𝅥 • | 𝅘𝅥 • 𝅘𝅥 • |.

ACTIVITY 3.4 *Listen to CD track 2-7 "West End Blues," past the beginning trumpet solo; in the first chorus the pianist clearly articulates the counts 1 2 3 4 | 1 2 3 4 |. Each chorus is twelve measures long; this is a perfect example of what is known as "twelve-bar blues," with each bar being four counts long. Do you feel the four counts in a bar being performed as 2 + 2?*

A three-beat unit, triple meter, is demonstrated by "Marieke" (CD track 2-8), most often associated with the late Belgian poet, songwriter, and cabaret performer Jacques Brel. The triple meter is articulated clearly in the bass with a primary stress on 1 but a secondary stress on 3 that anticipates the next count 1. In addition, **waltzes** are in triple meter; if you have danced a waltz, you have already embodied the feeling of it.

Meter is usually defined as a pattern of strong and weak counts. That definition is qualitative, rather than quantitative, telling you how you might expect the unit to be articulated. However, the stress pattern of the meter is not always so clearly performed, so that definition does not always work well.

Whether or not to articulate the pattern clearly is a musical option. CD track 2-9, the Waltz in C-sharp Minor by the Polish composer Frédéric Chopin (1810–49), for instance, is a waltz meant for concert presentation. Its speed is too fast for dancing, and there is considerable ebb and flow in the pace of the counts, as appropriate in the rubato performing style. If you were to listen to the entire piece, you would notice moments when the triple meter is hard to feel because it is not being articulated by musical stresses; it is still there however—in theory.

In fact, some musical practices that add rhythmic interest can confuse the sense of the metric unit. One of those is rhythmic syncopation. (With syncopation, the word "beat" is more usual than "count" or "pulse.") Once a regular beat is firmly established, rhythmic interest can be added by putting an accent in an unexpected place. If you count 1 AND 2 AND 3 AND 4 AND, stressing the AND, you have got the sense of "offbeat" syncopation. Another type of syncopation consists of accenting a beat where stress is not expected: If, in a regular grouping of four counts, you put stress on the "weak" counts 2 and 4 rather than the "strong" counts 1 and 3, that is a kind of syncopation sometimes called a "backbeat." If, as in CD track 2-10, the backbeat stress continues for very long, you can lose the sense of the "regular" beat. What defines the offbeat as offbeat is the framework that locates the strong "on" beat; because of that, syncopated music commonly combines strong downbeats with offbeat and backbeat stresses. Syncopation is a basic ingredient in African and African diaspora musics, but it occurs in many other musical traditions as well.

ACTIVITY 3.5   *To challenge your hearing of triple and duple meters, listen to CD track 2-11, Dave Brubeck's "Three to Get Ready and Four to Go," until you find it easy to count out the measures.*

The piece begins entirely in triple measures, with four phrases of three measures each, for a total of twelve measures. The piano gives the melody, while the bass plays on each count 1. Listen for the hi-hat (idiophone cymbal in the drum set) being struck offbeat, on count 2.

Phrase 1: 1 2 3 | 1 2 3 | 1 2 3 |
Phrase 2: 1 2 3 | 1 2 3 | 1 2 3 |
Phrase 3: 1 2 3 | 1 2 3 | 1 2 3 |
Phrase 4: 1 2 3 | 1 2 3 | 1 2 3 |

For the second chorus (from 0:12) the alto sax takes the melody. The metric pattern changes to phrases of two measures of triple plus two measures of duple (4) from that point to the end.

Phrase 1: 1 2 3 | 1 2 3 | 1 2 3 4 | 1 2 3 4 |
Phrase 2: 1 2 3 | 1 2 3 | 1 2 3 4 | 1 2 3 4 |
Phrase 3: 1 2 3 | 1 2 3 | 1 2 3 4 | 1 2 3 4 |
Phrase 4: 1 2 3 | 1 2 3 | 1 2 3 4 | 1 2 3 4 |

If you can count the pattern easily, you are very secure with duple and triple meter. If so, listen for another detail: It is in the duple measures that the instrumentalists take brief solos and play around.

Simple and Compound Meters.   Another quantitative characteristic of duple and triple meters is the way a count may be subdivided— whether into two or three parts. In exploring syncopation, we divided each beat into two equal parts by counting "1 and 2 and 3 and 4 and." Meters that divide each count or beat into two parts this way are called **simple meters**. The tune in CD track 2-12, a northeast Brazilian *forró*, is in a quick (simple) duple meter that you should be able to count in fast four-beat bars from the first downbeat (the fourth pitch you hear).

Compound meters divide each beat or count into *three* equal divisions. A compound duple meter, then, looks as follows:

Subunit: • • • • • •
Beat: •   •

In CD track 1-4, the Irish **jigs** "Tar Road to Sligo" (beginning to 1:31) and "Paddy Clancy's" (from 1:32) are both in compound duple meter, as shown with dots above. The beats are stressed musically in performance, so you should be able to feel them; saying "jiggity, jiggity" along with the music may help you feel the division. (A variant of the Irish jig not illustrated on the CD is the **slip jig**, in compound triple meter: three beats per measure, each divided into three parts.)

Assymetrical Meters. Quantitatively, when the total number of pulses in a measure is a number such as 5, 7, or 11 (rather than multiples of duple or triple), the subdivisions within the total number of counts will be **assymetrical**—2 + 3, 2 + 2 + 3, and so forth. This type of meter is often referred to as **additive meter**. This organization of time occurs in many musics, in jazz and in Russian and Balkan dances, for example.

In Paul Desmond's "Take Five"—a composition whose title gives away the total number of pulses in each measure—the meter is 3 + 2 (CD track 1-37). It is there in the initial drum introduction, but the Dave Brubeck Quartet performs it clearly when the piano and bass come in with a pitch pattern (pitches 1 and 5, see chapter 4) that articulates the subunits.

Counts: 1 2 3 4 5 | 1 2 3 4 5 | 1 2 3 4 5 |
Pitches: 1 • • 5 • | 1 • • 5 • | 1 • • 5 • |

The bass player is given the musical role of keeping the metric pattern through most of the piece, with that recurring 1–5 pitch pattern. It is reinforced by chord changes, at times on the piano. (Pitch—including chords—is explained in chapter 4).

In his volume in this series, Tim Rice translates the principle behind Bulgarian additive meters using the word "count" to describe the basic pulse and the word "beat" to describe the grouping of pulses within the measure. In a five-count meter, a measure has five counts but only two beats, of unequal length: long (three counts) and short (two counts). Similarly, a measure of seven counts with subunits of 3 + 2 + 2 is perceived as having three beats in the pattern long — short — short:

```
Counts:  1  2  3  4  5  6  7  |
         •  •  •  •  •  •  •  |
Beats:   long      short short |
         3 +       2 +   2
```

This is the meter on CD track 2-13, a melody for the *makedonsko horo* dance, played on a *tambura* (plucked lute). It is articulated by bowing on the drone pitches. For a transcription, see figure 3.1.

ACTIVITY 3.6   *To help you hear the assymetrical meters in both the jazz piece "Take Five" (CD track 1-37) and the Bulgarian makedonsko horo (CD track 2-13), practice them first without listening. Clap on the stressed counts while speaking the counts:*
For the 5: Clap on 1 and 4.
For the 7: Clap on 1, 4, and 6.
Since it is a bit awkward to count from 1 to 7 at the fast speed of the recording, try speaking it as
1 2 3 1 2 1 2 | 1 2 3 1 2 1 2 | 1 2 3 1 2 1 2 |, as Tim Rice does on the recording to get you started.
After a while, keep clapping but stop speaking the counts. Let yourself feel the short and long subgroups with a kind of swing.
Then put on the recordings and listen again. Figure 3.1 is a partial transcription of the makedonsko horo; it might help you hear the meter.

South Indian Tāla.   South Indian *tāla* (meter) shares with compound meter and assymetrical meter the importance of the quality of subunits. The subunits (*aṅga*) may all contain the same number of

FIGURE 3.1 *Bulgarian* makedonsko horo. Performed by Tsvetanka Varimezova (CD track 2-11). *(Transcription by Angela Rodel)*

counts, or they may be uneven. There are three types of subunit: a 1-count subunit, a 2-count subunit, and a subunit that can have either 3, 4, 5, 7, or 9 counts (or, as Karnatak musicians order them, 4, 3, 7, 5, 9, for a reason explained in Allen and Vishwanathan's volume on South India in this series). Most Karnatak *tāla*s consist of particular combinations of those types. The total number of counts in a *tāla* structure, then, depends on the number of counts called for in the subunits. The *tāla* most frequently drawn on for compositions is *ādi tāla*; its eight-count grouping is 4 + 2 + 2 (CD track 1-22)—subunits of four, two, and two counts, respectively.

ACTIVITY 3.7 *On CD track 1-22, T. Viswanathan sings a portion of a song, clapping out* ādi tāla *so that you can hear the strongest counts. Count it out as you listen. The first line of text is repeated several times, and you can get the tāla from it. Count 1 of the tāla falls on "Un" of "unnai."*

Count	1		2	3		4	5	6	7		8	
Subunit	4						2		2			
Count placement	•		•	•		•	•	•	•		•	|
Text			Unnai nambinen ayya caranam, nan									

"I worshiped you, lord, I prostrated at your feet."

Permit me to reiterate a point: When making music in all the types of meters discussed thus far—duple and triple, simple and compound, assymetrical, and South Indian *tāla*—performers and composers can choose whatever qualitative way they wish to make listeners aware of the metric structure (or to obscure it)—melody, harmony, instrumentation, drum pattern, dance pattern, hand clapping, or something else. Put another way: the means by which the meter is articulated is not part of what characterizes the meter. I pointed out to you that in "Marieke" (CD track 2-8) the triple meter is articulated by the bass stressing counts 1 and 3. In "Take Five," it is the bass, but also chord changes, that articulates the meter (CD track 1-37). In the Irish jigs performed on CD track 1-4, the violinist stresses many of the main counts by the technique of down-bowing. The Bulgarian *makedonsko horo* meter on CD track 2-13 is also articulated by bowing in the drone part. In "Unnai namibinen" the *tāla* is articulated musically by the text and its setting and physically by handclaps (CD track 1-22), but South Indian musicians relish the musical play of going against the metric structure.

Thinking more qualitatively, I now turn to structures in which a particular performance practice is an essential part of what characterizes the system for organizing musical time. This encompasses such systems as colotomic meter, rhythmic mode, and African polyrhythm.

Southeast Asian Colotomic Meter.   A clear example of an essential performance practice that articulates the metric structure is found in most Southeast Asian ensemble music: **colotomic meter**, in which one or more instruments in an ensemble is consistently assigned the musical role of articulating the metric structure. In Central Javanese *gamelan* music, the instruments assigned to do this are pitched gongs.

In the *gamelan* music of Central Java, the number of counts in a metric unit will be duple—8 or 16 or 32 or 64, and so forth. Interestingly, the *last* count of a grouping—count 8 or 16, for instance—is the most significant count. That beat is clearly marked by a stroke on the largest gong (*ageng*) in the ensemble; it literally holds together the metric structure.

ACTIVITY 3.8 *Feeling the last count as the point of greatest emphasis requires considerable reorientation for those of us who are accustomed to placing the stress on count 1. Without listening to music, count out cycles of eight beats, giving the greatest weight to the eighth beat by saying the word "*GONG*" in deep tones. If you do this while walking, you will get the sense of it quite easily. Also, putting a slight stress on beats 2, 4, and 6 as points of arrival will help you feel the approach of that important last count in the cycle. Do this until it feels right for the cycle to culminate in count 8.*

The roles of the instruments that articulate the colotomic meter are as follows:

- The *gong ageng* (G), a large hanging gong marks off the whole cycle (called a *gongan*)
  - • The *kenong* (N), a large kettle gong, subdivides the *gongan* into two *kenongan*:
    - ••• The *kempul* (P), a medium-sized hanging gong, subdivides the kenongan
    - ••• The *kethuk* (t) and *kampyang* (p), two small kettle gongs, further subdivide the *kenongan*. The *kethuk* is played with a damped stroke, usually two or three times in rapid succession. The *kempyang* is the highest-pitched colotomic gong.

These roles can be heard on CD tracks 1-35 and 1-36, which illustrate a particular colotomic pattern—that of the 16-beat **ketawang** form.

Because this same pattern is played over and over again through a musical composition, it is considered to be cyclical. The last count (here 16), functions as both a beginning and ending count, so the structure is cyclical in two senses of the word.

Collapsed into a single line, you can easily see that the only count on which there is no stroke in this colotomic pattern is count 4; a **rest** occurs there. Indeed, the only count where two strokes coincide is the last count of the cycle, stressing its structural significance. A piece will end with a stroke on the *gong ageng* that is a little delayed, for climactic finality.

16	1	2	3	4	5	6	7	8	9	10	11	12	13	14	15	16
N	p	t	p		p	t	p	N	p	t	p	P	p	t	p	N
G																G

ACTIVITY 3.9 *Speak the Central Javanese* gamelan *colotomic meter of it.* Ketawang, *saying "gong" for G, "nong" for N, "pyang" for p, "tuk" (as in "took") for t, "pul" (as in "pool") for P. You will feel the interlocking nature of it if you do it with friends, dividing the instrumental parts among you.*

When you have the flow of it, including the stress pattern, listen to CD track 1-9, a composition with that metric cycle of sixteen counts. You should recognize the beginning from listening to this selection before: the short nonmetrical passage played on the gendèr *(a metallophone struck with padded mallets).*

At 0:05 the gendèr *is joined by the drummer who begins to slow the pace.*

0:09 The first GONG stroke. From this point the other musicians begin to play. It will take a complete cycle through the colotomic meter for the speed of the counts to settle down and you may not feel the beat yet. But try: the most basic melody (played on a metallophone) is sounded only on the even-numbered counts in this piece. Under the guidance of the drummer, all gradually slow down through the first cycle. A female vocalist begins to sing at 0:27 as the end of the first cycle approaches.

0.31 The second GONG stroke. Try to feel the beats. Listen for Nong at 0:47 and Pul at 0:55. There, you can hear the vocalist and rebab *(bowed lute) player shift the melody to a higher pitch register and the end of the cycle approaches.*

1:04 The third GONG stroke. At 1:08 the male chorus enters. Keep trying to count and feel the beats. Listen for Nong at count 8 (1:20) and Pul at count 12 (1:28)

1:36 The fourth GONG stroke. Nong at count 8 (2:26). At 2:28 the drummer begins to give subtle cues to slow the pace further and bring the piece to a close. The last beat is stretched greatly as the musicians wait for the gong to sound before playing their last note.

2:50 Last GONG stroke

Because the gongs that perform the colotomic meter are playing pitches in the melody, the marking of the important counts is greatly submerged in the ensemble sound. If you were sitting in the ensemble, however, you would be consciously listening to or automatically hearing them.

Javanese colotomic meters are articulated qualitatively by other musical content as well: each meter is associated with its own drum pattern. This and Javanese colotomic meter in general are discussed at length by Ben Brinner in his book on Central Java in this series.

North Indian Tāla. North Indian *tāla* is another example of a metric system in which a given means of articulation is part of what characterizes a particular meter. Two North India *tālas* that are the same quantitatively—the same number of total counts and the same subunit structure—will be distinguished qualitatively—by a way they are articulated on drums. That way is through a one-cycle-long pattern of drumstrokes (a brief composition, really) called **theka.** A Hindustani musician, if asked to demonstrate a particular *tāla* will speak the *theka*, using syllables to indicate the strokes that would be played on the drum. The syllables have some relationship (though sometimes not much) to the sound that the stroke will produce on the drum.

For example, the *tāla* with a twelve-count cycle, with subunits of 2 + 2 + 2 + 2 + 2 + 2 and articulated on the *pakhāwaj* (a modified barrel-shaped, double-headed drum) is a meter called *chautāl*. A *tāla* with a twelve-count cycle, with the same subunit structure, but articulated on the *tablā* (drum pair) is *ektāl*. The *theka* of each is different, as shown here. Underlining indicates multiple syllables spoken in one count; a + indicates count one.

Chautāl (played on pakhāwaj) 2 + 2 + 2 + 2 + 2 + 2

+	0	2	0	3	4
dha dha	dhin ta	kat <u>dhage</u>	dhin ta	<u>tete</u> <u>kate</u>	<u>gadhi</u> <u>gene</u>

Ektāl (played on tablā) 2 + 2 + 2 + 2 + 2 + 2

+	0	2	0	3	4
dhin dhin	<u>dhage</u> <u>tete</u>	tun na	kat ta	<u>dhage</u> <u>tete</u>	dhin <u>dhage</u>

Furthermore, two *tāla*s with the same structure played on the same drum—*tīntāl* and *tilwāḍā tāla*, each sixteen counts (4 + 4 + 4 + 4) played on *tablā*, for instance—are distinguished partially by the *theka* through which they are articulated. (*Tilwāḍā* is used for slow selections, while *tīntāl* is used for any speed.) Here are those patterns as taught by Pandit Swapan Chaudhuri (slight variants exist).

Tīntāl (played on tablā) 4 + 4 + 4 + 4

+	2	0	3
dha dhin dhin dha	dha dhin dhin dha	na tin tin ta	ta dhin dhin dha

Tilwāḍā (played on tablā) 4 + 4 + 4 + 4

+	2
Dha -<u>kra</u> dhin dhin	dha dha tin <u>terekita</u>

0	3
ta -<u>kra</u> dhin dhin	dha dha dhin <u>terekita</u>

ACTIVITY 3.10 *Listen to those four* thekas *spoken on CD track 2-14 by George Ruckert, author of the volume on North India in this series. Then concentrate on* tīntāl, *as follows:*

(1) Team up with a classmate or two to speak the theka *syllables without worrying about counting numbers or thinking about subdivisions. Practice this by yourself and then do it with your classmates until you can all speak the* theka *easily. Ideally, memorize it.*

(2) Now you need to get comfortable with the quantitative structure of the tāla—*the feeling of counting out 16, coming to*

completion on a next count 1, and the subdivisions into groups of counts. To do this as Indians do, you will need to do physical motions to embody the pattern: for this tāla, clap three times—on counts 1, 5, and 13. Wave on count 9; as you will feel, that divides the cycle in half. Just do the motions until you are comfortable with the pattern.

(3) Once comfortable, speak the numbers of the counts as you do the motion.

(4) When you are comfortable speaking the theka, rather than the numbers, while doing the motion pattern, you will have really accomplished something.

(5) The final step is to hear the cycle in performed music. CD track 1-15 gives excerpts from a performance in tīntāl that features sitārist Ravi Shankar and tablā player Chatur Lal. You have 18 seconds to prepare yourself to hear the tāla: the first clear count 1 occurs at 0:19. To feel the beat from 0:05 to 0:18, you need to listen to the melody—not to hear the tune, but to sense beats that are just about a second apart. It will be impossible to feel the beat from the drummer because he is enjoying a quick moment for a virtuosic solo.

At 0:18-9 start speaking the beats: 1, 2, 3, etc., to 16. Count 1 comes again at 0:33-4, 0:48-9, 1:03. (A fade-out at 1:06 marks omitted improvisation after 1:06 in the full performance.) When you have listened to the first 1:06 several times and feel secure in the beat, speak the theka rather than speaking beat numbers. Do that several times as you listen.

Perhaps you have noticed this: while count 1 is (obviously) the first count in the tāla, it is also the count on which Hindustani musicians will bring a musical unit to an end. Count 1 is thus a beginning and ending point musically; because of this, North India metric practice is thought of as cyclical.

Notice in the theka that some of the syllables start with "dh" and some with "t." A heavier sound occurs for "dh" syl-

FIGURE 3.2 *Hindustani ensemble performing at the Julia Morgan Center for the Arts in Berkeley, California. From left to right: Abhiman Kaushal (tablā), Shujaat Khan (sitār), Sudev Sheth (tablā). (Photo by Shivang Rajendra Dave. Courtesy of Sudev Sheth.)*

lables because both hands strike the drums (Figure 3.2). Only the right hand produces the lighter "t" sound on the drum. To embody the feeling of this, produce imaginary drum strokes with your hands as you speak the theka. *Once you physically get that pattern, listen to the drumming on the recording. The drummer is free to vary the pattern a bit, so do not be surprised if he does not stick to the "textbook* theka.*" Just keep listening.*

After 1:10, my excerpting on CD track 1-15 resumes 13 seconds before the next count 1, so you have time to get ready. At 1:23, start counting 1 and try to follow the tāla. *The pace of the beats accelerates a bit. The next count 1 comes at 1:36, but Shankar is improvising through two cycles of the* tāla, *so you won't feel an ending. Shankar does end his improvisational passage at 1:49*

(count 1) and turns the soloist role over to Chatur Lal on tablā
for a one-cycle chance to shine. During that cycle, listen to the sitār
*for the beats because the two players have traded roles temporarily.
At 2:01 Shankar retakes the soloist role so you can listen to the
drum again. Keep trying to follow the* tāla *as the speed accelerates.
Counts 1 come at 2:14-5, 2:27-8, and 2:40-1—the end of the
performance.*

Middle Eastern Rhythmic Modes. The Arabic term **iqá** (*usul* in
Turkish) is usually translated as "rhythmic mode" rather than "meter,"
suggesting the qualitative nature of the rhythmic aspect of traditional
Arab and Turkish music. A **rhythmic mode** is a metric structure that
also bears particular expressive qualities. (Mode, as related to mood, I
discuss in chapter 4.)

So many rhythmic modes have the same total number of counts that
distinguishing them quantitatively makes no sense. Instead, each rhythmic mode is defined by the way it is articulated, that is, performed on
a drum. (You can see in this how Hindustani drumming was influenced
by the concepts and practices taken to North India by immigrant musicians from West Asia over a period of several hundred years, climaxing in the seventeenth century.)

In the Middle East there is a great variety of drums, each capable of
producing a variety of sounds. Only two sounds, however, **dumm** and
takk (Arabic language) are used to define the individual rhythmic
modes. *Dumm* is the deepest or lowest sound the instrument can produce. *Takk* is high pitched, the sound produced when striking where
the head meets the rim of the drum.

Each rhythmic mode is defined by a unique skeletal pattern of *dumm*s
and *takk*s that create a distinctive rhythmic quality. A comparison of
three different eight-count rhythmic modes should make this point
clear: *D* indicates *dumm*, *T* indicates *takk*, and a dash (−) indicates a rest.
The names of the modes here are those used in the eastern Arab world;
they are called by different names in different places.

Count	1	2	3	4	5	6	7	8
Maqsum	D	T	−	T	D	−	T	−
Masmudi saghir	D	D	−	T	D	−	T	−
Sáidi	D	D	−	D	D	−	T	−

ACTIVITY 3.11 *Listen first to CD track 2-15 to hear the three rhythmic modes drummed and also spoken by Scott Marcus, author of the volume on Egypt in this series. Then it's your turn: speak the patterns, making deep and high (heavy and light) sounds for* dumm *and* takk. *Do this at several speeds and you will feel the relative weighting of the mode caused by the defining strokes. Another way to feel the modes is to create a dance movement pattern for each one.*

Now listen to CD track 2-1. You are familiar with the non-metrical rubato *section that begins the ensemble introduction (*muqaddima*) to the song that will follow. The* rubato *section extends to 1:27, encompassing a beginning by full ensemble, followed by interaction between a soloist on* qanun *(frame zither) and the ensemble response. The next section of the introduction, starting at 1:28, is measured—in* **maqsum** *rhythmic mode. Listen particularly for the* **riqq** *(tambourine with jingling cymbals in the frame).*

In performing music in a rhythmic mode, drummers can make some substitutions or embellishments to the patterns in the interest of timbral and expressive variety, but the mode's defining weighting needs to be maintained. The extent of the embellishment should tastefully reflect the overall context in which the rhythm occurs—little, perhaps, when accompanying a slowly moving section of a lyrical song, and much, perhaps, when accompanying a rousing dance. Options, too, are part of what makes rhythmic mode qualitative.

The Arabian Peninsula, like Egypt, has a number of unique rhythms, including *sa'ûdî*, named after the country Saudi Arabia, and *'adanî*, named after the city Aden, in Yemen. In Iraqi music, the ten-beat *jurjûna* is a characteristic rhythm not generally found in music of the rest of the eastern Arab world (for example, Egypt or Lebanon). For Lebanese, Saudi, Yemeni, and Iraqi people, then, these specific rhythms play an important role in the creation, maintenance, and celebration of their unique cultural identities. For more on rhythms in the eastern Arab world, see the Egypt volume by Scott Marcus in this series.

Korean Changdan. Korean **changdan** are in some ways similar to Middle Eastern rhythmic modes. *Changdan* are rhythmic patterns that are drummed or in some other way articulated in musical performance: "a series of accented and unaccented strokes or beats" (Hesselink 1996: 152). Unlike any other time-organizing units I have presented here, some of the rhythmic patterns (*changdan*) occur in nonmetrical music and others in metered contexts.

The rhythmic patterns vary in length (total number of counts), but the number of counts in a unit is not emphasized as a particularly important distinguishing trait of a *changdan*. In this, the unit is more appropriately called a "grouping" than a "meter" (Lerdahl and Jackendoff 1981).

Two other defining characteristics of *changdan* are new in this discussion of time. One is speed; *changdan* are performed at specified (though relative) speeds. (Speed is of some consideration in Middle Eastern and North Indian *tāla*s but takes relatively less of a defining role there than in *changdan*.) Secondly, the amount of repetition of a particular *changdan* that can occur in a musical selection is another defining trait—free repetition or a set number of repetitions, for example. This extremely elaborate system for the organization of time indicates the importance of rhythm in Korean traditional music: most Korean ensembles, like Middle Eastern and Indian ensembles, include a percussionist.

Within a *changdan* drumming pattern an aesthetic sense of tension and release should be discernible. *Kutkori changdan*, for instance, is a pattern of twelve counts, with of four groups of three counts each. Drummed on the double-headed hourglass-shaped drum *chang-gu* (figure 3.3), you can feel gathering intensity from the first six beats, climaxing during beats 7–9, and letting down during the last three beats.

ACTIVITY 3.12   *To feel the triple rhythm of* kutkori *chang-dan, first count* **1** **2** **3** *slowly several times. Stand up to try this exercise. Korean musicians think of it as a rhythmic pulse based on breath (* hohup*), so you think the counts as you exhale on* **1** *and inhale on* **2** *and* **3**. *Continue to think* **1** **2** **3** *slowly.*

Now bend your knees so that you drop down slightly on **1** *and rise slowly on* **2** *and* **3**. *This is* ogum, *deep up-and-down movement of the body, coordinated with breathing. Do this exercise again several times, counting from 1 to 12 but keeping up the triple pattern. In this way you will feel the whole length of* kutkori changdan.

Now speak the syllables for the strokes on the chang-gu, proceeding through the kutkori pattern to feel the sense of the aesthetic cycle.

1	2	3	4	5	6	7	8	9	10	11	12
Dong		dak	Kung	[da da]	dak	Kung		dak	Kung	dak	

Dong *indicates hitting both heads at the same time.*
Dak *indicates hitting the right head with a thin, flat stick.*
Da *is a lighter version of* dak, *hitting with just the tip rather than the flat part of the stick;* [ ] *indicates filler strokes.*
Kung *indicates hitting left or right head with a wooden mallet.*

Now speed it up to about one-third faster than you've been doing it. (In kutkori changdan, each beat should be counted at approximately 92–108 beats per minute.)

Chungmori changdan *exercise*
A more stately rhythmic cycle, chungmori should be counted at 68–88 beats per minute and is usually taught with the following drum syllables. Make sure to emphasize the accent on the ninth beat; this is an essential identifying characteristic of the changdan. Also note that the "dak-i" pattern on the fifth beat should be articulated so that the "dak" lasts for three-quarters of the pulse while the "i" lasts only for one-quarter of the pulse. In contrast, the "dak dak" pattern on the sixth beat should be articulated evenly. "I" is another way to indicate a lighter "dak" stroke.

1	2	3	4	5	6	7	8	9	10	11	12
Dong	Kung	Dak	Kung	dak—i	dak dak	Kung	Dak		Kung		Kung

Like "da", "i" is another way to indicate a lighter "dak" stroke.
(Exercise courtesy of Donna Kwon)

As in Middle Eastern and Hindustani drumming, the drumming patterns that articulate Korean rhythmic units can be varied in performance. The extent and the ways in which a drummer can do that, of course, are learned within each tradition.

FIGURE 3.3 *Korean percussion ensemble. From left to right: Peter Kim* (puk drum), *Eunyang Kwon* (jing gong), *Patrick Chew* (chang-gu drum), *Donee Lee* (ggwaengwari gong). *(Courtesy of Donna Kwon)*

African Polyrhythm. **Polyrhythm** occurs in many musical practices around the world, but I am focusing on Africa. Here the sense of "a rhythm" is clearly delineated from "rhythm in general." **Polyrhythm** is the musical texture of performing multiple rhythmic patterns simultaneously. In much African ensemble music south of the Sahara desert, different instruments have their own rhythmic patterns that are repeated many times, in effect multiple rhythmic ostinatos. (An **ostinato** is a constantly recurring motive.) Each rhythmic pattern functions to mark off time spans in the musical flow. The patterns are not to be thought of in terms of meter, however: each is a grouping of beats without metrical accent.

In all polyrhythmic music, something has to hold it all together. It is helpful to listen for a steady pulse; I suggest you try that in CD track 1-5. In that Ghanaian selection—as indeed in West Africa generally, however, it is not the steady pulse, but one of the rhythmic patterns, that holds it all together. Twelve beats long, that pattern functions as a timeline. To be sure it can be heard among the percussion instruments and singing, it is played on a double metal bell or piece of iron whose timbre stands out clearly.

Musicians speak the pattern of the timeline (as well as others) in qualitative, mnemonic syllables that serve as memory aids. It is given here as spoken by Yoruba musicians of Nigeria (there are a few variants). Syllable-placement creates a 2 + 2 + 3 + 2 + 3 feel.

Pulse:	• •	• •	• • •	• •	• • •
Syllables:	Kong	kong	ko – lo	kong	ko – lo
Beat:	2	2	3	2	3

In ensemble practice, all the other musicians coordinate with the bell pattern and with each other. In performance, most of the musicians will repeat their pattern until cued to switch; the performers whose pattern remains constant are the players of the timeline. In his volume on Trinidad in this series, Shannon Dudley defines this rhythmic texture as featuring "a constant rhythmic feel or 'groove' that is created by the interaction of repeating and contrasting parts."

Ruth Stone, author of the book on West Africa in this series, writes:

> A former student of mine, Alain Barker, compared the use of some Western rhythmic patterns based on an organized down beat or conductor's beat to a house built on a concrete foundation. All parts relate to and depend upon that anchoring point in the ground. He contrasted that to African performance, which uses different organizing beats and is like a tent. The stakes in the ground hold ropes that depend upon tension between them to hold up the structure. African performance frequently depends upon multiple points of organization rather than a singular focus (Stone 2005: 84)

The second primary structuring principle in this African polyrhythmic music is that "contrasting part" mentioned by Dudley. In many African ensembles one individual is free to compose on the spot; that person is likely to be the most prestigious musician. In drumming ensembles, that would be the master drummer (figure 2.19). He (it is usually a man) is in charge; he will signal the other musicians when to switch rhythmic patterns in the course of playing. His organization of time through improvised rhythmic patterns is relatively freer than that of the other musicians, but he, too, feels that underlying pulse and interacts with the multiple ostinatos, including the bell pattern.

ACTIVITY 3.13 *The Ghanaian example on CD track 1-5 is an excerpt from "Atsiagbeko," a narrative dance depicting past acts of bravery in war and the blessings of peace. The master drummer dictates the form of the dance: a series of drum patterns, each of which has its prescribed dance movement. He signals the switch from one pattern to another. In this short segment, try to hear the master drummer, the double metal bell pattern, and the supporting parts played on three other types of drums. The player of a rattle keeps the basic pulse.*

The player of bell and each of the supporting drummers repeats his own pattern, as notated here. Pulses are separated by bars. The patterns are both rhythmic and timbral: the sequence of high (x) and low (•) sounds is as important as the rhythm of the stroke placement.

First, invent your own set of mnemonic syllables for speaking each of the patterns. They should be different for contrasting sounds made on each drum. Speak each pattern until it is easy.

Then listen to CD track 1-5 and try to follow each of the instruments. Listen for only one at a time.

| | • | | | • | | | | • | • | | | • | | | | • | | | | • | *double bell* |

| | | • | | • | | | | • | • | | | • | | • | | | | • | | • | *3 supporting* |

| x | x | x | • | • | • | x | x | x | • | | • | | • | *drums played* |

| x | | | • | | | • | | x | | | • | | x | | | • | *with sticks* |

Form an ensemble with classmates to perform these four patterns. You may want to designate one person to keep a steady beat as well. Keep repeating these patterns until you coordinate smoothly. Once that happens, someone stay with the double bell timeline, but others create your own polyrhythmic composition.

Ruth Stone identifies this rhythmic practice as one manifestation of an aesthetic idea, a love of what she calls "faceting." Each participant contributes a facet (a segment) to the whole.

As I talked to Kpelle musicians about what kinds of performance they most valued, they told me that the highest form of performance, from their viewpoint, was when musicians combined . . . short sound facets to create the synchronized whole. Such faceting was considered to be quite wonderful and much to be valued over everyone singing or playing in unison—that is, performing the same music together at the same time.

It's fascinating that as a ruler, such as a chief, appeared at an official function, his (there are a few women chiefs) bearing and presence were enhanced by the sounds that were played. A few chiefs had horn ensembles using carved ivory instruments, but more commonplace were the horns carved from a lightweight wood.

The audience that observed this spectacle had come to value the horn players who created a composition that required split-second timing and how the ensemble symbolized the ultimate in cooperation between multiple players. The most valued form of music was attached to the political leader who used these sounds to reinforce his status.

Strikingly, this most performative practice for the organization of musical time reveals ways in which people make music meaningful and useful in their lives.

Music in the African Diaspora.   A number of musical genres of the African diaspora organize time at least partially through the constant unchanging articulation of a rhythm pattern that is a grouping rather than a metric structure. In Caribbean and Latin American dance genres such as *salsa, rumba, tango,* and *cha cha,* the bell pattern is transformed to **clave.** In Caribbean and Latin American music, *clave* is the term for a rhythmic pattern that is repeated constantly and without change as a rhythmic foundation for a musical selection; it organizes the rhythmic feel of the music. In her volume on the United States in this series, Reyes discusses *clave* as a musical marker of ethnic identity: "Heard by itself or as part of an ensemble, it is immediately identifiable as Latino, or more specifically, Afro-Caribbean, by those who identify themselves as such."

A number of musical genres of the African diaspora—among them *salsa*—feature polyrhythmic organization of time. *Salsa,* with its three-drum percussion coordination plus other instruments, displays a thickening of the rhythmic texture beyond *clave.* Each instrument has a distinctive rhythm or rhythms (*ritmo*) to play. *Ritmo* refers to the quality of each one of them and also to the overall effect when they coordinate. The quality is defined by timing, volume, timbre, and the manner of blending with other rhythms. Perhaps most significantly, rhythmic thinking is crucial for everyone, because both melodic and percussion instruments are approached like drums. Musicians talk about playing *afincao* (i.e., locked together), meaning that if the rhythms are not happening "together," the music is "not happening." The quality of the rhythmic ensemble, which ultimately is all the ensemble, is of utmost importance (Marisol Berrios-Miranda, personal communication, 2001).

Revealing a synthesis of different musical ideas about the organization of time, Afro-Caribbean and Afro-North and South American polyrhythm is not held together by the African timeline; rather, its rhythmic groupings work within the context of meter. *Salsa* is in duple meter with measures of four counts, but it is a two-measure long *clave* pattern that really identifies it. On CD track 2-6, moments from a *salsa*, the *clave* can be heard played on the wooden idiophone called *clave*, whose timbre stands out from the drums and other instruments and voice.

With the evidence of just the systems discussed in this chapter, it is clear that the organization of time in music reveals the remarkable musical imagination of humankind. I shall now move to another element having to do with musical time—tempo, or speed.

SPEED

Musicians manipulate speed by two basic means: they focus either on the pace of the basic beat or on subdividing the basic beat.

> **ACTIVITY 3.14** *Compare the pace of the basic beat of your favorite dances or other types of music. What is the slowest? What is the fastest? To answer this you have to go back to that basic point: find the beat! The important question is this: Why did the musicians set the pieces at the tempos they chose?*

Once a speed is established for the basic beat, both **acceleration** (speeding up) and **deceleration** (slowing down) might be used in the structuring of time in a musical selection. You have already learned about *rubato*—ebb and flow in the pace of the basic beat. But tradition dictates that North Indian classical instrumentalists will gradually accelerate the beat of a selection; never falling back, they sometimes attain a breathtaking speed that requires incredible virtuosity (CD track 1-15). Conversely, gradually slowing down, **ritardando**, to end a piece occurs in many styles.

In the performance of "Marieke" on CD track 2-8, the effect of changing the pace of the basic beat is quite dramatic. Rather than slowing at the end, the speed accelerates. "Marieke" invokes images of World War I (1914–18) in the songwriter Jacques Brel's native Belgium. As a way of bypassing French defenses and attacking Paris directly, German forces marched across the fields of Flanders, resulting in some of the bloodiest fighting of the war. Buildings, roads, nature were completely destroyed, leaving only mud and leveled land. In the churned-up soil, wild poppies began to grow. Heralded in the poem "In Flanders Fields" by the Canadian poet John McCrae, published shortly thereafter, the poppies came to symbolize the tragedy and sacrifice of the war: "In Flanders fields the poppies blow/Between the crosses, row on row." In "Marieke" the loss of a loved one (a woman) is mourned (expressed in English), as is the damage to "my fatherland" (in Flemish), with its once-flourishing cities of Bruges and Ghent (in French) (figure 3.4). As if running to escape both memories, "the day is done" comes faster and faster until the song ends in shrill hopelessness.

Rather than accelerate the pace of the basic beat, musicians might create a sense of great speed by increasing the subdivisions of the beat; this is perception rather than acceleration. In the performance of South Indian music, for instance, the pace of the basic beat, once established, should not change (CD Track 1-22). For variety in the element of speed, therefore, musicians play with subdividing the basic beats. What changes is the rhythmic density; the speed of what fills each beat increases. To demonstrate this, on CD track 2-16, Matthew Allen, coauthor of the volume on South India in this series, speaks the syllables for a short drumming pattern "ta ki ta" in three speeds. He fits it into a three-beat *tāla* that he announces on the track; he claps on count one of each *tāla* cycle.

```
[first speed]
ta      ki      ṭa      ta      ka      di      mi
[second speed]
ta ki ṭa  ta  ka  di  mi-    ta ki ṭa  ta  ka  di  mi
[third speed]
t k  ṭ t  k d  m-t  k ṭ  t k  d m-t  k  ṭ t  k d  m-t k ṭ  t k  d m
```

"MARIEKE"

Ay, Marieke, Marieke, the Flanders sun
shuns the sky, since you are gone.
Ay, Marieke, Marieke, in Flanders Fields
the poppies die since you are gone.

Zonder liefde, warmede liefde	*Without love, warm love,*
wait de wind de stomme wind.	*wails the wind, the speechless wind.*
Zonder liefde, warmede liefde	*Without love, warm love,*
weent de zee, de grijze zee.	*Moans the sea, the grizzled sea*
Zonder liefde, warmede liefde	*Without love, warm love,*
Lijdt het licht, het donker licht.	*Suffers the light with darkening sky*
En schuurt het zand over mign land.	*And scours the sand o'er my land*
Mijn platte land, mijn Vlaanderen land.	*My leveled land, my Flemish land.*

Ay, Marieke, Marieke, the stars look down
So soon, so soon, the day is done
Ay, Marieke, Marieke,
The Flanders moon won't light your way,
The day is done.

Zonder liefde, warmede liefde	*Without love, warm love*
wait de wind, (c'est fini)	*Wails the wind (it's over)*
Zonder liefde, warmede liefde	*Without love, warm love*
Weent de zee (déjà fini)	*Wails the sea (already ended)*
Zonder liefde, warmede liefde	*Without love, warm love*
Lijdt het licht (toute est fini)	*Suffers the light (all is over)*
En schuurt het zand over mign land	*And scours the sand o'er my land*
Mijn platte land, mijn Vlaanderen land.	*My leveled land, my Flemish land*

Ay, Marieke, Marieke, the bells have rung
the echoes sound. The day is done
Ay, Marieke, Marieke. In Flanders fields
The echoes sound, the day is done.

Zonder liefde, warmede liefde	*Without love, warm love*
Lacht de duivel, de zwarte duivel.	*Laughs the devil, the dark black devil.*
Zonder liefde, warmede liefde	*Without love, warm love,*
Brandt mijn hart, mijn oude hart.	*Burns up my heart, my aging heart.*
Zonder liefde, warmede liefde	*Without love, warm love,*
Sterft de zomer, de droeve zomer.	*Dies the summer, the pitiful summer.*

En schuurt het zand over mign land.	*And scours the sand o'er my land,*
mijn platte land, mijn Vlaanderen land.	*My leveled land, my Flemish land.*

Ay, Marieke, Marieke, come back again
come back again, the day is done.
Ay, Marieke, Marieke, Reviens le temps
Reviens le temps
Bring back the days of Bruges and Ghent
de Bruges et Gand

Ay, Marieke, Marieke, come back again
Your love alone, the day is done
Ay, Marieke, Marieke, your love alone
Come back again, the day is done
Come back again, the day is done
Come back again, the day is done

the day is done

the day is done

FIGURE 3.4 *"Marieke." words and music by Eric Blau, Jacques Brel, Gerard Jouannest.* © *Copyright 1968 Universal-MCA Music Publishing, a Division of Universal Studios, Inc. (ASCAP) International copyright secured. All rights reserved. (Translation courtesy of Suzanne Lake)*

In both North and South Indian musics, a core of nine patterns provide musicians with a "repertoire" by which they can increase the rhythmic density within a single beat. "Ta ki ta" is among them. In the list below, items 2–4 constitute the basic subdivisions, then 5–9 use those again, in combinations. Capital T's make that clear.

1. Ta
2. Taka
3. Takita
4. Takadimi
5. TakaTakita (2 + 3)
6. TakaTakadimi (2 + 4)
7. TakitaTakadimi (3 + 4)
8. TakitaTakitaTaka (3 + 3 + 2)
9. TakaTakitaTakadimi (2 + 3 + 4)

ACTIVITY 3.15 *On CD track 2-17, you will hear George Ruckert recite the nine patterns. When you have listened sufficiently to follow what he is doing, experience this principle of increasing the rhythmic density yourself. Either speak it with Ruckert or set your own slower, steady beat. Clap to sound it out or ask a classmate to do it for you. If you find it too difficult to speak the syllables, substitute numbers. To experience this principle of increasing the rhythmic density, set a very slow, steady beat (•) and clap to sound it out. Then start speaking these patterns to fill in the beats, keeping the pace of the beat steady. If you feel really ambitious, carry it through the nine patterns.*

•	•	•	•
Ta	Ta	Ta	Ta
Ta ka	Ta ka	Ta ka	Ta ka
Ta ki ta	Ta ki ta	Ta ki ta	Ta ki ta
Ta ka di mi	Ta ka di mi	Ta ka di mi	Ta ka di mi
Ta kaTakita	Ta kaTakita	Ta kaTa kita	Ta kaTakita

Through subdivisions of the beat, musicians in an ensemble can play different instruments at different speeds, with all parts linked by a common basic pulse. Music played on the Central Javanese *gamelan*s demonstrates this clearly. The register (see chapter 4) on each instrument correlates with the rhythmic density of its musical part: the higher the pitch, the denser the part. When you hear an extremely slow basic melody in this music, listen for extremely fast playing on some instruments. To hear this, I refer you to CD track 1-9 and Activity 3.9.

In this chapter on the organization of time I have presented some ideas and practices by which musicians mark the passage of time through musical selections. Those ideas range from successions of unequal durations in freely floating rhythm, to a single regular unit—a pulse—to various kinds of meters, and to colotomic meter, rhythmic mode, and polyrhythm. Finally, I considered the element of speed, the pace of moving through time. In chapter 4 I take up the musical element of pitch.

Thinking about Pitch

∞

I treat the subject of pitch at some length in this book for two connected reasons: pitch is the fundamental element in both melody and harmony, and ideas about pitch need to be explored in order to understand how melody and harmony are cultivated in different traditions. Accordingly, I will start by analyzing pitch in basic terms—as single **tones** and in the formation of intervals and scales. Then I will proceed to the use of pitch in melody (thinking horizontally) and in harmony (thinking vertically). This specialized metaphorical use of "horizontal" and "vertical" comes from Western staff notation, where melodies are notated from left to right and harmonies are aligned vertically.

In its most generic sense, **melody** can be defined as any selection of pitches in succession. A particular melody will have one of several forms. It might be short—as in a **motive** (CD track 2-18). It might be relatively longer, as in an Irish tune (CD track 1-4) or a mariachi strophe (CD track 1-7), or even longer, as in a jazz riff of several sections or the solos of a Japanese *syakuhati* (vertical bamboo flute) player (figure 2.12, CD track 1-21). A melody can be easy to sing or play for those familiar with the melodic system, or difficult to remember.

In its most generic sense, **harmony** can be defined as pitches heard simultaneously. How the relationship between those pitches is understood differs from system to system.

PITCH

∞

"Ken McIntyre once commented that a great improviser could play an entire solo based on one pitch alone. Coincidentally, during an interview with a young drummer, a soft background recording featured flugelhornist Wilbur Hardin, who was gen-

erating tremendous excitement with a stream of single-pitched rhythmic patterns at his solo's opening. . . . The drummer suddenly burst out laughing and, with an apology for his distraction, added: 'Did you hear that? That's what our music's about. Listen to all that brother can say with one note!'"
(Berliner, 1994: 147).

∞

The term **pitch** as a relative quality of "highness" or "lowness" of sound is not limited to musical terminology: we speak of the high-pitched squeal of tires and the low-pitched roar of a powerful motorcycle engine. Musical pitch is a more focused idea, referring to a sound that is produced more purposefully in some area, high to low.

In terms of musical practice around the world, it is useful to think of a continuum of ideas about pitch placement. At one end is a sense of satisfaction when the pitch lies anywhere within an expected general compass. In his case study of East African music in this series, Greg Barz cites the distinguished Ugandan musician Centurio Balikoowa as saying: "The temperature in our country is sometimes a bit hot, and the instruments, apart from the flutes, they respond to the weather. If it's hot they go very high. If it's cool it goes very low. So people just play without thinking that this is [this pitch] or this is [that pitch as on a keyboard]." At the other end of the continuum is the ideal of precise placement, a pitch that results when a string, a column of air, or other sound-producing body vibrates at a particular **frequency** (rate) such as 440 cycles per second. I will return to this concept later.

Some instruments can produce clearer or more well-defined pitches than others. Wind, brass, and bowed string instruments have patterns of vibration that are periodic. The repetition rate, known as the fundamental frequency, determines the perceived pitch. Other instruments like wood blocks, snare drums, and cymbals do not produce periodic patterns of vibration, and although they may sound higher or lower, they do not have clear pitches. Periodic sounds have frequency components that fall along the harmonic series in that the constituent frequencies are integer multiples of the fundamental or repetition rate of the waveform. We say these sounds are harmonic. On the other hand, nonperodic sounds like those from many percussion instruments are said to be inharmonic. CD track 2-19 demonstrates the difference between harmonic and inharmonic sounds. The harmonic sound has frequency components at 220, 440, 660, and 880 cycles per second

(Hertz), whereas the inharmonic sound has frequency components at 220, 395, 678, and 845 cycles per second (Hertz).

The practice of harmony in Western music requires periodic or nearly periodic tones. *Gamelan* music from Indonesia, in contrast, uses percussion instruments that do not produce harmonic tones. In such music the Western notion of harmony does not apply.

Pitch Names. For communication about music and as an aid to memory (mnemonic), it is convenient to assign names to pitches. This has been done in various places around the world, using syllables, numbers, or letters. A few examples are given here.

Syllables. Syllables used to name pitches (and percussion strokes) are generically called by the term **solfège**. In India historically syllables have been assigned to seven pitches in ascending order as *sa, re* (in North India, *ri* in South India), *ga, ma, pa, dha* (in North India, *da* in South India), and *ni*. On CD track 1-32, those syllables are incorporated into vocal music as text for melody; this brief excerpt sung by the late great Pandit Amir Khan begins "*re—ni sa.*" Indian musicians notate music by writing those syllables, and they appear prominently in the case studies on North and South India in this series.

> **ACTIVITY 4.1** *Make a transcription of the pitch syllables from CD track 1-32. Then invent a notation to show the melody spatially—showing the contour. Once you have completely plotted the melodic contour, redo the notation to show indications of relative durations. Are some pitches prolonged rhythmically or sung relatively quickly? When you finish, try to sing with the recording from your notation.*

Solfège syllables have been used in European music since about 1600, as follows: *do, re, mi, fa, sol, la,* and *ti* (or *si*), in ascending order. The song "Doe, a deer, a female deer," from the Broadway musical *The Sound of Music*, plays with those syllables, as in "Ray, a drop of golden sun;/Me, a name I call myself." That song occurs as the nanny is giving the children a singing lesson. In fact, that system of solfège is used for teaching music around the world; it has been widely adopted throughout the Middle East, and musicians in Arab countries, Turkey, and Iran are masters at singing and sight-reading in solfège.

Numbers. Numbers are used in music in at least two different ways. One is to indicate pitch (*do* = 1, *re* = 2, etc.). The other use is technical, instructing musicians how to produce a particular pitch on an instrument. This is the case with the tablature for the Chinese *qin* (figures 1.8 to 1.11), where notation tells the player which string to pluck. In Javanese music, where basic melodies are played out on metal xylophone-type instruments, the slabs are numbered (figure 1.5). On the *qin* and the metallophone, the resulting melodies depend on which pitches the strings or slabs are tuned to.

Letters. In the European system, letters as well as syllables and numbers are used for identifying pitches. Adopted from Arabic in the early Middle Ages, the letters in ascent are A, B, C, D, E, F, and G. Interestingly, the present-day Arab world does not use this letter system, preferring either European solfège or traditional Arab or Persian names for the notes.

Setting the Pitch. Questions arise. Where is pitch *sa* or pitch 1 or pitch A? Who sets the pitch, and how?

Who Sets the Pitch. On many instruments the pitch is fixed in construction. During manufacture, a flute will have pitch holes drilled at some points. If, as in the case of the typical Tanzanian **filulu** flute, which is invariably played alone for one's own enjoyment, there is no need to worry about drilling holes to obtain pitches that will match some other flute's (Barz 2004:10). On a metallophone, the metal will be forged and then trimmed to produce a certain pitch when struck. Tuning a bar is accomplished by scraping or filing away different parts of the bar. If the pitch is too low, metal is filed off the end of the bar, thus decreasing its mass and raising its pitch. If the pitch of the bar is too high, metal is filed off underneath the middle of the bar, thus increasing the flexibility of the bar and lowering the pitch. On the metal surface of a steel drum discretely tuned spots will be hammered out (figure 4.1). On a chordophone, **frets** (perpendicular bars or strings running under several strings) are one mechanism for indicating the pitch placement; the player presses the string down to the fret (called "stopping the string") to indicate the place of other desired pitches. Most but not all fretted

FIGURE 4.1   *Steel drum with pitches labeled.*   *(Photo by Phuoc Truong)*

stringed instruments are lutes (figure 4.2); the zither-type Korean *komungo* has frets (figure 2.13, CD track 1-24). If they are to be fixed in place, the instrument maker will have to know the musical system in order to set the pitches properly.

If the pitches are not fixed on the instrument, the musician has responsibility for setting them. While a North Indian maker of *sitārs* (figure 3.2, CD tracks 1-14, 1-15) will put frets on an instrument, he will strap them onto the neck, rather than fix them in place, so that the player can set them according to the melody (**rāga**) to be performed. On the Japanese *koto* (figure 2.12), the player positions a moveable **bridge** under each string to set its pitch, and a player of a lute-type instrument, such as the *syamisen* in figure 2.12, tightens the strings to a certain basic pitch. Beyond that, fretless bowed and plucked lutes present great challenges for players. To obtain pitches beyond those on their open strings, all the musicians in figure 2.5 and the *syamisen* player in figure 2.12 (CD track 2-20) have to memorize where to press their fingers down on the strings along the neck. They must literally embody the sense of pitch as they train their muscles what to do.

FIGURE 4.2 *Salsa Band. Left front, Héctor Pérez (bongos); right center, Rafael Angel Irizarry (Puerto Rican* cuatro*); right front, Jorgé Martínez* (guitarrón); *right rear, Marisol Berrios-Miranda* (güiro); *rear left, Karim A. Imes (drum set); rear right, Allan Stone (bass). The bongo drums (front left) are tuned the interval of a fourth apart. Note the bridges on the sounding board of each of the plucked lutes, and the frets up the necks, as well as the tuning pegs on the guitar on the left rear.* (Photo by Kathleen Karn)

ACTIVITY 4.2 *If you know how to tune an instrument, artic-ulate that process to someone who is unfamiliar with it. In addi-tion, get someone to explain the process on an instrument you are less familiar with.*

Pitch Placement. At what sound levels pitches should lie is a matter of choice in a musical style, deeply embedded in tradition.

All musicians have an ideal of pitch precision, but the ideals differ widely. Indonesian traditions provide a good example of this. In Central Java, each ensemble (*gamelan*) of instruments is manufactured to have its own distinctive set of pitches (figure 1.5). No two ensembles are tuned alike, and the aesthetic effect of its tuning gives each *gamelan* a musical identity.

In Bali, precise tuning is done with pairs of instruments. However, the two instruments in a pair are tuned precisely *unalike*: the frequencies (the rate of vibration of the sound waves) of their pitches are very close but intentionally set far enough apart in order to produce **beats**. Beats occur when two sound waves with different frequencies overlap; what we hear are resulting periodic variations in loudness. This is demonstrated on CD track 2-21, with each instrument played alone, then the two instruments together. The practice of paired tunings creates the desired bright, shimmering metallic timbre that you hear in CD track 2-5. When played together, the higher instrument, known as the "inhaler," and the lower, the "exhaler," create this pulsing effect, metaphorically breathing and thus bringing the sound of the *gamelan* to life. When there is more than one of a single instrument, such as in the metallophone section of the *gamelan*, the inhalers are all tuned alike, and the exhalers are all tuned alike (Gold 2005: 33). The contrasting pitch ideals in the Central Javanese *gamelan* on CD track 1-9 and the Balinese *gamelan* on CD track 2-5 make the ensemble sounds unmistakably different. (I am assuming that you are remembering to take the initiative to listen when I refer to a CD track, even if I do not tell you to do so.)

In classical music in the European system the named pitches (A, B, C, D, etc.) are expected to lie at some precise place, that is, at a precise frequency: by agreement in recent times, the pitch called "A above middle C" vibrates at 440 cycles per second (with some preference also for the slightly higher pitch of 442 cps). Instruments with fixed pitch are manufactured to this standard, and instrumentalists without fixed pitch are expected to adjust to it. This adjustment can be witnessed and heard through the tuning practice that initiates an orchestra concert (CD track 2-22). Before the conductor of the orchestra comes onstage and the performance begins in a formal sense, the **concert master** (the male or female leader of the violin section, who acts as an assistant to the conductor) stands to face the orchestra and instructs the lead player of the oboe section to produce the pitch A. In turn, in a ritualized order the sections of the orchestra tune. From the cacophony that soon results, it is clear that this is also an opportunity to warm up onstage. Furthermore, the tuning cues the audience to settle into silence for the performance, a practice derived from and idiosyncratic of European classical music performance.

With a sense of "in-tuneness" firmly established in one's musical soundscape, playing against it can be an aesthetic choice. One need only think of the "bent notes" that play around with pitches' "in-tuneness";

modern keyboard synthesizers have wheels on them so the keyboardist can bend the notes. The *salsa* musician Gerardo Rosales insists that *salsa* is not authentic *salsa* unless the trombonist plays a little bit out of tune; not all *salsa* musicians agree, however (Berrios-Miranda 1999).

For a performer to produce pitches at the desired frequencies is known as "having good **intonation**." An ideal once held by musicians of European classical music was to "have **perfect pitch**," wherein one could identify or produce a desired letter-named musical pitch at its established frequency even if asked on the spot; now it is considered far more useful to "have excellent relative pitch." That is certainly the case if you want to enjoy music of traditions with different senses of intonation. A sensible, flexible way to think about "good intonation" is to appreciate musicians' exceptional ability to remember what they hear, in whatever pitch system they cultivate.

A finely cultivated sense of pitch is crucial also in the classical music of North India. Producing pitches that are out of tune with the expected pitch placement is sufficient in contemporary times to ruin a musician's reputation, but it has always been so; from the *Nāradīya Śikṣā* (c. fourth century C.E.): "Wrong musical intonation is a crime in which one risks one's life, one's progeny, and one's cattle" (te Nijenhuis 1974: 36). Flexibility is embedded within the system, however: there is no standardized pitch frequency (cycles per second) for the pitch called *sa*. *Sa* can be placed anywhere a singer is comfortable placing it—not so high or so low as to prevent reaching all the pitches desired in the improvisatory moments to come.

ACTIVITY 4.3 *Experiment with singing a straight ascending row of pitches, calling them* sa re ga ma pa dha ni sa re ga ma. *Start the* sa *on several different pitch levels and listen and feel the difference. Finally, find "your* sa*," a place to start where it is most comfortable to sing up that number of pitches.*

All of the preceding discussion about pitch assumes that a pitch is a discrete entity, a sound. To musicians in some traditions there is much more to it. In Korean musical aesthetics, for instance, the moments of the sounding are just part of the aural experiencing of a pitch. Its dying away, its decay as a string gradually ceases to vibrate audibly, is at the heart of the aesthetic sense, as well: the beauty of "sound into silence." This should be clear to you from listening to CD track 1-24— the fretted zither *komungo*—particularly through the first minute and a half. The player creates vibrato with his small bamboo rod (figure 2.13) until the sound of the plucked string dies away; the decay is even more obvious when a pitch is allowed to die without vibrato.

THINKING HORIZONTALLY

Intervals. In the discussion above I focused primarily on single pitches, but here I want to move to thinking about pitches in relationship to each other. That relationship can be horizontal—that is, a succession of pitches, as in melody—or vertical—that is, in some kind of harmonic simultaneity. In either case, it is the distance spanned between pitches that comes into play. The English-language term for that distance is **interval**. The matter of intervals is more important in music in the European system than in any other, because that system cultivates harmonic relationships. Nevertheless, I shall approach intervals first as pitches occurring one after another (horizontally), as in melody.

Naming Intervals. So important are intervals in European music theory that they are given names. Two factors are involved in the naming. One is the number of pitches that the interval spans. Figure 4.3 depicts a keyboard with the white keys labeled A, B, C, D, E, F, and G.

Ascending from A to B involves two pitch letters; the interval from A to B is thus called a second. Going up from A to C spans across A, B, and C (i.e., three pitch letters), so the interval is called a third, and so forth. The interval from one note to another note with the same letter name spans eight pitch letters and is called an **octave** (*octo-*, "eight"), as in A to the next higher (or lower) A.

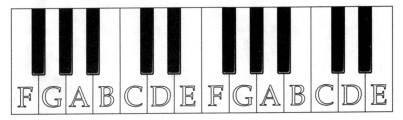

FIGURE 4.3   *Keyboard with white keys named.*   (Chart by Viet Nyugen)

ACTIVITY 4.4 *Practice singing and naming intervals in both ascending and descending order: second, third, fourth, fifth, sixth, seventh, octave. Say the letter name of the pitch as you sing it. For example: to sing an ascending fourth from A, sing A, B, C, D, then sing the two outside pitches back and forth—A and D, D and A—to get the feel of it.*

The second factor involved in the naming of intervals in the European system is the type or quality of the interval. There are different types of seconds, thirds, fourths, and the like. Looking again at the keyboard (figure 4.3), you can see two types of seconds. Between pitches B and C (the interval of a second) and E and F (also a second), there is no intervening key. Between F and G (also a second), however, there is an intervening key. The size of the second between F and G is wider: it is called a **major second**. The interval between E and F is the smaller second, called a **minor second**.

Seconds are named in another way as well: the major second is called a **whole step** (in figure 4.4 labeled *W*). The minor second is a **half step** (in Figure 4.4 labeled *H*). Figure 4.5 shows how, on the piano keyboard, the interval between any two adjacent keys is a half step.

Just as there are two types of seconds, there are two sizes of thirds—major and minor thirds. To explore these, see Activity 4.5.

ACTIVITY 4.5 *On the keyboard, count the number of half steps in the third from C to E. You should find four. This is a major third. Or think of it this way: two whole steps make a major third.*

Now count the number of half steps in the third from E to G. There are only three half steps (or, a whole step and a half step). This is a minor third.

Major and minor thirds are crucial intervals for you to hear and feel. One way to do it is to sing the familiar melody of

FIGURE 4.4 *Two ways of naming the interval of a second.* *(Chart by Viet Nguyen)*

FIGURE 4.5 *Half steps on the piano keyboard.* *(Chart by Viet Nguyen)*

"Frère Jacques" (CD track 2-23): the melody on just those two first words of the song outline a major third, first in ascent and then in descent. You might know this as "Are you sleeping?"; in that case, the major third occurs on "Are . . . sleeping." Sing it several times. Once you have that interval in your ears, try to lower the pitch on "Jac/sleep" by a half step; the melody will sound very different with a minor third.

Microtones. Many musical systems use intervals smaller than the half step, the smallest named interval in Western music; resulting pitches at such intervals are sometimes called **microtones. Quarter tone** is another term that is frequently used in a rather loose manner to describe many different "types" of pitches that do not fall into the Western scale. For example, microtones/quartertones are a feature of Arab music, which is based on a theoretical scale of twenty-four pitches per octave. The system includes all the twelve pitches per octave that coincide with those of Western music, but achieves its additional twelve notes per octave by subdividing the intervals into quarter steps. One obtains thereby half-flat" intervals–a half-flat second, half-flat third, and the like. No musician would ever play the twenty-four notes in succession; rather, the system just supplies a great variety of possible pitches from which scales may be derived. **Maqam Rast**, a melodic mode explored in depth in Scott Marcus's volume on the music of Egypt and the eastern Arab world in this series, features a half-flat third and a half-flat seventh (CD track 2-1).

> **ACTIVITY 4.6** *Listen to the beginning of CD track 2-1, the instrumental introduction to a song by the great Egyptian singer Umm Kulthum. In the melodic unit (phrase) that immediately follows the downbeat given by the double bass, the second note is a half-flat third. The penultimate note of that phrase is a half-flat seventh. The phrase repeats. Listen to the opening section several times, up to the beginning of the* qanun *(plucked frame zither) solo.*

Scale. Theorists and practitioners in a number of musical systems think about melodic material in terms of pitch sets—groups of pitches. One clear way to articulate a set of pitches is to present them as a scale, in straight ascending or descending order. (Note: this is not appropriate for some types of pitch sets.) When one hears a scale, the focus can be on the pitches or on the intervals formed by the distances between the pitches. In Indian music theory, for instance, the focus is on the pitches, while in the European system the focus is on the intervals. I shall sample a few scale types and illustrate how scalar material might be used in melodic practice.

The Chromatic Scale. Sounding all twelve pitches in an octave on the piano in ascending or descending order produces what in English is called a **chromatic scale**.

ACTIVITY 4.7 *Find a keyboard and use figure 4.5 to position a finger on pitch C, in about the middle of the keyboard. Play each key in succession (both white and black) up to the next pitch C. You have created a chromatic scale of twelve pitches.*

A dramatic example of the chromatic scale in melody is the opening of the famous aria "L'amour est un oiseau rebelle," from *Carmen*, an opera by the French composer Georges Bizet (1838–75). Much of the first part of the aria consists of a descending chromatic scale. (This aria is more commonly called "Habanera," which is actually the Cuban song form that supposedly served as the stylistic basis for the aria.)

ACTIVITY 4.8 *At the point in the story of the opera* Carmen *that is recorded on CD track 1-31, a number of women factory workers mill about onstage, trying to attract the attention of soldiers who wait instead for the sensually flirtatious heroine, Carmen. The excerpt begins as she finally enters. Carmen is interested only in a soldier whom she does not see.*

First listen to CD track 1-31 all the way through, for the purpose of following the French text (even if you do not know French).

The quick orchestral introduction to the aria begins at 1:02. In repeated listenings, focus on the chromatic scale at the beginning of the aria and through the selection. Occurrences of chromatic melody are underlined in the French text. You will hear it better if you try to sing along with the soloist. Keep listening, because that melody repeats.

(Carmen enters)

0: 05 **All**

La voilà!   *There she is!*

0:17 **Men**

Carmen, sur tes pas,   *Carmen, we're all at your feet!*

nous nous pressons tous;
Carmen, sois gentille, au
moins réponds-nous,

Carmen, be kind and at least
    answer us,

Et dis-nous quel jour tu
    nous aimeras.
Carmen, dis-nous quel jour
    tu nous aimeras.

and say that one day you'll love us!

Carmen, say which day you will
    love us!

0:33 Carmen
Quand je vous aimerai?
Ma foi, je ne sais pas.
Peut-être jamais,
    peut-être demain,
Mais pas aujourd'hui,
    c'est certain.

(after a quick glance at Don José)
When will I love you?
Really, I don't know.
Perhaps never, perhaps tomorrow,

    but not today—that's certain.

1:08
L'amour est un oiseau rebelle
que nul ne peut apprivoiser.
Et c'est bien en vain
    qu'on l'appelle,
S'il lui convient de refuser.
Rien n'y fait; menace ou prière.
L'un parles bien, l'autre se tait;
Et c'est l'autre que je préfère.
Il n'a rien dit, mais il me plait.

Habanera
Love is a bird wild and free
    whom no one can tame;
And it's useless to appeal to him,

    if he's in the mood to refuse.
He heeds no threat or prayer.
One speaks well, the other is silent;
    and it's the other whom I prefer.
He has said nothing; but he
    pleases me.

1:36 Chorus
L'amour est un oiseau rebelle
que nul ne peut apprivoiser.
Et c'est bien en vain qu'on
    l'appelle,
S'il lui convient de refuser.

Love is a bird wild and free
whom no one can tame;
and it's useless to appeal
    to him,
if he's in the mood to refuse.

1:37 Carmen
Amour, amour, amour, amour!
L'amour est enfant de Bohême,
Il n'a jamais, jamais
connu de loi.
Si tu ne m'aimes pas, je t'aime.

(first line overlapping with chorus)
Love, love, love, love!
Love is a gypsy child
who never, never heeds
any law.
If you don't love me, I love you;

Et si je t'aime,
prend garde à toi!

And if I love you—
ah then, beware!

2:05 Chorus

Prends garde à toi! Ah then, beware!

Continue to listen for repetition of the last three lines and the verse from the beginning of the "Habanera."

Long chromatic descents and ascents and quick three-pitch chromatic motives comprise much of the melodic material in the contemporary piece "Mini Overture" by the Polish composer Witold Lutosławski (1913–94) (CD track 2-4). This is a snappy fanfare for brass quintet. Within seconds of the start, the first trumpeter gives out a descending chromatic alarum, which is taken up in turn by the horn and trombone players. Immediately after, the trombonist initiates the idea of repeating three-pitch chromatic motives, answered very quickly by the second trumpeter and then the horn player. From that point you can hear rapid three-pitch chromatic motives that seem to be everywhere: 1:02 to 1:35 is thick with them, also at 1:55. The long chromatic line recurs at 2:35, recalling the beginning at the end.

Diatonic Scales. **Diatonic scales** comprise some arrangement of half steps and whole steps. If you have grown up hearing music in the European system, and you just sing the most natural scale that comes into your head, you will no doubt sing one of them—the **major scale**. You have learned it by osmosis. It is the scale you sing on the text syllables "Doe, ray, me, far, sew, la, and tea" in "Doe, a deer" (that is, the solfège syllables *do, re, mi, fa, sol, la,* and *ti* or *si*). Figure 4.4 shows a major scale that begins on pitch C. You can see there the arrangement of whole steps and half steps within an octave: W W H W W W H (CD track 2-24).

ACTIVITY 4.9 *Other CD tracks you have listened to thus far have melodies that use a Western major scale. Listen again to identify at least two of them. This is a good moment for you to be certain that you have added all the references to all the CD tracks thus far in your cumulative accounting for them.*

Another important diatonic scale in the Western system is the **natural minor scale**. Its arrangement of whole steps and half steps is W H W W H W W. Major and minor thirds play the most significant part in distinguishing the major and minor scales.

The "Oriental" Scale. Perhaps you will immediately recognize CD track 2-25 as a Spanish flamenco song—by the vocal style perhaps, or by the guitar style. The scale in the melody might also sound familiar to you; starting on C, its pitches are C D♭ E F G Ab B. You have not yet encountered in this book the interval between pitches 2 and 3, and between pitches 6 and 7; because it spans two letter names, it must be a second of some kind, yet it encompasses three half steps. Larger than a major second, this **augmented second** distinguishes this scale from a diatonic scale and establishes its "difference." The music of the excerpt on CD track 2-25 is so particular to flamenco that the scale is strongly associated with the Roma, who developed the style. Linking the Roma (gypsies) and Spain and nondiatonic melody is logical. The Roma have a long history in Spain. So, too, did peoples of the Near East (more properly called "West Asia" now) of non-Christian faiths (Muslim and Jewish) until 1492, when Ferdinand and Isabella expelled them. Left behind were assimilated elements of those peoples' cultures—including music. Even today, some musics of southern Spain suggest some cultural retention through the centuries.

Non-Romani composers have used this and similar nondiatonic scales to suggest not only the Roma but also other exotic people and places in "orientalist" fashion (Said 1978). For that reason, this scale is sometimes called the "**Oriental scale**." Begging for further exploration here are the words "orient," "oriental," and "orientalist" in order to begin to understand why the adjective "exotic" is frequently attached to nondiatonic—i.e., different—scales in the European perspective. (I can tell you from personal experience that North Indian musicians find the minimalist selection of scale possibilities in the European tradition to be quite "boring"; they find nothing "exotic" in the difference.) In the European imagination in the period of world exploration, "the Orient" meant—not Asia as a totality as one may think—but particularly the "Near East"—as lands of Arab and Indian cultures were called in reference to their location relative to the colonial powers to "the West." "Oriental" is the adjective form of "orient," pertaining in that terminology to characteristics of peoples and their cultures in the Arab and Indian worlds. "**Orientalism**" is what Edward Said dubbed the imaginative construction by European powers of a view of Arab (and

Indian) culture as the "exotic Other" for purposes of the colonial project. (See Chapter 6.) Because the word "Oriental" now connotes derogatory colonialist attitudes, English speakers today use the term with
caution.

Nevertheless, that one musical scale heard in CD track 2-25 in particular continues to suggest the generalized "exotic other," and the use
of it may outlast the use of the word "oriental." I recently heard it
employed in Ken Burns's documentary series, *The War*—first a soulful
violin line based on that scale over a vague "harmonic" steadiness
behind the telling of the bombing of Pearl Harbor, a musical underlining of the otherness of the Japanese to Americans, and then again as the
genocide of the Polish Jews—Hitler's other—is narrated. From the earlier discussion of microtones/quarter tones, you can realize what an
essentializing connotation has clung to that particular scale. However,
many types of nondiatonic scales exist and in many musical systems
around the world.

Number of Pitches in an Octave.   To consider scales on a worldwide basis, it is useful to think in terms of the number of pitches that
lie within an octave. There are numerous **heptatonic** (seven-tone) scales,
of which the European major scale is one (CD track 2-24). From the perspective of the total number of pitches within an octave, Arab music
scales, too, are all heptatonic—selections of seven pitches from the
twenty-four possibilities mentioned under "Microtones." The scale on
CD track 2-1 is an example. **Pentatonic** (five-tone) scales are also numerous, such as the scale of "Auld Lang Syne" (C, D, E, G, A), sung to mark
the beginning of a new year.

ACTIVITY 4.10   *To experience music with two different pentatonic pitch selections, first sing "Auld Lang Syne." Then listen to CD track 1-9, a selection in a Javanese tuning system
called* sléndro, *which is pentatonic. While the pentatonic scale
of "Auld Lang Syne" has a clear "gap" between pitches E and
G, Javanese* sléndro *positions the five pitches more or less equidis-
tantly within an octave.*

*Listen to the Irish ballad on CD track 1-8 again. Try to make
out the pitch selection and make a scale from the pitches.*

While "we" usually think about pitch selections in terms of pitches within an octave, there are other possibilities. One is the concept of **tetrachord** as an analytic tool. A tetrachord is a four-note scalar segment whose first and fourth pitches are separated by the interval of a perfect fourth (for example, C to F, D to G). On CD track 2-27, you can hear the heptatonic scale on CD track 2-26 as the combination of a lower tetrachord and an upper tetrachord. (See Marcus 2007.) Modern Arab music theorists usually recognize nine different tetrachords, each with a unique intervallic configuration, each named. On CD track 2-27, you hear the tetrachord named **rast** as both the lower and upper tetrachords. CD track 2-28 gives you *rast* and two others—**nahāwand** and **hijāz** for comparison.

Pitch Functions.   Whether you have a set of five, six, twelve or some other number of pitches in a set, the idea of assigning some particular function to one or more of them is widespread. A South Indian classical *rāga* (**melodic mode**) is likely to have a beginning pitch, an ending pitch, and "life-giving tone(s)" on which the melody pauses and dwells.

An extremely common musical practice is to establish a **pitch hierarchy**; that is to say, some pitch in a pitch set is given more importance in melody than other pitches. Ethnomusicologists have called it various things: a **tonal center**, a base note, a fundamental, or a primary pitch. One can often sense a tonal center in listening to melody, perhaps because the pitch occurs frequently or because the melody comes to an end on it. The best way to locate a tonal center is simply to listen and let it emerge in your hearing—and not worry if you cannot sense it at first.

ACTIVITY 4.11   *Try feeling the tonal center in these selections: CD track 1-2, Trinidadian steeldrum; CD track 1-3, Chinese ensemble, "Moderate Tempo Six Beats"; CD track 1-6, "Ballad of César Chávez"; and CD track 2-23, "Frère Jacques" ("Are you sleeping").*

In the European tradition the tonal center is called a **tonic**, and the system of music that is organized around having a functional tonic is called **tonal music**. It is appropriate to think of "tonic" as a "home pitch" because in tonal music aesthetics there is a definite sense of finality associated with returning to the tonic pitch to end a piece. You can feel this clearly on CD track 2-7, "West End Blues."

Any pitch in the European system can be the tonic of a major or minor scale. The resulting tonality is identified as a **key**: the key of A major (A is *do*) or the key of A minor; the key of D major (D is *do*) or the key of D minor. Keys are useful in several ways, one of which is performing music at a pitch register that is comfortable for your voice or on your instrument.

> **ACTIVITY 4.12** *Find a comfortable pitch for yourself, from which you can sing a major scale up, covering about an octave. Identify your comfortable key by finding the starting pitch (the tonic) on the piano.*

Hierarchy is so important in tonal music that three other pitches in a key are designated as more important functionally. The important pitch that is five pitches up from the tonic is called the **dominant**; in "Take Five" (CD track 1-37) the bass player articulates the metric structure by alternating between the tonic and dominant. The pitch located four pitches up from the tonic is the **subdominant**. A third important pitch is generally called the **leading tone**; located a half step below the tonic (or, in the less common case of the "upper leading tone," a half step above tonic), it is used to create a feeling of going toward the tonic.

Mode. Beyond the rather abstract idea of pitches and their functions, intervals, and scales is another way of thinking about what constitutes fundamental melodic material on which compositions and improvisation are based. That is **mode**, an idea about pitch and melody that encompasses both explicitly musical practice and extramusical associations. European major and minor scales are modes, in that there is sometimes a mood associated—a sense of major as "happy" and a sense of minor as "sad." "Association" is the operative word here. Tom Turino points out how, unlike in North America where the minor scale that begins with a minor third is associated with sad, somber, or serious emotions, it has no such emotional meanings for indigenous Andean people of South America. Rather, it is speed that bears an association with moods: slow tempos communicate more serious or profound sentiments, and fast pieces are associated with upbeat emotions (2007). In addition to mood (or instead), it is musical practice that distinguishes modes. Rajna Ledoux has described the way she learned about mode in Turkish music, there termed **makam**.

Every Tuesday morning I would meet my teacher, Yusuf Ömürlu Bey, for my lesson. Each time, he would have ready two identical binders containing select vocal and instrumental pieces in one *makam*. With these binders on his desk—one for him, the other for me—introduction of a new *makam* would commence. As he is browsing through the sheets deciding which tune we will start our lesson with, Yusuf Ömürlu Bey is humming in free rhythm a vocal improvisation, a *seyir* of a *makam* I am about to learn. This little ritual is followed by his explanation of the properties of the *makam*. He would write a scalar formation of a *makam*, clearly defining its tonic and dominant with whole notes, delineating its tetrachord and pentachord with arches, showing acoustical relationships between adjacent notes with standard symbols [letters] and also the general melodic progression of the *makam*.

Up to this point, Yusuf Ömürlu Bey's instruction is very systematic and does not depart from the explanations one can find in textbooks on Turkish music theory. His instruction is musically mute, my teacher never finding any reason to demonstrate either the scale or those nuances with his voice.

From that point, however, Yusuf Ömürlu Bey's instruction departs to the more illusive and poetic realm of "colors" [*renkler*] or "fragrances" [*kokular*] of the *makam* in question. This is where his passion for Turkish music and Turkish melody becomes obvious. As he demonstrates with his voice these *colors and fragrances in the form of characteristic motif, change in register, shift to important functional degrees, and melodic alterations that give particular identity* to the *makam*, his facial expressions depict *the emotional feel* of the *makam* that puts it into the realm of poetry. He frequently describes them with poetical tropes such as melancholy, happiness, and so forth. As a conclusion, Yusuf Ömürlu Bey hums another vocal improvisation demonstrating discussed features of the *makam* for that day, and segues into singing several vocal and instrumental compositions from the binder. (Klaser 2001: 62–4)

In the quote, I have italicized those characteristics—particular expressive qualities—that make mode a more encompassing idea about melodic material than even the composite of pitch and pitch function, interval, scale, and key.

To pursue *makam* (Turkish spelling) a bit with a musical illustration, I turn to *maqam* (Egyptian transliteration) Rast that is featured throughout Scott Marcus's book in this series on Egypt and the eastern Arab world. For pitch selection, *maqam* Rast will be performed with the *rast* tetrachord in the lower position, but with any of the three tetrachords (CD track 2-28) in the upper position. It will take sharp listening to hear the quick shifts among them in the melody of CD track 1-37, but with a listening guide, you can at least get the principle of the melodic practice, with a focus on *hijāz* tetrachord.

0:05–0:11	The initial rubato phrase starts with the notes of a *hijāz* tetrachord (G-Ab-B-c),
0:33–0:38	That again.
0:55–	The *qānūn* solo reasserts the *hijāz* tetrachord.
1:26–1:30	With the entry of the percussion, a quick alternation, here *nahāwand* tetrachord
1:30–1:36	*hijāz*
1:36–1:37	*nahāwand*
1:37–1:39	*hijāz*, before falling to the tonic. A tonic pitch is a characteristic of modal practice in the *maqām* system.

The words "mode" and "mood" are linguistically related and musically articulated. "If you take any set of notes and continually play only these notes, then a mood is built up. After a long period of hearing only these notes, adding a new note creates a shock. Similarly, by playing only a different set of notes, a different mode is created" (Scott Marcus, personal communication, 2001).

Musicians in North India consider many of their melodic modes (*rāga*) bearers of special expressive capacity to communicate moods. Some historians explain that capacity by citing the ancient connection of music and drama, where the shifting moods in a play would be expressed musically. Other historians connect it with the shifting natural moods in a day, from meditative in the early morning hours, to energetic in midmorning, tantalizingly tentative at sunrise and sunset, and serious in the late night. Others explain it through the different contexts and functions of music in a complex court culture in which India's classical music was cultivated—music for religious worship, light after-dinner entertainment, serious discussion deep in the night. Perhaps it is a combination of nature and culture. Whatever the reason, meditative *Rāga Āsāvarī*, with all its particular modal characteristics, is best performed in early morning. Rag Jog, featured in CD tracks 1-14 and 1-15 is a relatively recent melodic mode, best played late at night from midnight to 3:00 a.m. The Malhar *rāga*s are best performed in the monsoon season, when, perhaps, they might relieve the oppressively humid atmosphere by causing a cloudburst (or by bringing a beloved, who is as awaited as the rain).

Melodic mode with all its characteristics and associations is fully explored in the Egypt, North India, and South India volumes in this series.

THINKING VERTICALLY

In the discussion above, I focused on pitch as the fundamental material for melody. Here I shift to thinking about pitches that are heard simultaneously (vertically), bringing harmonic orientation into play. The amount of focus on vertical relationships and the nature of them differs from music to music; no musical system cultivates verticality as much as does the European music system. In the discussion below, I present a few examples of ways in which musicians practice music with a vertical orientation.

Naming Vertical Intervals. The term **interval** in harmonic thinking has the same meaning as in melodic thinking: the distance between two pitches. Several intervals may be heard on CD track 2-29; their names in European music theory are as follows: minor and major second, minor and major third, perfect fourth, augmented fourth/diminished fifth and perfect fifth, minor and major sixth, minor and major seventh, and octave. Intervals that exceed the octave are called ninth (i.e., an octave plus a second), tenth, eleventh, and so forth. The vocal duo on CD track 1-6 are singing in a style that is characteristic of the Mexican *corrido*—in parallel thirds. Neither voice carries "the melody"; they sing pitches at the interval of a third a part—sometimes a minor third, sometimes a major third.

Dissonance and Consonance. The quality of the sound produced by a vertical interval is spoken of as **dissonant** or **consonant**. A widely held idea in European music theory has been that those intervals which are mathetically simple regarding the ratios of their frequencies (an octave is a simple 2:1 ratio) are "consonant." The consonant intervals are the first five of the natural overtone series: the octave, the fifth (3:2), the fourth (4:3), the major third (5:4), and the minor third (6:5). Complex intervals, on the other hand (a major second is 9:8) are "dissonant."

According to this theory, dissonance produces tension, whereas consonance offers relaxation, by release of tension.

ACTIVITY 4.13 *When a pitch is produced, we hear it as a single entity, but in actuality it is a composite of the fundamental frequency plus a set of mathematically related overtones—the* **overtone series**.
Find a stringed instrument with which to experiment. (The strings inside a piano will do, or guitar or violin strings.) To obtain the first natural overtone of the pitch to which one string is set, sound the string while lightly touching it right in the middle of its length, producing a simple 2:1 ratio; do not press so hard that you touch the sounding board. Doing so should result in a ringing pitch an octave higher than the string's pitch when played normally. To get the second overtone, experiment with finding a spot where the string is divided into three equal parts. When you find it, the pitch a fifth higher than the first overtone (i.e., an octave and a fifth higher than the string's normal pitch) will result. To get the third overtone (a fourth higher than the second overtone and two octaves higher than the starting pitch), find the spot one-fourth the length of the string.

Venturing beyond that mathematical concept of consonance and dissonance takes us into the subjective realm of musical aesthetics. For example, we find entirely different aesthetic ideas about the interval of a second: to Bulgarian women in the area of Sofia, the second is "pleasant and smooth"—in effect, consonant. In an example presented in Timothy Rice's volume on Bulgaria in this series, one woman sings the melody; another sings a part that zigzags between the tonic pitch and the note below it (CD track 2-30). They are striving to make their vertical intervals "ring like a bell" by narrowing them, especially on long-held notes, to somewhere between a major second and a minor second until they get the desired effect, an intense "beating" that is reminiscent of that produced on the paired Balinese instruments (CD track 2-21). The tension of singing is released at the end of a verse with a cry on the syllable "eee," leaping melodically up a seventh or an octave, and sliding down.

Nor is the idea about dissonant seconds and sevenths maintained in a good deal of contemporary composition, whether written in the tonal system or not. Lutosławski 's "Mini Overture" abounds with minor seconds; they contribute part of the energy of the piece (CD track 2-4).

Functional Harmony. Intervals stacked vertically in tonal music are usually understood to form **chords**. A certain chord built on pitch 1 (*do*) of a key is the tonic chord (written in Roman numerals, I); likewise, a certain chord built on pitch 5 is the dominant chord (V), a certain chord built on pitch 4 is the subdominant chord (IV), and so forth. Not surprisingly, those chords constitute a hierarchy analogous to the pitch hierarchy discussed above: the tonic chord is all-important; the dominant chord and subdominant chords are important, in that order. This use of chords is called **functional harmony**.

Chords in the tonal system consist of three or more pitches. The most basic is a **triad**, so called because it consists of three pitches, the upper two of which are stacked a third and a fifth, respectively, above the bottom pitch or root of the chord.

ACTIVITY 4.14 *To do this activity you need to gather at least two friends. Together count as you sing up from pitch 1 to 5 (starting anywhere that is comfortable for all of you), then sing just 1, 3, and 5 (leaving out 2 and 4). Sing 1–3–5–3–1 (ascent and descent) until it feels easy; those are the pitches of a triad. Then split up the pitches among you so that someone is singing each of the three pitches. When you sing them simultaneously, you are producing a triad. Build more triads, stacking thirds above any pitch.*

A sequence of chords is called a **chord progression**. In much tonal music a common practice guides which chord is likely to follow a given chord. The subdominant chord (IV) is likely to be followed by the dominant chord (V) or the tonic chord (I), for instance, and the dominant chord (V) is likely to lead to the tonic chord (I). Chord progressions of countless songs use just two or three of those chords.

ACTIVITY 4.15 *With the recording on CD track 2-31, sing this progression of these pitches:*
1 4 5 1 4 1 5 1 4 5 1
If you were to build chords on each one of those pitches, your chord progression would be I IV V I IV I V I IV V I. The pitches are called the root pitches of the chords.

The *corrido* "Ballad of César Chávez" (CD track 1-6) uses the tonic and dominant chords in a clear fashion. The guitar player anticipates the change with finger picking. Here I have rewritten the first two verses, with the chords indicated.

(Guitar intro settles on I.)

En un día siete de marzo, Jueves Santo en la mañana,

   I   V   V   I

Salió César de Delano, Componiendo una compaña.

   I   V   V   I

(Brief guitar interlude stays on I.)

Companeros campesinos   Este va a ser un ejemplo

   I   V   V   I

Esta marcha la llevamos   Hasta mero Sacramento.

   I   V   V   I

A genre of music that uses the I, IV, and V chords to the fullest is the blues. In most blues pieces, a chord progression that repeats in every verse provides stable underpinning for the flexible parts that swirl around it. Stripped to its simplest form, that chord progression is as follows.

I   I   I   I

IV IV I   I

V   V   I   I

ACTIVITY 4.16   *Listen to the* corrido *on CD track 1-6 and try to sing the tonic and dominant pitches that undergird the chord progression.*

If you succeed at that, proceed to CD track 2-7, "West End Blues," a 1928 Louis Armstrong hit. Try to follow the blues chord progression when the theme begins, just after Armstrong's famous introductory trumpet solo.

The first task is to feel the tonic. Listen through the selection until you are sure you have that. Then focus on chord changes. You should expect to get all the way through the blues chord progression in the length of one chorus.

0:15 Listen to the chords in the piano through the first chorus.
0:50 The second chorus features a solo by trombonist Fred Robinson.
1:24 Armstrong sings scat syllables through the third chorus, alternating with Jimmy Strong on clarinet.
1:59 The fourth chorus features a piano solo by Earl "Fatha" Hines.
2:33 The final chorus starts with a long-held high pitch on the trumpet before Armstrong takes off again.
The piece ends on a clear, comfortable tonic chord.

One of the effects of the global circulation of popular music, particularly from the Americas and the Caribbean region, is the widespread presence of functional harmony—or, in some cases, what seems to be functional harmony. On CD track 2-32, there are moments from a selection of new Egyptian music, featuring someone playing chords in rhythmic patterns that match the rhythmic modes played by the percussion section. While these chords often match those of Western harmonic practice, they also frequently follow a non-Western harmonic grammar. Said Kadry Sorour, "We generally don't hear the chords as establishing a Western sense of harmony. Rather, they add color to the *maqām* that is being played (personal communication to Scott Marcus, cited in Marcus 2007:173). In CD track 2-32, the *maqām* is again Rast, with the *rast* upper tetrachord.

Tone Clusters. Complex tone clusters occur in Japanese *gagaku* music, played on an aerophone called the **shō**. (It is the first instrument heard on CD track 2-2, and the players of *shō* sit at the rear right in figure 2.18.) A **tone cluster** is a vertical set of pitches, without the functional implications of chords in the tonal system. In the *shō* part in this musical tradition, the bottom pitch of the cluster and the occasional single pitch correspond to melodic pitches. The effect of the *shō* cluster is that of a complex chord played on an organ, sustained for several counts, and gradually changed to another cluster. The *shō*'s part is important to the sound of the ensemble; without it the texture becomes sparse, as you can hear in CD track 2-2 when its part ceases.

THINKING HORIZONTALLY AND VERTICALLY

Now I want to consider the interplay among musical parts when groups of people make music together. The variety of melodic and harmonic practices can be heard as lying along a continuum, at one end of which is music with no vertical dimension and at the other is music in which the vertical dimension is paramount. Musical relationships among the various parts result in what many music analysts call **texture**. For a good deal of music in the European system, it is possible to classify pieces according to categories of texture, and I refer to those categories below. Many pieces, however, are not easily categorized, and when one considers musics outside of Europe, the number of possibilities for ensemble relationships burgeons, causing many ethnomusicologists to avoid analyzing music in terms of texture altogether. In this section I shall explore some of those many possibilities, starting with ways a group of musicians might perform one melody.

Performing One Melody.
Solo and in Unison. A musical texture consisting of a single melodic line and nothing else is **monophony**, literally "one voice." Melody is monophonic if sung or played by a single person alone (**solo**), as on CD track 1-1, Islamic Qur'ānic recitation; on CD track 1-21, a *syakuhati* solo; and on CD track 1-8, an Irish ballad. The texture is still monophonic if that single melodic line is sung by a group of people in **unison**, either on the same pitch or in octaves. (Note: singing pitches an octave apart is musically thought of as singing "the same" pitch.) The Navajo song (CD track 1-10) is started as a solo, then the individual is joined by others in unison. For the first thirty-four seconds of CD track 2-33, the four-

Sumer is icumen in.
Lhude sing cucu,
Groweth sed and bloweth med,
and springth the wude nu.
Sing cucu.
Awe bletheth after lomb,
Louth after calve cu;
Bulloc sterteth, bucke verteth
Murie sing cucu.
Cucu, cucu.
Wel singes thu cucu,
Ne swik thu naver nu.

FIGURE 4.6. *"Sumer is icumen in."*

teenth-century song "Sumer is icumen in" ("Summer is a-coming in") is presented in unison by a mixed chorus. (The Middle English text is provided in figure 4.6). Various signs of summer are noted—seeds growing, female animals with young, and the male animals restless— but the recurring reference is to the cuckoo, whose call is imitated melodically.

Interlocking Parts. Another way of performing a melody communally is to split it up among several musicians, assigning a single pitch or a few pitches only to each person. The melody is the sum of the parts. (This performance style was known as **hocket** in music of the late medieval period of Western history.) If you listen closely to the Peruvian panpipe selection (CD track 1-33), you can hear that two players combine pitches to make the melody in each part. This performance practice of **interlocking parts** occurs frequently in Balinese music also; on CD track 1-25, players of a group of *gangsas* create a single melodic line with pitches subdivided between them, interlocking in intricate rhythmic patterns, playing at rapid speed. From the beginning of the CD selection to 0:36 you can hear one of the two parts alone, from 0:36 to 1:03 the second part alone. From 1:03 to the end, the two parts join in a complete interlocking pattern (**kotekan**) to form the melody. These examples have demonstrated interlocking parts as melodic, but the same practice occurs in rhythm. On CD track 2-34, multiple players of bottles interlocked and alternated, together creating the resulting rhythm.

Rounds. Along the continuum from horizontal to vertical orientation is the performance practice of singing a melody as a **round**. As you must know from singing rounds yourself, music makers begin the melody at systematically different spots, thereby overlapping. It is challenging, because you have to concentrate on singing the melody yourself—thinking horizontally—while at the same time hearing the combined voices vertically. The total effect can be so busy that one must listen carefully to be sure that just one melody is being rendered. On CD track 2-33, "Sumer is icumen in" is sung as a round from 0:36 to 1:34; in this performance the women start the round and the men join.

A melody sung as a round is just one type of a texture called **polyphony** (literally "multiple voices") in European music terminology (see further discussion below). When each singer imitates the melody of other singers (rather than simultaneously singing a different melody), the result is **imitative polyphony**. In a round (also called **canon**) the imitation is strict; everyone sings the melody just alike.

ACTIVITY 4.17 *Reach back in your memory for a round you sang when you were young. Try to sing that melody or another that you remember with a friend or group of friends—first in unison, then in multiple parts. Perhaps "Frère Jacques" ("Are you sleeping?") is one of them; its melody is on CD track 2-23.*

Heterophony. In **heterophony** (literally "different voices") multiple musicians perform one melody, but each musician might render the melody somewhat differently. In Arab music, for example, a lute player and a flute player might give slightly different renditions of a melody, in part because of the idiomatic capabilities of each instrument. The flute player might insert frequent trills, or the lute player might insert rapid and repeated plucking of a single note. When played together, the two different renditions create a highly valued heterophonic texture (CD track 2-1).

Heterophony is widespread in Asian musical traditions. On CD track 2-35, the classical Japanese composition "Yaegoromo," the sung melody at the beginning is self-accompanied on *koto* and further accompanied on *syamisen* and *syakuhati* (figure 2.12). A heterophonic texture is created by the somewhat different timing and pitches as the three instrumental parts and vocal combine to present "the melody."

ACTIVITY 4.18 *To test your hearing and understanding of different practices for performing a single melody, listen to these tracks on the CD and decide whether each is an example of monophony or heterophony: tracks 1-3, 1-17, 1-18, 1-24, 1-26, 1-30, 1-34 and 2-1.*

Performing One Melody with Another Part. A single melody can also be performed with one or more other parts that use pitch (as opposed to a nonpitched drum, for instance) but whose function is not melodic. Such a relationship among parts takes a number of forms in music throughout the world; I mention only two here.

Melody and Drone. A widespread manner of performing a single melody with a pitched but nonmelodic part is to put it over a **drone**—sustained tone. A drone is usually thought of as being one pitch that undergirds the melody by being sounded in a persistent fashion, as in Scottish bagpipe music (CD track 2-36).

However, there are multiple varieties of drone. On CD track 1-14 and 1-15, North Indian *sitār* (plucked lute figure 3.2) music, the pitch *sa* is sounded intermittently on a string designated on the instrument for a drone; while the sounding of *sa* on that string is far from constant, its function is heard as a drone. A drone might also consist of multiple pitches. When the drone in India's music is kept on **tānpūra**, a chordophone devoted solely to that role, it consists of multiple pitches that are sounded in succession constantly from the beginning to the end of a performance selection (CD track 2-37). The metal strings of the *tānpūra* provide a lush sound quality that contrasts with the vocal timbre.

Homophony. Perhaps the most widespread practice of performing a single melody—thanks to the dissemination of American popular music worldwide—is to back it up with functional chords. The term for this texture is **homophony** (literally "same voice"). Chords undergird the melody, and the melody is conceived in terms of the harmony; in that sense, they are "the same voice." Because the term is so linked with tonal harmony, the label "homophony" is most applicable in such music. Examples can be heard on CD tracks 1-2, 1-6, 1-7, 1-31, 1-37 and others. In some homophonic music, such as choral renditions of hymns and patriotic songs, the harmonizing parts move in the same rhythm as the melody—another sense in which they are the "same voice."

Performing Multiple Melodies.

Polyphony.   When multiple melodic parts are performed together, the texture is termed **polyphony** ("multiple voices"). The singing of rounds, the type of polyphony discussed above, is a musical practice in which one melody is taken up in turn by multiple musicians. Here, I discuss another type of polyphony: the texture achieved when multiple musicians perform different melodic parts simultaneously. But what constitutes a "melodic part"? Because they work with such a variety of musical traditions, ethnomusicologists who want to use the term "polyphony" consider any number of things to be a melodic part—anything from a short ostinato to a full tune. In his volume on Bulgarian music in this series, Rice considers a two-part woman's song to be an example of polyphony: one woman sings "a melody" while the other sings a second melodic part, but not one he identifies as "a melody." Rice's idea of "melodic part" is typically flexible.

Melody and Ostinato.   Some scholars consider an **ostinato**—that is, a constantly recurring melodic, harmonic, or rhythmic motive—to be an extended form of drone.

A performance of "Sumer is icumen in" is not complete until the melody, which you have already heard performed in unison and as a round (CD track 2-33), is complemented by not one ostinato but two ostinati (called *pes* in medieval terminology). Each of them is a melodic motive. The text of ostinato 1 is "Sing cucu nu, sing cucu"; the text and melody of ostinato 2 reverse the two phrases: "Sing cucu, sing cucu nu." The two ostinati can be heard on CD track 2-33, from 1:28 to 1:57.

When all parts of "Sumer is icumen in" are performed together, a full polyphonic texture is created. From 2:01 to the end of CD track 2-33, you can hear the rich texture that results from the combination of the two ostinati and the melody performed as a three-part round. For performers and listeners, this piece demands simultaneous horizontal and vertical musical orientation.

In this chapter I have discussed pitch as the foundation for both melody and harmony, offering perspectives from music theory as well as practice. I also explored a variety of ways in which musical parts are made to relate. In the next chapter I shall discuss processes for structuring a musical selection.

CHAPTER 5

Thinking about Structuring

∞

The topic of musical structure has arisen several times in earlier chapters: from the perspective of instruments in chapter 2, in the section "Ideas about Ensemble"; from the perspective of the organization of time in the second half of chapter 3; and from the perspective of texture in Chapter 4, in the section "Thinking Horizontally and Vertically." In this chapter I shall present several additional ideas about structures that musicians have found useful and meaningful.

Ethnomusicologists are interested in exploring not only *how* music is structured but also *why* it is structured the way it is. Accordingly, in this chapter, I consider a selection of structuring processes in composing and musicking that result in musical forms. It may help to think of musical **form** as architectural design in sonic form.

IMPROVISING AND COMPOSING

Pertinent to thinking about structuring as a process is the ongoing lively discussion regarding what is encompassed by the two terms "improvisation" and "composition." That discussion has been particularly crucial in ethnomusicological study for several reasons. Much of the music discussed in this book involves the process of interweaving musical material that is given with material that is being newly created even as one listens. That process is generally called "improvising"; ethnomusicologists understand it also as "composing."

There are two misconceptions about improvisation that we in ethnomusicology have to counter regularly. One is that improvisation is inevitably completely "free," implying that music being newly created during performance is not based on anything preexisting. Ethnomusicological research has not confirmed that idea. Rather, we usually see musicians using something musical that already exists—an idea about ensemble relationships, a rhythm pattern, the pitch selection in a mode, or something else—as the basis for new music.

The other misconception is that improvisation is not composition—or, put another way, that the process of creating music during performance is intrinsically different from the process of creating music before a performance. This distinction involves a bundle of assumptions. First is the idea that the timing of the creative activity is crucial—that composing necessarily precedes performing. However, it is widely recognized now that composing is a cognitive process that can be taking place in the mind at any time—including while performing.

The idea that composing must precede performing accompanies the supposition that composing means writing something down (or, conversely, that if music is not written, it must be improvised). This interpretation does not take us far when we consider that much music is created in the world, but relatively few people are interested in notating it. For example, writing is not required for Indonesian musicians to remember enormously complex, lengthy compositions. (See Brinner 1995). In addition, notation systems are invented to suit the purposes of a particular musical tradition and may have little to do with what happens to the notated item when it is performed. (See "Transmission," in chapter 1.)

It is also sometimes assumed that the result of the compositional process is an item, a thing—a *piece*—which can be performed again and again in a relatively intact form. This idea about "a piece" is viable for a good deal of music, particularly if the modifier "relatively" is kept in mind: pieces in the European classical tradition, songs in the South Indian classical tradition, Irish dance tunes, Mexican American *corridos*, and many other repertoires are transmitted in a relatively intact form. However, the corollary—that composing has not taken place if the process of creating music does not result in a relatively fixed product—is an assumption that ethnomusicologists do not find viable. Improviser/composer Myra Melford suggests that we think of a continuum of ideals from thoroughly composed to thoroughly improvised—or, in reality, as free as possible (personal communication, 2007).

Beverley Diamond found a somewhat similar continuum among the Inuit. "In Nunavut, the songs are most often carefully composed and privately rehearsed before they are presented at a drum dance. The line between "composition," "song reception," and "improvisation," however, is not rigid. One singer whom I recorded in the 1970s improvised a verse about the visiting woman who was collecting songs. Some songs are received in dreams or in that half-awake state that one is in early in the morning after a night's sleep. Some songs may remain static, or composers may add to a song when new experiences warrant a new verse" (Diamond 2007: 39).

∞

The Ugandan musician Centurio Balikoowa, cited in Greg Barz's volume on East African music in this Global Music Series: "In most African musics we have this idea of the expectation and anticipation of the music always being developed within a performance. There is that idea that listening would be boring if we didn't continue to add things into the performance. When we have an ensemble of three endingidi, two will play in contrasting keys, while the third player will be expected to improvise and put in something different so that they don't play the same thing."

∞

More meaningful than defining in systematic ways what is "composed" and "improvised" is exploring the wide range of musical flexibility that exists in music around the world. The amount of flexibility and the nature of the flexibility that is exercised in the performance of given material varies widely from music to music. When an Irish dance tune (CD track 1-4, 1-26) or a Mexican American *corrido* (CD track 1-6) is performed, the community expects some degree of change—but not too much—to occur in each performance; this results in recognizable variants and is known as "the folk process of re-creation." Some flexibility—variations in phrasing, in speed, in dynamics perhaps—is expected in the performance of a good deal of notated music in the European classical tradition as well; this is called "interpretation." In a Middle Eastern ensemble performance, repetitions of precomposed music in the course of a performance are anticipated moments for variation, when the musicians are likely to add their own melodic ornaments or heterophonic realizations of the composed passages (CD track 2-1). In much music of Africa and the African diaspora, one primary structural principle assumes a particular form of flexibility—the contrast of something that varies with the more or less "fixed" patterns that make up a polyrhythmic texture (CD track 1-5).

Urged to define the term "improvisation," I suggest this. **Improvisation** is a compositional process in which a musician exercises relatively great flexibility with given material during a performance. The "given material" might be a tune, a chord progression, or a rhythm (twelve-bar blues or a drumming pattern), for example.

ACTIVITY 5.1   *Search your personal collection for recordings of two versions of one popular tune. Use those performances to analyze the degree of flexibility in the particular style of your selections. Think about the expectation for flexibility and the musical results. How would you define "composed music" in this context? Would you be tempted to call anything in the selection "improvisation"?*

Consider, too, where the ideas of "an arrangement" and "a cover" fit in here.

When I assigned Activity 5.1 to a class, I added to it an invitation to critique in writing my suggested definition of improvisation. Student Kirk Danielson responded to the assignment from his experience playing and listening to jazz, as follows:

> I think this is a pretty accurate representation of improvisation. However, I think there might need to be a clause about how improvisation is already somewhat pre-thought, or previously constructed or practiced. Usually there is some kind of structure or arrangement or organization to the song, especially when many players are involved. Often in jazz, which is generally characterized by improvisation, there is a set of chord changes, a melody or "head," and a form, usually AABA or ABAB2 or twelve bar blues. The players will interpret the melody by playing in their own characteristic way, and then "solo" or "improvise" over the changes by playing lines, riffs, and arpeggios. These are part of the player's vocabulary, and it is just as if he were speaking. It is not as if he is reinventing the wheel, or discovering something new every time he plays, but it is as if he or she were to speak and the scales and riffs were his or her alphabet. Perhaps the definition should be: Improvisation is the compositional process in which a musician exercises relatively great flexibility with given material during a performance, but often with a pre-construction notion of the structure or arrangement of the song, particularly when other players are involved. (2007)

Responding to the question about covers in Activity 5.1, student Max Ghenis chose to focus the assignment on the Beatle's song "Norwegian Wood," which he had experienced in an arrangement for a marching band.

I choose this piece in awe of the value of instrumental covers, and as an advocate for the cover band as a unique and valuable musical category. Arrangements as intricate as Buddy Rich's "Norwegian Wood" show the extent to which covered material can be as original as any other music form. The reality is, cover bands and arrangers do the same thing all other musicians and composers do; they're just more overt about citing their sources. (2007)

Student Natasha Dagys made the point that different types of flexibility are expected in different contexts of performance of the same song. Her example was two versions of the song "When You Believe" on the soundtrack to the motion picture *The Prince of Egypt*. The first version was sung by the (cartoon) characters in the course of the movie, while the second plays during the credits sung by pop singers Whitney Houston and Mariah Carey.

In the movie version of the song, the performance is more structured and sung similarly to an actor saying his lines; it follows strict cues, and the vocalists appear to be singing exactly what is written on a score. The pop version, however, exemplifies a more flexible style that begins very structured yet includes an improvised (or ad lib) section. The vocalists express emotion as well as showcase their vocal skills through variations in phrasing, timbre, and pitch. In this context, this type of flexibility is expected, since the attention is on the singers themselves, unlike the movie version, where the focus is on the lyrics and how they relate to the plot. (2007)

Composing Persons. Thinking about the process of structuring music also brings up the matter of who is doing the composing. The question arises of just who a "composer" is in the eyes of a community. Is "a composer" necessarily a different person from "a performer"? In many musical traditions, composer-performers are commonplace. In Japanese music for traditional instruments, for instance, the practice of composers who are not *koto* and *syamisen* and *syakuhati* players writing for those instruments was introduced along with other Western practices, so most of the traditional repertoire is by composer-performers. The composer of "Yaegoromo" on CD track 2-33 was a *syamisen* player, writing in 1804 for voice and *syamisen*; the other parts were probably added later by other composer-players. Recently, a new second-*koto* part for the solo instrumental section was composed by Keiko Nosaka, a contemporary koto artist. (See Wade 2005.)

I have often wondered if it is the prevalence in most European music since the eighteenth century of the custom of the composing person being a separate person from the performing person that has contributed to thinking about composing and improvising as different processes. Think, for instance, of Johann Sebastian Bach (1685–1750), who was a master improviser even of complex polyphony, and of Wolfgang Amadeus Mozart (1756–1791), who improvised cadenzas within compositions and entire compositions on the spot.

Think, too, about the number of composers at work on one musical selection; it is not always a single individual. The example of jazz presents a quintessential case of groups of persons composing "a selection" together. Tom Turino observed a different sort of communal compositional process in the Peruvian Andes (CD track 1-33):

> The night before most festivals in Conima, the core musicians of a given indigenous community ensemble come together to compose between one and three new tunes for that year's event. They do so within the established characteristics of a given genre which limit, and thus guide, the compositional process. . . . Pieces are composed collectively in a kind of "brainstorming" session. Sitting in a circle, the core [panpipe] musicians softly blow motives or sections of pieces simultaneously as they think of them. Musical ideas that do not seem promising are simply ignored. If someone comes up with an interesting musical idea others will listen and gradually join in playing it. At this point, if the original idea does not seem to have promise, individuals gradually stop playing it and go back to square one riffing new ideas. If the motive or section still seems promising the group will then brainstorm the next section of the AABBCC form based on this germinal idea. After an entire tune has been roughed out—by adding the additional sections bit by bit, playing them together, deciding whether they work, and brainstorming new ideas for portions not deemed attractive—group members will then fine tune the piece by suggesting small changes here and there and then playing through the piece with the new alterations. What was miraculous to me was that this whole process took place with hardly any discussion or even words being said. . . . By the end of the composition process the input of a number of people is combined into a finished piece and "the community" is considered the composer. Interestingly, group consensus decision making proceeds in much the same manner; verbal ideas are either simply ignored or are repeated by new speakers, perhaps with modifications or additions, until the contributions of a number of people are combined into a finished decision that the community fashions together. (2007)

Ben Brinner describes another sort of collaborative compositional endeavor in the Central Javanese gamelan tradition (CD track 1-9).

There are certainly individual composers. However, when a Javanese musician composes a new piece, he or she does not determine every detail or expect to have others replicate the piece precisely. Musical compositions are frameworks for playing that can be worked out in different ways depending on the context and musicians' desires. "Astonishingly little of this music is truly fixed, only to be performed in one way. This does not mean that anything goes—far from it—but a Javanese musician is constantly adapting both to the circumstances at hand and to fellow performers. Audiences are aware of this at some level and appreciate the smoothness with which musicians work things out" (Brinner 2008:22). Understanding the flexible ways of making music, then, is how one needs to understand what constitutes TMI—the music itself.

Now I turn to discussion of a selection of principles by which music has been structured. Priority is still given to why music may be structured the way it is, that is, structuring as a process in music making.

PUTTING SOMETHING SIGNIFICANT FIRST

Easing gradually into a musical selection is a formal strategy that is preferred in a number of Asian musical genres. In North Indian classical music, a vocalist or instrumentalist will start a major selection in a formal concert by introducing the characteristics of the melodic mode (*rāga*) and establishing the mood through nonmetrical, carefully shaped improvisation called *ālāp* (CD tracks 1-14). The drummer in the ensemble, not yet playing, sits onstage listening; he is like a member of the audience, responding with a shake of the head or a quiet exclamation to particularly creative moments in the *ālāp* (figure 3.2). The *rāga* provides the given melodic material for an entire performance selection.

At the opposite extreme of easing into a piece of music is the clear announcement of an important motive right at the beginning.

ACTIVITY 5.2 *In European classical music, that opening motive is often the primary **theme** or subject matter of the entire piece. Try to identify two of the best-known beginnings in European classical music on CD tracks 2-18 and 2-38. If you recognize them, assist a classmate who does not.*

Though those two ways of beginning a selection are entirely different, they share a musical purpose crucial to the shaping of the whole selection: the most significant musical material is put first.

ACTIVITY 5.3 *Listen to the beginning of several selections by your favorite performing group or artist. Is there a consistent style for beginnings? If so, why, do you suppose? If not, why not, do you suppose?*

North Indian Instrumental Form. The beginning *ālāp* section asserts the primacy of melody in the hierarchy of music elements in the Hindustani tradition. In the most expansive musical form that comprises a performance selection of North Indian instrumental music (*ālāp-joṛ-jhālā-gat-gat-jhālā*), however, a gradual sequence occurs that systematically shifts focus to other elements of music (figure 5.1). Following the *ālāp*, the instrumentalist begins to add pulsating rhythm to the melodic improvisation (*joṛ*). Then, creating interesting rhythms with a combination of melody and drone pitches (*jhālā*), he or she accelerates the speed of the playing. The first real break in the sequence occurs as the drummer enters the selection; at that point a composition (*gat*) is presented, adding a metric cycle (*tāla*) and a tune in the *rāga* to the "given materials" that form the basis of further improvisation. The

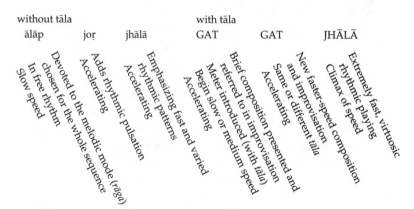

FIGURE 5.1 *Hindustani instrumental sequence.*

desire for gradual acceleration (see the section on speed in chapter 3) is turned into a structural principle when a composition in slow or medium speed is followed without break by a second composition in fast speed. This is a practice in Hindustani classical vocal music, as well. Indeed, this slow beginning and acceleration to a rapid conclusion is characteristic of Hindustani *rāga* development in general and is known as the **badhat** (pronounced "bar-HOT"), which means "growth." The maintenance of the picture, feeling, and design of the slow and steady growth of the *rāga* is a highly prized and aesthetically satisfying aspect of the performance of mature musicians, one that suggests the growth of a plant from seed to full flowering.

ACTIVITY 5.4   *To demonstrate the Hindustani instrumental performance sequence, I have chosen moments from a nearly twenty-nine-minute recording in Rāga Jog. Excerpts from the* ālāp, jor, *and* jhālā *sections are on CD track 1-14, and excerpts from the* gat *section are on CD track 1-15. The artist, sitarist Ravi Shankar, chose to play only one composition (gat) and not to proceed at the end of that into a final* jhālā. *Listen to them, with this guide.*

CD track 1-14

From the beginning of CD track 1-14 to between 3:17 and 3:45, you will hear ālāp. *Shankar presents the pitch selection and melodic nature of Rāga Jog in three ways.*

0–0:11   He gives you pitch Ṣa, *the tonal center (Activity 4.3). Try to match it, get it in your head. In these initial seconds also he will run the nail of his little finger (right hand) quickly down the sympathetic strings that lie under the playing strings to cause the shimmering timbre on the* sitār. *That is a Ravi Shankar signature moment.*

0:12–0:33   Shankar gives us the pitches of the rāga *in short phrases—too quickly to catch them unless you really know what to listen for.*

0:36–1:57   He begins improvisation in free rhythm and a slow speed. First he will improvise downward, until he reaches low pitch Ṣa. *Try to hear some phrases that are characteristic of Rāga Jog, as follows.*

A very short motive is used cadentially, that is, to end a melodic unit.

is a phrase that occurs several times.

Enjoyable in Jog is the inclusion of two forms of Ga (pitch 3, here E^b and $E^{\natural}$). But you will not hear them in chromatic sequence (p. 114). The higher Ga ($E^{\natural}$) is used when the melody ascends upward—to the next pitch up—Ma (pitch 4) or higher. The lower Ga (E^b) occurs when the melody descends from it—in the motive Sa-Gab-Sa, for instance.

The pitch Dha (6) does not occur at all in Rāga Jog.

Short fade-out 1:57 The anticipated shape of a formal ālāp is that the initial descent to a lower register will be followed by melody that ascends gradually through the middle register and up into a higher register. You hear a bit of that improvisatory climb in this short excerpt from 1:59 to 2:27.

Short fade-out, then 2:31 to 3:01. The ālāp has gone on for a while, but here you should perceive it coming to an end with the Ni Ni Sa motive. Immediately, the jor section begins. Pulsation gives a regularity to the rhythm, but, since there is still no drum being played, you know there is still no meter. The rhythm is still "free."

Short fade-out, then 3:03 to 4:36 The jor section becomes quite fast, and the playing very excitingly virtuosic. When you hear the constant strumming of Sa on a drone string from about 3:40, you are hearing jhālā. This ālāp-jor-jhālā sequence ends with a melodic tihāī (see p. 141).

CD track 1-15

This track continues the performance sequence, still in Rāga Jog. The drummer, Chatur Lal, begins to play tablā, by which you can be certain that the music is now in a meter (tāla); this performance is in tēntāl (see p. 87).

0:00–0:19 Listen to the melody to feel a beat. From 0:05 to 0:19 Shankar plays the gat tune. The first eight beats of the tune are the clearest, as shown here, but it is more important for

Pa	Pa	Pa	Ma	Ma	Pa	Ni (Ni)	sa	sa ga ma...	
5	5	5	4	4	5	7 (7)	1	1 3 4...	
G	G	G	F	F	G	B♭ (B♭)	c	c e f...	

you now to feel the articulation of the beat through that tune than it is for you to follow the tune itself. Listen again and again to this initial passage until you feel beats just about a second apart.

Once you have the pace, start at 0:00 again, but this time focus on the drummer. He announces his entry into the performance with a flourish—a one-tāla cycle-long solo. This is customary.

0:18–0:19 Start counting the beats: 1, 2, 3, and so forth, to 16. Count 1 comes again at 0:33–4, 0:49–9, 1:02–3.

1:06 A fade-out marks omitted improvisation after 1:06 in the full performance. My excerpting resumes thirteen seconds before the next count 1, so get ready.

1:23 Start counting 1 and try to keep the tāila (see p. 87). As expected, Shankar is accelerating the pace of the beats.

1:36 This is the next count 1, but Shankar is improvising through two cycles of the tāla, so you won't feel an ending here. His improvisational passage ends at

1:49 and he turns the soloist role over to Chatur Lal on tablā for a one-cycle chance to shine. During that, Shankar repeats the gat tune, effectively "keeping the tāla" with its now-clear beats.

2:01 *Shankar retakes the soloist role. Try to keep the* tāla *as the speed accelerates. Counts 1 come at 2:14-5 and 2:27-8. The cycle beyond that consists largely of a* tīhāī, *to end the performance.*

If you listen to this track sufficiently to be secure in the tāla, *you may also listen for the small ways in which Chatur Lal varies the* theka *pattern with which he articulates the meter. And you can enjoy switching your listening to Ravi Shankar's improvisation.*

| | : | A | : | | : | B | A' | : | | Optional ending |
| | | Exposition | | | | Development | Recapitulation | | | Coda |

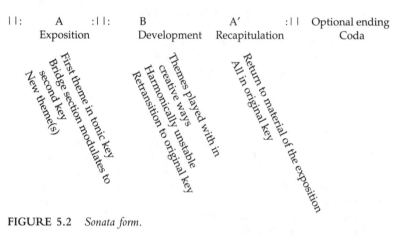

FIGURE 5.2 *Sonata form.*

Sonata Form. In many pieces in the European classical tradition, the opening theme is thoroughly *developed*—subjected to transformations that generate new musical ideas and moods—as the selection proceeds. One important form in European classical music in which that happens is **sonata form**. Sonata form features an opening section (A) that introduces one or more themes and includes a **modulation** to another key, a development of the themes in the middle section (B), and a return to the original key and recapitulation of the themes in the last section (A'; see figure 5.2). (Because the sonata form has three sections, it is also called ternary form.) Developed by Viennese composers and used in almost all the first movements of their symphonies, sonatas, and other genres, sonata form became extremely significant in European classical music in the eighteenth and nineteenth centuries.

Modulation, the shifting from one tonal center to another that is a crucial characteristic of sonata form, constitutes an important practice in structuring a good deal of music created in the tonal pitch system. As its occurence in "Marieke" (CD track 2-8) shows, it can be used to dramatic effect.

> **ACTIVITY 5.5** *Listen to CD track 2-8, "Marieke." A modulation occurs about three-quarters of the way through this performance. Try to catch the timing at the moment when it happens. It will help to try to hear the tonic pitch through most of the song, then listen for a shift. Once you identify where it happens, try to articulate why it occurs where it does.*

TELLING THE STORY

In many instances the demands of telling a story musically are significant factors in the structuring process. In this section I offer a few examples of different responses to those demands.

Music for the Moment. As a *dalang* (puppeteer) in Indonesia weaves his story with shadow puppets, he sends cues to musicians who instantly respond with music appropriate for the moment—battle music, walking music, meditating music (figure 1.5). While the music with which they respond is pre-composed, the musicians cannot know in advance what will be called for when. In any given performance, the plot is usually not the main focus. Rather, the elaborations, digressions, and manner of execution of well-known stories take precedence. This is discussed in detail in Lisa Gold's book on Bali and Ben Brinner's book on Central Java in this series.

Contrasting Instrumentation. In forms of music drama in numerous cultures, shifting instrumentation (including voices) is exploited fully. In the short section from the opera *Carmen* on CD track 1-31, the interplay among instruments, men's chorus, women's chorus, and heroine (Carmen) provides a kind of structure by instrumentation that heightens the sense of the text and moves the drama along.

> **ACTIVITY 5.6** *Make a photocopy of the text given in Activity 4.7 and follow it as you listen again to CD track 1-31 to refresh your memory of the scene (p.115).*
> *This activity focuses on the instrumentation. Listen to the whole selection to identify and list as many of the instruments as you can—remembering to include voices in your list—a male solo voice,*

a female solo voice, a male chorus, a female chorus, a mixed chorus, if you hear those. Each constitutes a musical part in the instrumentation. On the photocopied text, mark what you hear in terms of shifting instrumentation. Note who sings, with whom or alone, unaccompanied or accompanied, with what instrument, and the like.

When you have completed your listening, write an analytical summary of the way Bizet uses instrumentation in structuring the scene. For example, think about how changes in instrumentation heighten the sense of the text and, even when the text repeats, create a kind of dramatic motion.

Through-composed Music. In "telling" the story of the battle in 202 B.C.E. between the monarch of the Ch'u dynasty and his challenger from what would become the Han dynasty in China, the music in "The Great Ambush" (CD track 2-37) continually changes. Because the musical content changes from beginning to end of the selection, the form is called **through-composed**. Also, this particular example is programmatic, that is, an instrumental rendering of "a text." The piece opens with the *pipa* (figure 5.3) imitating the powerful and martial sound of drums in the high register; that is followed by highly dramatic effects produced by means of different playing techniques, speeds, **dynamics** (use of volume), and the like. Some of the music imitates sounds of a battlefield, while other passages only suggest thematic content.

ACTIVITY 5.7   *Listen to CD track 2-39, the first two minutes of "The Great Ambush" performed by Tsun-yuen Lui.*

Several versions of the program have been published, each listing the events of the battle. This one suggests eighteen sections: massing of troops, the line up, drum beats, the signals, artillery barrage, bugle calls to open a gate, calling the generals, taking battle stations, the dispatch, the ambush, the skirmish, the cannonade, shouts, the charge, the siege, the call to retreat, the Ch'u army routed, the suicide of the Ch'u leader.

Plot on a timing chart where the programmatic sections come in the piece in order to answer this question: Is the program clear, or not?

FIGURE 5.3 *Tsun-yuen Lui playing Chinese* pipa. *(Courtesy of the UCLA Ethnomusicology Archives)*

Strophic Form. **Strophic form** provides an excellent design for telling a story. The word "strophe" (stanza or verse) usually refers to the text, but it has been adapted in musical terminology to refer to a song tune that is repeated while the text changes. That is the form chosen for *corrido*s. The melody of "The Ballad of César Chávez" (CD track 1-6; figure 1.4) is strophic: the same melody is repeated for each stanza of text. Often, when there is considerable musical repetition, you need to focus on what is changing.

	Text lines	Melody lines
Verse 1	A B C D	A B C D
Verse 2	E F G H	A B C D
Verse 3	I J K L, etc.	A B C D, etc.

ACTIVITY 5.8 *To try your hand at plotting the patterns of repetition in a strophic song, return to CD track 1-8, the Irish ballad. Make a chart similar to the one just presented, with a column for text lines and a column for melody lines. In addition, note the rhyming pattern because that is another kind of repetition.*

The selections on CD track 1-37 "Take Five," and CD track 2-7 "West End Blues," are both in strophic form, though their "verses" or "stanzas" are called "choruses." Make a listening chart for each, in which you articulate what changes and what stays the same. Go to your cumulative record of information for some guidance.

∞

It is Sunday morning at the Power of Jesus Around the World Church located along the outskirts of Kisumu, Kenya.... The congregation is invited to begin the service by laying their hands on a group of members who recently lost a family member. Before long, one of the service's leaders begins to speak in tongues. The bereaved members all fall to the ground as they too begin proclaiming in unintelligible statements. Within minutes a large portion of the congregation is swept up in the spirit and the emotion of the moment. . . . After an extended period of time one of the pastors begins the call of a well-known chorus known in North America as "Kumbaya" [CD track 2-40], singing into a generator-powered microphone. The give and take between the soloist and the congregation builds up gradually. The spirit healing session "cools" down after a half hour or so, and the performance of "Kumbaya" reunites the community, giving them back "language" while at the same time bringing them back to their seats. (Greg Barz, in the volume on East Africa in this series)

∞

RESPONDING TO THE CONTEXT

In many instances, musical selections are structured in response to something in the context, broadly conceived—from sacred to secular, from ritual to concert, from formal to casual, and the like. Limitations or opportunities provided by technologies are a sort of context; the short time available on early recordings, for instance, caused musicians to curtail what would have been longer selections. In addition, aesthetic values are a sort of context to which musicians may respond in the structuring of music. Composing for a particular opera diva causes a score to have more arias for one character than others. If a cathedral has balconies on either side from which choirs might sing or instrumentalists might play, a composer might write interactive music to surround the worshipers with affective sound. Below, I sample a few contexts to demonstrate this point further.

Expectation for Audience-Performer Interaction. In an improvised performance such as the Hindustani performance sequence described in figure 5.1 (CD tracks 1-14 and 1-15), audience response can play a big part in how the soloing musician proportions the music he or she is creating. If the audience notes approval with "wah! wah!" or with a shake of the head, then the musical idea that drew the response might get prolonged, repeated with subtle changes.

Audience-performer interaction can also shape performances by some larger groups such as the Middle Eastern ensemble on CD track 2-1 (figure 5.4). Arab audiences react in the moment, participating in a shared performer-audience feedback system. The lively interaction can be heard at several points even in the short portion of a selection reproduced in CD track 2-1: at the beginning, during the *rubato* section

Muqaddima (Ensemble introduction) - - - - - - - - - - - - - - - - - -Song

Rubato section - - - - - - - - - - - - -Section in rhythmic mode - - - -Song	
(rhythmic ebb & flow)	(from 1:28) (at 3:02)
Full ensemble, followed by	Full ensemble
Qanun solo with ensemble	Melody played 5 times, at
responses (from 0:58)	1:27, 1:46, 2:02, 2:19,
	2:35
	Ending phrase repeated
	quietly as transition

FIGURE 5.4 *Egyptian performance structure.*

(to 1:27), and beyond. This audience reaction reveals an aesthetic value in eastern Arab music whereby a premium is often given to musicians and listeners alike achieving an ecstatic state, *tarab*, during performances. A number of musical features facilitate the creation of *tarab* in art music contexts, including the focus on one *maqām* (melodic mode) at a time, which allows the mood of the *maqām* to reign over the occasion.

Here is where the *tarab* aesthetic comes into structuring: while aspects of overall progression are worked out in advance, much is typically left to be decided as the performance unfolds. Repetitions (when and how many) are often determined in the moment, allowing the performers to react to the existing mood and energy. Furthermore, a song or instrumental composition can be stopped at any number of points in response to the urge to shift to one of several improvisatory genres. To help build the overall mood, audience members are supposed to show their immediate reactions to the music by gesturing in a variety of ways and by calling out any of a number of traditional phrases (Marcus 2007: 115).

The eastern Arab aesthetic feedback system invokes a different behavioral expectation than the internalized individual aesthetic reactions by audience members that characterize practices in some Western concert-going contexts—that is, remaining silent and unmoving, revealing reaction only at the end of a piece. (Exceptions to this are rife, of course, such as opera performances). Balinese audiences, too, recognize the desired inner state of divine inspiration that may overcome a *dalang* (master puppeteer) during a *wayang kulit* performance (Gold 2005: 90). While the Western art music practices will not affect the structuring of the music being listened to, the eastern Arab and Balinese practices may affect the shaping of the drama.

Audience-Performer Interaction in Storytelling. The Liberian Kpelle "epic pourer" is completely in charge as he narrates the story of the hero Womi, a superhuman ritual specialist (CD track 2-34), but interaction with the audience is crucial to the telling. Ruth Stone sets the stage from her fieldnotes:

> In a backyard, not too distant from the market street, Kulung, an epic singer was preparing to begin his performance of the Woi epic, a story that is familiar to Kpelle people because in earlier years it was routinely performed in Gbeyilataa and other village communities around Liberia. A soft mat had been placed on the ground, and he knelt there

as he made sure that his supporting performers were in place. The people from Gbeyilataa, some eight miles from Totota, formed the bulk of the crowd. One man agreed to be the questioner, while two young men began to tap the bottles to form the interlocking background rhythm for the performance. Four more young men and women from the assemblage sat together on a bench where they formed the chorus that, together with the instrumentalists, created the backdrop for the epic performance (2005: 22–23).

The "epic pourer" voices all the characters in the story, sings, responds to a volunteer questioner from the crowd, and directs a group of supporting listeners who also provide the musical backdrop. The structuring process within which he works is **part-counterpart**, in which one or more supporting parts interact. In the Kpelle epic genre, that structuring process is played out in several ways simultaneously. Repeating what could have been one rhythmic part, two musical supporters tap bottles to form an interlocking rhythm. Another four or more young people form a chorus; what could have been one extended choral phrase is segmented between the two groups. The narrator and all the musicians together articulate a form in which the narrator's part is flexible, while the supporting group's parts are fixed. In addition, the narrator and the questioner articulate a form; in that case, both parts are flexible.

When an Indian or Pakistani *qawwālīyā* sings in a Muslim Sufi gathering, he watches the participants for signs of going into trance in order to encourage it musically. In this instance, the "performer-audience interation" is enacted within a ritual process and a devotional response structure the music (Qureshi 1987). The shaping of music in response to a ritual situation happens all over the world.

The Need for Intra-ensemble Interaction.   Interaction among members of an ensemble are at play in the Egyptian selection on CD track 2-1 from 1:28, when the full ensemble launches into a melody in rhythmic mode. The number of repetitions of that melody will depend on the context; in this instance it is played five times. As the ensemble performs this precomposed introduction, the singer, Umm Kulthum, would traditionally be sitting in a chair in the center of the ensemble semicircle. When she is ready to sing, she stands up; on CD track 2-1, that happens during the fourth time through the melody (between 2:19 and 2:35), and you can hear the audience responding with applause. Her ensemble, understanding her signal that it is time to move on in the composition, responds by softening its sound a little. But in this performance, she must not have been quite ready to start singing. Seeing her signal that unreadiness with her hand, the *qanun* player (the leader of her ensemble) must have signaled to everyone else because we hear the ensemble energized. It repeats the melody again. The whole introduction (*muqaddima, p.150*) ends with a small phrase played quietly over and over so that focus shifts fully to the singer. Everyone waits, as she decides when the moment is right to begin singing.

Now the audience-performer interaction intersects with intra-ensemble interaction. Umm Kulthum sings the first phrase of the song "Aruh li min" (at 3:02), and the audience responds with a huge wave of applause. So strong is the applause that she stops singing. She has stopped for at least two reasons: she needs to acknowledge the applause, and she also needs to make sure that she does not lose control of the crowd. Whenever the audience response got "over the top," Umm Kulthum would stop and politely wait for the audience's energy to dissipate. Toward her audience she was respectful and appreciative but always in control. What do the ensemble players do? They keep playing, but they have not yet figured out what to do. Their interaction with the singer continues as they await the signal to proceed (Scott Marcus, personal communication, 2001).

In this one selection of Egyptian music, then, we see that the precomposed piece has a set form (a *rubato* section that includes space for an elaborating *qanun* solo, a full ensemble section in rhythmic mode, and a song), but the execution of that form in performance is shaped by the musicians, responding in a flexible manner to cues from the audience and from each other. The entire selection by the famous singer Umm Kulthum and her ensemble can be heard on the CD of Scott Marcus's book on *Music in Egypt* in this series; Marcus devotes considerable attention to the stirring performance and the artiste who held an extraordinary position as a female singer in the Arab world.

Echoes of a Ritual Practice.   Revealing their origin in shamanistic ritual, several concert performance genres of Korean music use a progression through a series of *changdan* as the single most important structuring principle (see chapter 3). Effecting a gradual buildup of tension that is reminiscent of the progress of a ritualized seance (*kut*), the rhythm patterns change in a series of sections. That is the structure of the important solo instrumental genre of **sanjo** (CD track 1-24). Not only does the rhythm pattern change, but the speed of the basic beats also gets gradually faster from the beginning to the end of a piece.

> **ACTIVITY 5.9** *Track the succession of* changdan *through the selection on CD track 1-24, portions of a solo instrumental performance genre called* sanjo. *Here it is played on* komŭngo *by Han Kap-deuk (figure 2.13) and, on* chang-gu, *by Hwang Deuk-ju. Note the gradual increase in speed.*
>
> Chinyangjo changdan *(through three and one-half times: second time at 0:53, third time at 1:38, fourth time at 2:19)*
> *(24)* • - - - - - - - - - - - - - • - • • - • | • - - - - - - - - - - - - - •
> - - • - • |
> • - - - - - - - - - - - - • - - • - - | • - - - - - - - - - - - - •
> - - • - • ||
> 2:42 Chungmori begins (see p.93)
> *(12)* • - - - - - - - - - • - - - - • - - - • - • - - - • - • - - - • - - -
> - - - - • - - - |
> 4:53 Onmori *begins (fade-out at 5:00)*
> *(10)*

Call and Response. The part-counterpart relationship spoken to earlier between the performer and the audience comes into play in interaction between members of an ensemble as well. One type is **call and response**, with which you may be familiar. Call and response is sometimes taken generally to imply the juxtaposition of solo with group, sometimes more pointedly referring to a musical repartee among parts. In either case, it is deeply significant in African music, for example. Almost as soon as they could talk, the Liberian Kpelle children heard in CD track 2-41 would sing in ways they had heard adults sing; this counting song is a clear instance of the call and response structuring process. As they had heard adults in their context, the child soloist varied her line, while the others performed without fundamentally changing their part. The words are "One, two, three, try it again. Fence two, three, try it again." ("Fence" is a term that often refers to ritual, since many rituals are performed within an enclosure that is fenced in to keep noninitiates out (Stone 2005:66). The same intra-ensemble inter-action is at play as the master drummer or singer creates one part to which an ensemble of instrumentalists or singers responds, when one player in a xylophone duo leads and the other responds, when listen-ers encourage a praise singer with a response. Transported to North America in the era of slavery, that structuring process could be heard as one worker led in song, with fellow workers responding. In con-temporary gospel a lead singer embellishes a solo with support from the choir; in the blues there is the same sort of interplay between singer and instrumentalists as well as among the instrumentalists.

> **ACTIVITY 5.10** *The structuring process of solo-group instru-mentation and part-counterpart musical interaction are heard in music all over the world. With that idea as a focus, review the variety of musical practices that are offered on the CDs. Listen to each selection again, for the purpose of finding those structures. This is a good time for you to double-check to be sure that you are up-to-date on your cumulative record of all the references to the tracks on the CDs.*

Music and Movement. Straddling the boundaries of dance, music, and sport is Brazilian *capoeira*, a "blurred genre" that can be described as a game or martial art with music, a form of dance with vocal and instrumental accompaniment, as a drama, and as mentioned in Chapter 2, a philosophy and worldview that emphasizes liberation and embodies reciprocity (Murphy 2006: 55). The capoeira ensemble typically com-prises a singer and chorus who interact with call and response; this can be heard on CD track 1-19. In addition, there are three *berimbaus* (musi-cal bows, at three different pitch levels), *pandeiro* (tambourine), *agogô* (double metal bell), *reco-reco* (notched bamboo scraper), and *atabaque* (large drum resembling a conga). The ensemble forms the polyrhyth-mic backdrop. Competing within a circle of spectators, two contestants use athletic leg thrusts to throw each other off balance. As physical play changes, the music should change accordingly, and if the music changes, the contestants should respond in kind. *Capoeira* players depend on the lowest-pitched *berimbau* for specific melodic-rhythmic patterns, called *toque* for the tempo of play, and for specific phrases that suggest the timing for movements. During a long period of apprenticeship, players learn to integrate their movements with the sound and rhythms of the *berimbau*, using what could be described as full-body hearing. Players use the groove established by the *berimbau* to choose unexpected moments in which to launch an attack on their opponent (Murphy 2006: 61). "The musicians [all *capoeristas* themselves] create the atmosphere within which the game comes to life; they make the game possible, and the game, in turn, gives meaning to the music" (Lewis 1992: 134).

When music is meant for dance, it is important to coordinate the form of the music and the dance. Thousands of Irish dance tunes have a **binary form**—A and B sections (CD track 1-4). Each section is eight measures long. The two sections are usually repeated in performance, creating a tune that is thirty-two measures long.

ACTIVITY 5.11 *On CD track 1-4, "Tar Road to Sligo" is played for one minute and thirty-one seconds before the musicians move on to the second jig ("Paddy Clancy's") in a medley. The band consists of fiddle (Becky Tracy), mandolin (Stan Scott), and whistle (Dora Hast). The tunes move in compound duple meter at a fast clip. The first section (A) is repeated exactly. The B section varies the pattern a bit: In the repeat, the first four measures are retained exactly, but the last four measures are slightly different (B'). The total structure is: A A B B' A A B B' A A B B', with each segment taking about eight seconds.*

Listen to CD track 1-4 and identify what changes, in the midst of so much repetition.

The bipartite structure of dance tunes in the British Isles and in associated traditions in North America are closely linked to the designs of the dances. Many Irish, Scottish, and English set formation dances feature a setting section (dancers remaining in place) followed by a traveling part. Anyone who has participated in North American square dances will recognize this form; one section of the tune is used when the active couple dances a figure with another couple in the square, then returns to place; the second section corresponds with the promenade or traveling part. The influence of dance design on the performance of dance tunes can still be heard when the tunes are played in a listening context such as a concert or a *seisun* (session) like those described in the Scott-Hast volume on Irish music in this series (figure 5.5). The form of tunes remains the same, but the tunes are grouped in different kinds of medleys, as in CD track 1-27, to maintain musical interest without the dance (Peggy Duesenberry, personal communication, 2001).

Close coordination between movement and music occurs also in the Balinese dance form of *topeng*; the best illustration of the necessity for extremely tight coordination is the element of sudden interruptions (*angsel*) in the flow (CD track 2-42). Short *angsels* are usually only one- or two-beat interruptions and are always syncopated. The long *angsels*

FIGURE 5.5 *Session at Gleeson's of Coore, near Miltown Malbay Co. Clare. The session has been a feature for decades, catering to musicians and dancers alike. In this photo the musicians are Ita Crehan (keyboard), Eamonn McGivney (fiddle), Conor Keane (accordeon), Michael Downes (fiddle), P. J. Crotty (flute, mostly hidden), Angela Crotty-Crehan (concertina). The set dancers include singer Peggy McMahan and singer/concertina player Kitty Hayes. Musicians Junior Crehan and Annette Munelly are having a break at the bar.   (© Peter Laban, Miltown Malbay Co. Clare)*

consist of a sequence of events. The dancer cues the drummer with a movement particular to long *angsel*. This occurs immediately following a short *angsel*. The drummer then responds by playing louder, filling in the space following the short *angsel* (otherwise empty). The rest of the musicians know to reenter instantly, rather than wait until midway through the metric cycle as they would in following a short *angsel*. There are short *angsel*s at 0:28, 0:34, 0:52, 1:15, 1:38, and 1:44. They are immediately followed by a series of swelling dynamics: the melody is continuous, becoming soft and loud several times until the dancer cues the final *angsel*, at which point the musicians break, as in the short one. The music and movement are tightly coordinated: as the dancer bends his knees, swaying from side to side, the music becomes softer. He straightens his knees and raises his arms high, and the music becomes loud. He jerks his hand suddenly, elbow high and bent, and freezes as the music abruptly stops. As he does this, the drummer makes the *plak* stroke with his left hand, so that the dancer appears to have made the sound (Gold 2005: 108.) This is all easy to imagine as you listen to CD track 2-42.

COMING TO AN END

The musical term for an ending is **cadence**. "Cadence" encompasses not only what happens at the very end but also how the ending is approached. The use of speed is another possible practice for coming to closure. Listening again to "Marieke" (figure 3.4, CD track 2-8), you can hear how acceleration is used to approach the ending. In a good deal of music, slowing down occurs to mark the ending.

In most tonal music the ending is a matter of harmonic practice: we expect the last chord to be the tonic chord. The *corrido* and blues selections (CD tracks 1-6 and 2-7) demonstrate this cadential practice clearly. There is also a common practice in the choice of chords that lead up to the tonic and cause us to expect the ending. In the *corrido* and blues and in a great deal of other tonal music, the V (dominant) chord will immediately precede the tonic. Melodically, in tonal music pitch 7 (*ti*) or 2 (*re*) often functions as a lower or upper leading tone respectively, causing us to expect resolution to the tonic pitch.

Musical practice for creating an ending might involve rhythm and the metric structure. As was pointed out in Activity 5.4, in North Indian improvisational practice, musical units will usually end on a count 1. Because the improvising musician could decide to stop at any count 1 and needs to signal the accompanists to create an ending simultaneously, musical cues must be sounded leading up to that ending on count 1. One type of cue is a *tihāī*—a melodic or rhythmic pattern that is performed three times, with the last repetition ending on the cadential count 1. A *tihāī* brings the performance on CD track 1-15 to an end.

ACTIVITY 5.12 *On CD tracks 2-43 and 2-44, George Ruckert demonstrates two* tihāī *that can be created, for example, from the drumming stroking phrase: Tete kata gadi gena dha. In the first one (CD track 2-43), he chooses to put one count between the first two repetitions; that becomes part of the pattern. Played (or spoken) three times, then, it consumes 17 counts (including the final count 1). Speak the pattern several times, saying "rest" for the counts after dhas. The* tihāī *comes to an end on the final dha, so you don't need to repeat "rest" there.*

Tete kata gadi gena dha -
Tete kata gadi gena dha -
Tete kata gadi gena dha

Tihāī *occur within a tāla cycle, and Ruckert chooses to put his into* tīntāl, *the cycle of 16 counts that you spoke while studying Chapter 3 (see p. 87, CD track 1-15). To fit this first* tihāī *into* tīntāl *and come to an end on count 1, he needs to begin it on a count 1. On CD track 2-43, he begins the recitation by speaking the* tīntāl *theka and then goes right into the* tihāī. *Listen to this several times and then speak it all with him.*

To create the tihāī *on CD track 2-44, Ruckert chooses to speak the pattern right through without any count between the repetitions. That consumes only 15 counts—not a full cycle of* tīntāl. *So he has fun with it: he puts two counts after the third dha and makes that the pattern. He keeps on going with the principle of three times through until the final dha comes out on a count 1. Speak that three times (without thinking about* tīntāl), *saying "rest rest" for the two-count separations.*

Tete kata gadi gena dha/ Tete kata gadi gena dha/
Tete kata gadi gena dha —Tete kata gadi gena dha/

Tete kata gadi gena dha/ Tete kata gadi gena dha —
Tete kata gadi gena dha/ Tete kata gadi gena dha/
Tete kata gadi gena dha
On CD track 2-44, Ruckert again starts with the theka *and*
then recites the whole tihāī. *Listen to this several times and then*
speak it all with him. Enjoy!

Finally, if you want really to struggle, try speaking both tihāīs *with*
Ruckert while doing the hand motions of the tāla. *(See p. 87.) Good*
luck!

Especially when music is structured in response to a fluid context, consideration of cadential practice (i.e., how something ends) needs to be complemented by considering why the music is brought to an end. The story is finished, the performance time runs out, the artist is ready to quit, the audience loses interest, the person in trance returns to consciousness—all these and more can bring about musical ending.

ACTIVITY 5.13 *Listen to two musical selections of your* *choice. Analyze and articulate how the ending is created and con-* *sider why.*

AESTHETIC CHOICE AND INTELLECTUAL PLAY

The aesthetic values held by people about music constitute one of the most meaningful of contexts. Any number of musical forms can be understood as results of aesthetic and intellectual decisions. Here are two examples.

Polyrhythm for fun. In Inuit communities across the whole of Arctic Canada and Alaska, women and children in particular have created games that bring joy and laughter to indoor space. Widely known are juggling games, in which the changing meters of a song "counterpoint" the steady rhythm of juggling three or more balls. The rhythm of juggling must be consistent. The action of tossing a ball with one hand and

qu-luk-pa qu-luq-qu-luq-pa   tu - nit tu - nit tu - nit__   a - ya - ya

a - ja - ju - ni   a - ja - ja__   a-ja-ju - ni   ka - mang-u - kua ka-

mi - u - taa - li   puq - ta - llaq - si - ruq - tik   au - mik

au - mik   qa - nung - mik   tak - ta - lat - ti - vuq

a - liq-qang-ma u - na   ti-vu-a-li u-na   a - na-ngni-tu - a - luq-ju - aq

va - ta - li va - ta - va - ta - li   a - li-qat - tia-nga   u - va - nga - lu   *etc.*

FIGURE 5.6

catching it in the other creates a 1-2 pattern. In Figure 5.6, a partial transcription of a juggling game on CD track 2-45, however, you can see
how the word rhythms create groupings that constantly shift from 3 to
2 to 5 or 7. While the jugglers would not think of these different word
groupings as changing "meters," this European convention can be useful to represent the song. To sing the changing patterns and juggle in a
consistent duple one at the same time is a challenge (Diamond 2008).

Contrasting Rhythmic Modes.   In Middle Eastern music, with its systems of melodic modes and rhythmic modes, the deep value placed on

the power of music to express mood is seen in aspects of musical form. One of those is the juxtaposition of different rhythmic modes. As composed by Riyad al-Sinbati, the selection on CD track 2-1 is in *maqsum* rhythmic mode beginning at 1:28. Contrasting with that, the song (3:02, just as the track ends) starts in *wahdah* rhythmic mode: Dumm – – Takk – – Takk –. The composer's reason is a change of mood, as *wahdah* is weightier and more appropriate for a serious song. Marcus features this song in his volume on Middle Eastern music in this series.

SOCIAL VALUES

In this chapter, I have taken the ethnomusicological approach of exploring not only *how* music is structured but also *why* it might be structured the way it is. As a further example, I shall demonstrate how one social value held by different groups of people is played out musically in different ways. The shared value is this: the conduct of cooperative, supportive social relationships within a group is prized above individual achievement.

As observed by Santosa and cited in chapter 2, the Central Javanese tradition of *gamelan* music (CD track 1-9) is a practice that conserves relations not only among patrons and the musicians but also among members of the community; it is a communal practice in which no one individual stands out. This can be heard in the homogeneous nature of the sound ideal. Furthermore, no one instrumental part stands out from the others in any sustained manner; the marking of the important colotomic structure on multiple instruments is embedded in the ensemble melody. Even in the modal introduction, the one section of a piece in which a single "voice" might be heard as an individual, the constraints of brevity and conventional instrumental patterns keep the expression of individual musicality in check. The music expresses community.

Jazz, in comparison, is a musical practice that, above all others, symbolizes throughout the world the African American identity that emerged from within difficult human circumstances. Even when jazz is practiced by people of other groups—as it is, all over the globe—its meaning is remembered and resignified (CD track 1-37). Performance practice in jazz is of a group, for a group, expressing a cause held in common or remembering that cause. Rather than submerging the individual musicians within the group in the musical structure, however, individual creativity is featured in two ways—cooperatively, in that individual players take the spotlight in turn, and competitively, as musicians engage in fierce cutting contests that display and stretch their explicitly jazz-style musicianship. Through musical practice, a global musical community is created even as the historical and culturally-specific senses of community continue.

In this chapter I have discussed how and why the structuring of music contributes to making music meaningful and useful in people's lives. Aspects of earlier discussions—of instruments in ensembles, of rhythmic, of melodic and harmonic practice—have been recycled, to put the pieces together, in a manner of speaking. In the final two chapters, I shift the focus explicitly to ethnomusicology as an intellectual field and research practice.

CHAPTER 6

Thinking about Issues

∞

When the moment came to write this chapter, I was in French Polynesia, following the lure of the South Pacific to celebrate a significant birthday. In this beautiful place, I wondered, how can I concentrate on writing about the topics that unify the case studies in this series—such matters as globalization, identity, and authenticity? I need not have worried, for the issues were all around me. Globalization, for instance: the music that newly made Polynesian friends wanted me to send them upon my return home was American—ranging from rock 'n' roll and rhythm and blues to the latest styles. By no means, they said, was American popular music meant to replace "their own" music; it was just that the global availability of American music presented a range of choices. I, on the other hand, especially wanted to experience "their music," something different that would permit me a glimpse even as a tourist of another culture. And, frankly, as an ethnomusicologist with a historical bent, I wanted to reassure myself that the cries of alarm heard for years over inevitable "gray-out," or homogenization, of the world's cultures in the face of unmitigated global flow had not erased the beautiful Polynesian music that is audible on recordings distributed in the United States. I need not have been so concerned; "the local" lives on.

What I had not really focused on before I got to Tahiti was that it is *French* Polynesia. French Polynesia is not a nation-state; its residents have voted to continue its status as a territory although it is thousands of miles from France. Tahiti's political status serves as a reminder of the long era of colonialism, when European nations (and relatively more recently, the United States and Japan) asserted claims over a substantial portion of the earth. Colonialism forms the backdrop for numerous new nation-states and the sense of nationalism therein. Here around me, I now realized, were the ever lively topics of the nature and effects of culture contact and the formation of senses of identity and relations of power—all topics important in the study of music.

In this chapter I shall discuss a selection of those topics, but first a commentary on two rubrics is needed: "music in global culture" and "world music." "Global culture" suggests that there are ideas, systems of production, and products circulating among peoples to the extent that something is widely shared. As one reader of the first edition of this book in manuscript form put it, in the twenty-first century there are no completely isolated musical communities any longer; something connects all musical production and permits music to be simultaneously global and local: global in its production, distribution, and consumption by audiences, while local in its performance aesthetic and situatedness in a coherent cultural milieu. In response, a reviewer of this book for the second edition countered quite rightly: "Conversely, nothing is truly global, i.e., used, consumed, produced or understood in the same way. Even those 'things' that are most universally human are understood in different ways. Nothing is only local . . . nothing is totally global." Tahitian music can then claim cultural space anywhere it is listened to (likewise American popular music), but its place is still an island in French Polynesia. "There's a sense that geography doesn't have to equal destiny. . . . Many new global artists have the curiosity to wander the earth with their music and the integrity to stay connected to their homelands" (Farley 2001: 7).

The rubric "world music" was first coined (as far as I know) by ethnomusicologists in the early 1960s to categorize instruction in traditions other than those of European classical music. It became an industry-sponsored term, a convenient label for the marketing of those traditional musics. "The most exhaustive guide to them, *World Music: The Rough Guide*, looks at 'ethnic' musics in particular places; here, the editors are concerned mainly with what they perceive to be 'indigenous,' 'authentic' musics. And they are marketing their book primarily to those western consumers who want to buy what they believe to be the authentic, the real" (Taylor 1997: 16). (Read on for a discussion of authenticity.)

In time, "world music" came to include popular music produced around the world. The term had always carried the sense of "Other," and the rubric "world beat" took on the same connotation. In his 1997 book *Global Pop*, Tim Taylor points out that while "world music" and "world beat" are putatively labels for musics, they are more often used to label musicians: "If it seems that the world beat category refers to music that is somehow exotic, different, fresh, and North American/ British pop/rock oriented, it is also true that musicians who make this— or any—music that sounds mainstream will be categorized by their ethnicity rather than music" (16–17). Writing for *Time*, Christopher Farley asserts: "The old-school term world music is a joke, a wedge, a way of separating English-language performers from the rest of the planet. But there has always been crossover . . . in 1967 Frank Sinatra recorded an album of songs by Brazilian composer Antonio Carlos (Tom) Jobim. . . . Such music became world music only when darker-skinned folks sang it" (2001: 7).

It is, I think, time for us to move on from the term "world music." The title "Global Music Series" for this set of textbooks is intended to encompass the study of music as it flourishes in some places in the globalized contemporary world—whether that music springs from a particular long tradition or results from global interaction.

Throughout this book, in the course of introducing you to numerous ways of thinking about basic elements of music (instruments, organization of time and pitch, and structuring), I linked the concepts and practices to ways in which people make music meaningful and useful in their lives. In so doing, a number of perspectives arose—for example, the ways in which cultural and social status and value come into play with regard to music, the relationship of music with senses of community, the importance of context, roles and responsibilities of those involved with musicking as well as their relationships with their communities, the effects of colonialism and globalization, and many others. All these have had to do with fairly broad ways of understanding what "the music" is; they are all core in the ethnomusicological study of "music" (see chapter 1).

In ethnomusicological parlance, however, the word "perspective" is likely to be replaced with the word "issue." "Perspective" implies a viewing point, whereas "issue" is more like the word "topic." More than the rather neutral word "topic," however, "issue" implies something that is important to debate or discuss. Discussion of an issue assumes the likely deliberation of multiple perspectives—experiences and observation of multiple people, practices, and histories, for example. The word "issue" also assumes possible disagreements and some degree of complexity. In this chapter, I invite you to think about the perspectives offered earlier, but within the framework of issues.

The choice of issues pursued in this chapter has been guided by three criteria. The most significant criterion is the aim of deepening your thinking about the material presented in chapters 1–5. Whereas I presented most of it on a musical practice-by-musical practice basis (as in "here is this and there is that"), the issues approach provides more potentially connective tissue. The second criterion is the purpose of this book as a framing volume for case studies in the Global Music Series;

each of them is conceived around three or four themes that the author considers to be significant for the musical communities and their practices. The issues featured here lay the groundwork for many of those themes. The third criterion is a desire to divulge something of the intellectual history of the field of ethnomusicology when it is pertinent. The resulting discussion provides, I hope, a backdrop for thinking about the conditions of music and the study of it in the twenty-first century.

ENCOUNTERS AND IDENTITIES

From the earliest days of ethnomusicology in American universities, music has been studied through the lives of people. The first work was undertaken from the 1920s by scholars trained in anthropology and located in tribal cultures—primarily American Indian and also African. Ethnographical studies by Alice Fletcher, Helen Roberts, George Herzog, David McAllester, Alan Merriam, and others explored how music functioned for groups and interpreted repertoires as reflections of values and social structures. As the field has developed, numerous scholars have written about the processes of and responses to contact between groups with different music.

A Focus on Influences.   Having witnessed considerable change in the musical traditions of the groups they studied, anthropologists in the 1930s developed a theory of change, termed "**acculturation**." In 1961 a statement of the theory was carefully crafted by the International Musicological Society: "Acculturation comprehends those phenomena which result when groups of individuals having different cultures come into sustained first-hand contact, with subsequent changes in the original culture patterns of either or both groups" ("Criteria for Acculturation," 1961). Specific elements of that statement should be noted: individuals within groups are credited; the nature of the contact being considered is first-hand (i.e., not mediated) and sustained; and change might result for either one or both groups. Unfortunately, the term "acculturation" became applied to studies that skewed this theory: Groups became lumps of people (whole tribes or immigrant groups, for instance). Furthermore, the change that was noted in acculturation studies was primarily in the culture of dominated groups, as the theorists belonged to what was perceived as and was in reality a dominating group (as in "the West" and "the rest"). A habit developed of essentializing the culture of whole groups—that is, citing one or a set of traits that one can easily forget are enormous generalizations, sometimes with historical political roots, such as the biologically racialized assertion that all Africans have a good sense of rhythm.

A Focus on Boundaries. The introduction by Fredrick Barth to a collection of essays titled *Ethnic Groups and Boundaries: The Social Organisation of Culture Difference* (1969) contributed to a shift of scholarly focus from acculturation—the influence of one group on another—to the construction and maintenance of boundaries between people. The term "ethnic group" was introduced, reflecting the anthropological concern with classification (Stokes 1994: 6). Significantly, this meant a shift to greater inclusiveness: rather than viewing culture mostly from the perspective of a dominant group, all groups were potentially given voices by analysis of social action, called "social performance" by the French theorists Pierre Bourdieu (1977) and M. de Certeau (1984). Ethnomusicologists began exploring musical practices as evidence of people's using music in the construction and maintenance of boundaries between themselves and other groups. Whether the Other is a dominating group or another dominated group, a large proportion of these studies focus on relations of power among peoples. Many studies have appeared under the rubric of "identity study," that is, the examination of musical practices that express, if not assert, difference through the construction of an identity of some sort.

The National Community. A great deal of attention has been focused on expressions of national identity, with music playing important roles. The word "nation" is used in two senses. In the sense of culture, the term "nation" is applied to some subgroups within a geopolitical nation—an African American nation and American Indian nations being two examples. In Canada, the term "nation" is the norm with reference to First People (the rubric preferred to "American Indian" or "Native American") because of the important long-term goal of parity of governments. (The word "tribe" is generally regarded as derogatory north of the border, but acceptable in the United States.) In the geopolitical sense, the term "nation" is applied to an independent political area with geographic boundaries. The term "nation-state" adds to that latter sense the state, an apparatus for management, a mechanism for the maintenance of an internal community and the conduct of relations with other nations. The modern nation-state as a political reality came into being in Europe in the eighteenth century and gathered momentum with world events in the nineteenth and early twentieth centuries.

Nation-states developed as the site for processes of modernization, wherein the growth of the capitalist economic system spawned urbanization, commercialization of culture, and the intensified use of technology as in industrialization and in print culture. To consolidate and communicate changing values, public school systems were instituted, and the use of multiple mass media for communication expanded as a basic tool. European and then North American processes of modernization then became synonymous with "progress." To put it succinctly, modernizing was and is "a euphenism for adopting capitalist ethics and worldview" (Turino 2008: 98).

A basic component of the economic success of the modern European nation-states (and then of the United States and Japan) was the extension of their geographical boundaries for political control of a substantial amount of the world's land and population. As the tools of modernization were applied in colonized areas, they became coupled with the inexorable influence of Western culture on Others. In the cultural sphere this could mean, for instance, instruction in European music in new public school systems and the transmission of music through the media of the new music industries. The case study by Marcus on music in the Middle East considers westernization and modernization in relation to contexts for music making, instruments and ensembles, attitudes toward music, music in the schools, and pedagogy.

Another set of words is worth thinking about. Cultural encounters in the course of colonizing the Middle East and India had given rise to a discourse about "the Occident" and "the Orient," adhering to a rationale that Edward Said termed "orientalism." In Said's words, orientalism is "a system of knowledge about the Orient, an accepted grid for filtering through the Orient into Western consciousness" (1978: 6), a "cultural enterprise, a project whose dimensions take in such disparate realms as the imagination itself . . . the spice trade, colonial armies . . . a complex array of 'Oriental' ideas (Oriental despotism, Oriental splendor, cruelty, sensuality), many Eastern sects, philosophies, and wisdoms domesticated for local European use" (1978: 4). Lest we associate this discourse only with the British and French who dominated "the Orient" from the early nineteenth century until the end of World War II, Said reminds us that since that time America has dominated the Middle East and approaches it (and East Asia also) as France and Britain once did. In chapter 4 I examined a microscopic manifestation of orientalism— "the Oriental scale," with its lingering reference to sensual Otherness.

To modernize, then, meant for all intents and purposes "to westernize." "The West," however, is a rubric that is so all-encompassing as to be incautious, unclear, and potentially misleading. Thinking geographically, what is "the West" taken to include? Europe, surely, but all of Europe? For the Bulgarians in Eastern Europe until the late nineteenth century, for instance, "the West" did not include themselves but meant Central Europe owing to the Bulgarian political situation as part of the Turkish Ottoman Empire for three hundred years. Not until the end of World War II and the establishment of a communist government in Bulgaria in 1944 did modernization (read "westernization"), in the form of urbanization, massive industrialization, and widespread high school education, become the norm there (Rice 2004: 7). Are North America, South America, and the Caribbean included in references to "the West"? I frequently hear African American and Latin American musics—surely situated in "the West" geographically—referred to as "non-Western music" when an explanation is being made by nonethnomusicologists to characterize which musical practices are likely to be encompassed within the purview of ethnomusicological study.

ACTIVITY 6.1 *With good maps of the world handy to you, answer these questions. Thinking geographically, what is "west" of China, Japan, India, the Philippines? Where does Asia end and Europe begin in that enormous, continuous landmass? Where do the demarcations into western and eastern hemisphere lie? Within the hemispheres, where does the continent of Africa fit?*

Thinking culturally about "the West," what does the rubric mean? Even just the European cultures are very different from each other, are they not, and the encounters of other cultures with them differed accordingly. Historians of European musics are likely to be careful to write about the various repertoires in terms of a single country or city or court—Italian opera as opposed to German, for instance, madrigal at the court of Ferrara, the Viennese symphony, and the like. To what do you refer when you say "the West"?

"The West" is a rubric that is likely to be used (often unintentionally) geopolitically, is it not? Categorizing African American and Latin American musics as "non-Western" musics is a habit of speech that suggests marginality with respect to structures of power. When Asian scholars write "the West," they are usually implicating the hegemonic wielders of political, economic, and therefore cultural power in the colonial era, as well as the musical practices of particular peoples and institutions who bore and still bear that power. I have been careful about the rubric of "the West" in this book. However you choose to use the rubric, "the West," I hope that you will be careful, too. Words are very important.

Embedded in discourses of both Orientalism and modernity was the assertion of the superiority of "the West." "Drawing on earlier social-evolutionist theory which defined the 'modern' industrialized countries (civilization) as the present and 'traditional' societies (the savage and barbarian stages) as the past, the discourse of modernity defines itself as the all-encompassing present and future, and all alternatives ('the traditional') as an outmoded past" (Turino 2000: 6–7).

In dealing with the power of "the West" in the nineteenth century, Japanese leaders invested in the belief in the superiority of European music—a legacy of the colonial era—in their process of modernization. And the Japanese transmitted it to Koreans, whom they colonized in the early twentieth century. The dilemma this assertion has caused for musicians of indigenous traditions in those countries is serious and ongoing (CD tracks 1-17, 1-21, 1-23, 1-34, 2-20, and 2-35). The situation in Japan and Korea is quite striking when compared to that of India: political leaders and musicians alike in that former jewel in the crown of the British empire have been unswervingly confident of the superiority of their classical music, with its long history, intellectuality, and spirituality (CD tracks 1-14, 1-15, 1-22, 1-32, 2-14, 2-16, 2-17, 2-37, 2-43, and 2-44).

World War II (1941–45) effectively disrupted the paradigm of global (imperial) colonialism; a number of new nations came into being in the ensuing decades. Several independent nations also emerged near the end of the twentieth century from the dissolution of the Soviet Union. Not surprisingly, nation building—and therefore music and nationalism—is a topic that persists in ethnomusicological study.

Processes other than modernization and westernization also are at work in nation building. Among them are the construction of a united community, the choosing of emblems of representation that all citizens may share, and the assertion of some sort of difference by which one nation-state can be distinguished from others. Music can be important in each of them. To demonstrate these processes, I shall continue to move between historical and present time and continue to draw on case studies in this series for examples.

One of the first tasks in building a new nation-state is to create a united community—an "imagined community" (Anderson 1991)—even when the population is heterogeneous in some way. In French Polynesia the diversity is ethnic, with Tahitians and multigenerational resident Chinese, Japanese, Europeans, and Americans. In addition, occupants of the territory's several islands have long traditions of distinguishing themselves from each other. If French Polynesia were to become a nation-state, it would need to deal with the inevitable claims of multiple groups and construct a national identity.

For colonial Americans of the eighteenth century, the new identity could not be an outgrowth of shared language, beliefs, customs, traditions, and norms the way it was in European nation-states. Americanists point out that the United States may be the only nation in the world that was invented from an idea, lacking any foundation in a defined territory, a religious authority, a common culture, or a single people. Indeed, the Indian tribes, the country's earliest inhabitants, were themselves separate nations, each with a language and culture of its own. Until 1871, when congressional action ended the practice, those nations, their sovereignty recognized, could separately negotiate treaties with the U.S. government. These political conditions, combined with the multiplicity of cultures that Indian nations represented, made it highly unlikely that support for an overall American national identity might have been constructed on an Indian tribal base.

The creation of even an "imagined" united community in the United States (as in *e pluribus unum*) has been and always will be extremely challenging. (Look at the unfinished pyramid on the one-dollar bill, suggests Adelaida Reyes.) Declaring independence from British colonial power was just one major step. As Reyes eloquently discussed in her volume on America in this series (2005:68 and elsewhere), for more than a hundred and fifty years after the nation declared its independence, power—social and aesthetic—stood firmly on a Europe-derived base. Even to the 1950s, 80 percent of those who immigrated to the United States were of European ancestry. Americans had to travel a long road through two world wars and earn status as a superpower before they could take their independence from Europe as a *psychological* reality (p. 30). Only then could they break free of their habitual deference to Europe. This was due in no small part to the resistance of the new Americans to assigning otherness to those to whom they were still bound by deep historical, cultural, and personal ties. America thus chafed against, but nonetheless emulated, those whose cultural hegemony it found difficult to escape. And even as those ties were loosened by time, the fact remained that the principal threat to identity is not what one differs from most obviously but what one resembles enough to be mistaken for (pp. 63–64). Reform of immigration laws in the 1960s widened the range of diversity throughout the country as nothing had before. In that decade also, the black power and civil rights movements laid the groundwork for the rise of ethnic pride among African Americans, Native Americans, Latinos, and other groups. With the influx of Asians and formerly locked-out populations, diversity built up enough of a critical mass to mount a multiculturalist challenge to the then-dominant Anglo-European melting-pot assimilationist ideal (p. 30). The recognition of a boundary that distinguishes America's music from other musics, Europe's in particular, was the necessary prelude to formulating an American musical identity.

From the 1870s the Japanese government found European music useful for nation building. Once they made the decision to follow the European and American models for including music in their new public education system (established expressly as a tool in the modernization process), they faced a dilemma: the various indigenous traditional genres had such deep class and other type of group associations that none could satisfy the community-building task for which music was needed. The solution was to adopt a different (i.e., non-Japanese) music that could be transmitted in such a way that it would be shared by all Japanese. As a result of the continuing emphasis on European music for over 130 years, Japan's traditional music has become exotic to most of its citizens. To counteract that, national cultural policy enters the picture again. Among the steps taken, the government's National Theater fosters the preservation of those forms deemed most important. (See my case study on Japan in this series.)

In time, governments around the world have established a variety of national cultural policies to meet the challenges posed by both internal heterogeneity and the forces of westernization. In Malaysia, the government's effort to promote national unity among a disparate ethnic population has resulted in the promotion of a newly created music that is based on traditional Malaysian music but incorporates Western influences (Chopyak 1987). The approach in China has been similar. In his volume in this series (2008), Frederick Lau discusses such nationwide institutions as the symphonicized Modern Chinese Orchestra and the music conservatory. On the other hand, he notes that regional and local musical styles are widely appreciated. Interchange, dialogue, even confrontations between those national institutions and local traditions have produced many of the new developments in Chinese music.

"Music nationalism" is the use of music specifically to assert the all-important sense of united community within a nation-state, and also to assert some sense of difference to citizens of other nation-states. The national anthem is the most obvious example of the powerful medium that music can be. Think of broadcasts you have seen of the Olympics and consider the sight of the gold medal winners, standing under their nation's flag, listening to their national anthem. That focused moment of music nationalism is meant to announce the winner with a musical signal, to set the victor apart from the other contestants, and also to engender a sense of pride among citizens of the medalist's nation.

Most new nation-states have a flag and an anthem; many of them also have an emblem. The emblem may be anything—something from nature such as an eagle, something material such as an airline, something cultural such as a musical instrument, or even a composer. Frédéric Chopin (1810–49) is a case in point: the great Polish composer (CD track 2-9) and pianist was successfully redefined by the Polish intelligentsia in terms of the changing contexts of Polish nationalism. Chopin had little experience of his country's folk music; rather, he was an international composer in the European tradition, stranded in Paris by political circumstances and personal choice. His late romantic style came to denote revolution and the struggle of the individual against the world. By the early twentieth century he had posthumously become a cult "Pole" in Paris, which, in turn, was part of what made him valued in Poland, a genius representing a distinctly Polish contribution to Europe's international culture. In socialist Poland, however, Chopin was celebrated for his adherence to his roots and his refusal to conform to the bourgeois aesthetics of romanticism. One way or another, he remained emblematic of the Polish nation.

One type of music that has been crucial historically in the construction of new nation-states is folk music. Its connection with nationalism and national identity is discussed below in the section on authenticity.

ACTIVITY 6.2 *Other than the national anthem, is there any music or musician that you consider to be emblematic of your nation? If so, articulate the reasons why that is, and how it or they are used.*

Regional Identity. Another sense of boundary expressed through music that emerges as significant in several of the Global Music Series volumes is the layer of regional identity within national identity. In Fred Lau's *Music in China*, where identity is one of the overarching themes, we get a sense of the huge importance of the meaning of regional musics in that huge nation. In one sense, Chinese music is made up of many regional genres, and one usually needs to identify the region from which a music originates; for instance, CD track 1-3, **jiangnan sizhu** ensemble music is from the area south of the Yangtze River around the city of Shanghai and CD track 1-30 is opera from the Gwangchou (Canton) region. In a similar vein, a person's identity is invariably defined in terms of ancestral place of origin—not the nation but the region—and social class. Regardless of where one lives, the sense of identification with the place of one's origin and not one's birthplace is an important notion that grounds an individual. This tie to a specific region is manifested in multiple ways, such as dialects, cultural practice, food, and music, that, as a complex of practices, become emblems of a regional identity. However, in the modern context, regional music is often used as one of the necessary ingredients that make up what is generally called "Chinese music," a collective category that is tied to the emergence of modern nationalism. Regional versus national music turns out to be a complex issue.

So important is it in Brazil (another huge country geographically) that John Murphy organized his volume through it; CD track 2-12 gives you a taste of music from Northeast Brazil. Such music has been crucial for articulating the nostalgia felt by northeastern migrants to the large cities of the south and, indeed, in the 1940s played a crucial part in the very invention of the concept of the northeastern region of Brazil, even to the point of becoming a symbol of an "authentic" Brazil (2006: 100).

Gender.   Another kind of identity that has been explored in the case study volumes and in ethnomusicology in general is that of gender. Studies that focus on gender are about the ways maleness and femaleness are constructed. (Gender is a cultural category, while sex is a biological category.) Concerning gender, you can find observations scattered throughout this book; in chapter 2, for instance, I explore the gendering of some musical instruments.

Historically in ethnomusicological writing, as in other scholarly disciplines, gender has usually gone unnoted unless the musical practice being studied is particularly associated with females. Otherwise, maleness is taken for granted, and male spheres of cultural action have received the lion's share of attention.

Focus on women and their musical practices is burgeoning, however. In the volume on South India, for example, Vishwanathan and Allen remark that despite women's participation in artistic life from time immemorial there, written accounts of South Indian music and literary history have tended to concentrate on the contributions of men. When work by or about women musicians, authors, or composers has been published, in some cases it has been deliberately altered, in effect erased and suppressed (2004: 74). Unfortunately, the same could be said for women musicians in many places. A variety of perspectives are being taken—woman musicians as symbols of a nation, as players of gendered roles in a community, as forces for social or cultural change, as political spokespersons, as inter-cultural negotiators, and as individual artists. Relating directly to a cultural icon featured in this book, for instance, is Virginia Danielson's excellent ethnographic biography of the great Egyptian singer, Umm Kulthum (CD track 2-1). I think also of Jane Sugarman's book on wedding music in the Balkan country of Albania (1997) and Ellen Koskoff's study of a Jewish community in New York City (2001), for other instances. Ideally, whether the focus of our study is musicking by males or females, and particularly when the focus is on both, we should remark on gender because of its many implications for understanding musical practice.

Performance in public, as apposed to private, spheres has been a thorny issue in many places. Women who brave the possible consequences of having their music received as performed sexuality rather than expressive artistry have been pioneers. In Middle Eastern cultures, for instance, the respectability of a female performer must be carefully negotiated; the stardom of a singer such as Umm Kulthum in Egypt is quite remarkable in light of that reality (CD track 2-1). In both South and North India female vocalists of classical genres have in the past found the refusal to accept payment for performance as a means of maintaining unquestionable respectability. Performances on radio— heard but not seen—presented a new and respectable context for women singers.

In so many instances, the performance of a particular musical genre is a gender role. Exploring the reasons for that can reveal much about the culture and its history. In Japan, for instance, the musico-dramatic form *kabuki* has been performed exclusively by males for several centuries, although it originated with female performance. In America women instrumentalists still find it difficult to break into the predominantly male world of jazz instrumental performance.

The control of musical knowledge is another arena where gender considerations often arise. In India, whether the learners are male or female, most teachers have been men. In contemporary Japan, while there are a few famous male performers of *koto*, instruction on the instrument has passed almost entirely into the purview of women (Figure 2.12).

Likewise, the authoritative role of leader in musical ensembles is often subject to gender considerations. North American women are making their way increasingly into the ranks of professional choral conductors (figure 1.1). In the orchestral world, however, the gender barriers are tall and thick; there are still few professional women orchestral conductors.

Ideas about masculinity and femininity can be understood by considering the matter of performance style. In her book, *Engendering Song*, Jane Sugarman explores social and musical practices among the Préspa Albanian community. She writes:

> Throughout a wedding celebration, men and women gather to sing in ways that strongly differentiate them by gender. . . . While women sing softly and "thinly" of courtship and marriage, sitting with great composure deep within the host family's house, men sing loudly and "thickly" of heroism and romance, drinking and toasting boisterously in the family's courtyard. (1997: 252)

Social attitudes in South India early in the twentieth century also provide a good example of this, with gendered style affecting "the music" as well. Women were discouraged from performance mannerisms that were considered male, such as the keeping of *tāla* on the thighs. (Note: in Chapter 3, I gave you the way of keeping *tāla* with fingers.) Moreover, concerts by women singers stressed harmonious ensemble performance, rather than the jousting improvisational back-and-forth affiliated with improvisation and gendered as male musical behavior (Vishwanathan and Allen 2004: 73–74).

Conversely, it is important to note when the gender of a performer is explicitly not the point. In some traditional Japanese vocal music, it is difficult to tell whether a man or a woman is singing, so ungendered is the style; an expressive rendering of the text is the most important criterion for performance style. In Chinese opera, the way gender is represented in musical drama is more important than the sex of the performer (CD track 1-30). The dramatic role of a refined woman, for instance, may be played by a woman or a man; either will meet the expectations for sound quality and presentation that are "given" for the role. Likewise, in traditional Balinese theater, certain dance *styles* are strictly male or female. Blurring the two is a third style, known as *bebanci* (androgynous), which is enacted when a male dances a female or effeminate role, or vice versa, and when certain dances consciously combine elements of male and female styles. These three—male, female, and *bebanci*—overlap with the portrayal of the refined/coarse (*halus/ keras*) dichotomy: male or female dances can be either refined or strong and coarse. *Bebanci* dances tend to be a combination of the two or to fluctuate between them (Gold 2005: 95).

  Culture change with regard to gender and music has become a prominent issue in research. The emergence of a star system in the past two decades in many places appears to be changing the situation for women musicians. While a female Javanese singer (*pesindhen*) in non-*gamelan* contexts may perform in a style with prominent overtones of sexuality, in the context of *gamelan* she must mask those overtones (CD track 1-9). Cultural knowledge of the association of the *pesindhen* and sexuality, however, makes her presence ever intriguing, and her status has risen. At present in Indonesia, the amount of attention that should be accorded her is a dilemma.

Multiple Identities.   The focus on boundaries in ethnomusicological study has led us to understand "identity" in a number of ways—not only "types of identity" such as national, regional and gender, but from many perspectives. Tom Turino reminds us: It is generally understood that social identities are always multiple and situationally relative. The same person can identify with her family, community, school, region, with others of the same gender or social class, as well as with an 'ethnic' designation or country depending on the goals and salient nodes of identity within a particular situation (2008: 4). To demonstrate this, I invoke the steelband, or pan (CD track 1-2, Figure 1.2), which was officially proclaimed the national instrument of Trinidad and Tobago. The emergence of the steelband as a symbol of national identity draws us into stories of other types of identity—social class, ethnicity, race, gender (as told by Dudley in his case study in this series). An instrument of the lower class originally, pan began as an ingenious creation of poor people who made the most of meager resources; around 1940 people began to tune different pitches on the surface of metal containers such as paint cans. Untrained musicians took pride in mastering the musical language of the educated class. When, in the nationalist movement of the 1940s and 1950s, the collection and promotion of folk music and dance was considered important, some intellectuals in Trinidad held up the steelband as an example of "urban folk" creativity. Its cultural status gradually ascended, and middle-class youth began to play in bands; by the 1960s women even began to play. During the 1970s schools all over Trinidad began to include steelband in the curriculum. When the prime minister declared it the national instrument in 1992, some Trinidadians of East Indian descent protested that such a symbol favored the status of Afro-Trinidadian culture over Indo-Trinidadian culture. But proponents of pan countered that the steelbands had come to include people of diverse ethnicities and classes. Regardless, Trinidadians could claim to have developed the instrument entirely on their own, and furthermore, because it had achieved international recognition, it was an ideal emblem for a unified national community.

As people have multiple sensibilities, musical practices can have multiple "identities" as well. For those of Mexican heritage, for whom the connections among race, ethnicity, and social hierarchy result in social alienation in United States society, mariachi music takes on a dimension of value that is necessarily different from that in Mexican society (CD track 1-7). Emerging from its rural roots in several states of western Mexico, the music of mariachi ensembles was seized upon in the early twentieth century by Mexican media and officialdom as an important expression of Mexican national identity. Mariachis appear with campaigning politicians, as "folkloric" entertainment for tourists, and in government-sponsored representations of Mexico to the international community. Mariachi musicians, however, often are quick to express the disjuncture between being glorified by officials as a source of national identity and pride on the one hand and being neglected or victimized by class prejudice on the other.

In the United States, the Mexican American movement beginning in the 1960s and the emergence of mariachi-in-schools programs heightened the position of mariachi music as a positive signifier of cultural identity. Mariachi music's social value increased dramatically among Mexican Americans when popular singer Linda Ronstadt, of Mexican American background, launched her national tour and *Canciones de Mi Padre* album in 1987. Ronstadt brought a new spotlight of public attention to the music and made it "cool" to like mariachi music. Her promotion of the music put it in a new social light—it was worthy of the American popular mainstream, not marginal, and it was contemporary, not outmoded—and Mexican Americans flocked to it. Thousands of young Mexican Americans enthusiastically have taken up mariachi music as a closely held badge of personal and group identity. As discussed in Daniel Sheehy's volume in this series, Mexican-born mariachi musicians point to the respect and appreciation shown to them by American audiences.

ACTIVITY 6.3 *Pursuing the idea of multiple identities, turn your thoughts to yourself, the identities you embody by birth or have chosen to construct. How do these identities enter into the way you live your life? Do you keep them more or less separate, for instance, or do they overlap and shift rather seamlessly? Think as well about how you express these identities—through clothing, through forms and styles of speech or movement, by choice of associates and activities—and most important here, through music and dance.*

AUTHENTICITY

The association of music with national, ethnic, and other types of identity gives rise to one issue that just does not go away. In fact, concern with it is due largely to nationalism. As observed by Peter Wade in his *Music, Race, and Nation* on music in Colombia:

> The notion of the modern homogeneous nation in Latin America owes a great deal to European models, not just for the structures of the nation-state, but for the basic cultural values of "civilization" espoused by elites. This has led to debates within Latin American political and intellectual elites about "imitation" and "authenticity": some nationalist currents have felt that a "proper" nation cannot simply be a copy of some other (notionally original) societies and cultures; there must be some authentic cultural traditions to create originality, difference, and hence identity. (2000: 11–12)

The linking of authenticity to music came about through the thinking of the Prussian preacher Johann Herder from the late eighteenth century. Herder argued as follows (as summarized in Taruskin 2001): Language makes humans human, but it must be learned socially, in a community. Since thought is based on language, human thought is a community product. Each language manifests unique values and ideas. When the concept of language was extended to learned behavior or expressive culture—customs, music, and so on—they too were seen as essential constituents of a precious collective spirit. Expression of the collective spirit became an explicit goal of the arts. Distinctive culture could serve both as a marker of difference in external relations and a symbol behind which the citizenry could rally as a community. Thus was born the concept of authenticity as faithfulness to one's essential nature.

Authenticity became a thing as well as a quality. Where was it to be found and in what forms? Herder placed authenticity with the folk: folklore was authentic wisdom, folk music the true music of a people. With folklore elevated in value, its appropriation by elite culture to express national identity began to flourish.

The ambitious collecting of items of folk expressive culture began with Herder himself. The collecting of folk music—songs particularly, due to the value accorded to language—became an important activity of prominent figures in the history of ethnomusicology and of European music such as the Hungarian composers Béla Bartók (1881–1945) and Zoltán Kodály (1882–1967). Post–World War II socialist nations' collecting was and is state-sponsored, with the focus on archiving songs as items—the possessions of a nation, or of a region within a nation, or some other distinguishable group. Composers also collected in order to have new material for their creative work.

Questions of authenticity and folk music remained closely linked, and aspects of Herder's thinking resonated still in the publications of Maude Karpeles, an important figure in folk music research in the first half of the twentieth century. In the *Journal of the International Folk Music Council* in 1951, Karpeles defined authenticity in folk music: developing unconsciously, evolving through a process of continuity, variation, and selection, and transmitted orally. While the word "authenticity" does not appear, and her "developing unconsciously" became "springing from the creative impulse," Karpeles's hand can be seen in a resolution of the IFMC in 1953, in which folk music is defined as a "thing" that exists owing to certain creative processes:

> Folk music is the product of a musical tradition that has been evolved through the process of oral transmission. The factors that shape it are: (i) continuity which links the present to the past; (ii) variation which springs from the creative impulse of the individual or the group; and (iii) selection by the community, which determines the form or forms in which the music survives. (*Journal of the IFMC* 5 [1953]: 23)

Even very recently, where the words "authenticity" and "authentic" appear in writing about music, they are likely to refer to one or more elements in that definition of folk music. I shall focus on each of those elements in turn.

The idea of a product occurs twice in the IFMC definition: "Folk music is [a] product," and then "the form or forms in which the music survives." Whether one calls them "objects," "items," or "forms," "products" are thought of as possessing (or lacking) authenticity. In the flurry of 1980s research and argument about authentic performance practice of European music before 1750, for example, the aim was to perform as authentic an object (a piece of music) as possible—using period instruments or new instruments modeled after them, trying to learn from written sources how ornaments would have been produced, and the like.

In this way of thinking about authenticity, the act of performing also becomes an object (or, as Taruskin puts it, a text). It is happening, for instance, when, in the interest of "authentic performance," a conscientious conductor of a non-Bulgarian choral group works with the singers to achieve a sound as close as possible to that of a traditional Bulgarian chorus (CD track 2-30). Whereas the authenticity movement in musicology was a historical project, contemporary multicultural projects are more likely to try to produce "authentic performances" modeled after performance as it is heard in recent times.

Authenticity is also thought of as residing in a person who has acquired the knowledge that permits him or her to perform authentically or to evaluate "authenticity" as a critic. Here, "authenticity" resembles "authority." As Taruskin states it: "Authenticity . . . is knowing what you mean and whence comes that knowledge. And more than that, authenticity is knowing what you are, and acting in accordance with that knowledge" (1995: 56). Taruskin's "you" puts the emphasis on a person's individual identity. The matter of authenticity's residing in a person emerges for ethnomusicologists who seriously pursue the practice of a contemporary music as a means of doing research. A lively debate persists with regard to those persons' "authenticity" as performers if the music is not one they grew up knowing. Often the debate is about whether it is "really" possible to be bimusical or multimusical (equally "authentic" in more than one tradition of musical practice), or whether someone who is not native to a culture can possibly be an authentic culture bearer of the music of another culture—knowing something inside out, in a manner of speaking. The debate usually arises because some individuals consider themselves to be authoritative in a non-native musical practice, while others doubt the authenticity of that identity. You can pose the same question about performers of early European music who did not live at the time and therefore in the culture of the music they are performing.

> **ACTIVITY 6.4** *Discuss these questions with your friends: Do you think a non-native musician can be an "authentic" performer of Indian classical music? Can a Japanese musician be an "authentic" performer of jazz or European classical music? Can a white person be an "authentic" performer of black music? Can a black person be an "authentic" performer in the European operatic tradition?*

"Authenticity" becomes easily paired with the idea of "tradition" as in the IFMC definition: "Folk music is the product of a musical tradition." Even in this definition, however, "tradition" is difficult to define. It appears to be a style of performance, or a musical genre—something within which items evolve. David Coplan defines tradition as "dependent upon a symbolically constituted past whose horizons extend into the present" (1990: 40). For the purposes of this discussion, the key idea is that a tradition links the present with the past.

The nature of "the past" to which tradition is linked has been a subject of much discussion in the humanities in recent years. In her study of the American genre of country music, Joli Jensen found that enthusiasts locate "the past" in whatever they believe to be disappearing in modern life and find the expression of nostalgia in country music to be useful in facing the realities of the present:

> I believe that we ratify the conflicts of modernity by ascribing to country music the authenticity we see evaporating in the present. . . . Country music, and its burden of maintained authenticity, is a way to address, obliquely but intensely, unresolvable conflicts in modern life. . . . Various markers designate country music's "realness": natural origins, spontaneous production, communal performance, heartfelt lyrics, sincere performers, and loyal fans are among the aspects invoked to prove that country music is more real than other forms. (1998: 160–61)

"Natural origins [if she means creative impulse], spontaneous production, communal performance"—these phrases resonate with the ideas in the IFMC definition of folk music.

Nostalgia pervades the sense of the past of youth in Bulgaria, who conceive "traditional experiences" as those that precede modern experiences (see Rice's book on Bulgaria in this series). They yearn for music that does not use the most obvious devices of modern popular and classical music such as loud electronic instruments and percussion. I will return to other ideas about "the past" below.

Commercialization and the media are two realities of modern life that emerge in discussions of "authenticity." Often it is in the context of the consideration of change, or "variation," as it is put in the IFMC definition of folk music. That folk music changes is not at issue: change or variation is taken to be natural and is still generally accepted as part of the folk music process. It is the reason for the change that causes concern about authenticity. Karpeles argued in 1968 that "genuine folk song" is not possible in modern industrialized society ([10]), and that idea still lingers, with commercialization, mass media, and other characteristics of modern life being regarded as negative forces. Jensen comments on this, with respect to the audience for country music.

> When country music changed in the 1950s, many attacked the shift as commercialization. The fear was that country music, infected by outside forces like the media and big business, was becoming less authentic, less real, more commercial. This draws on claims of the mass culture debate and on metaphors evident in the production of culture perspective. It imagines music as representing and offering authenticity and imagines the media and the marketplace as outside forces—polluting, contaminating, inauthentic. (1998: 161)

Jensen herself, however, responds that country music has been fundamentally commercial in origin and purpose since at least the 1920s. In the language of cultural studies, the scholar of popular music Richard Middleton would likely denounce the reactions of Jensen's informants as bourgeois attempts to devalue urban industrial working-class culture, attempts rooted in a romantic critique of industrial society (or more generally modernity) (1990: 130, 168–69).

In fact, commercialization is part of the reality of a good deal of music that is considered to be "traditional." In his volume on Mexican and Mexican American music in this series, Dan Sheehy explores this with regard to mariachi music (CD track 1-7). Mariachi music is at once a music rooted in over 150 years of tradition, a commodity governed by market considerations, and a dynamic, evolving musical stream of activity. It is shaped and expanded by tributaries of musical innovation and social meaning from the American side of the border. According to Sheehy, a key to knowing mariachi music "from the inside out" is understanding mariachi musicians as a community linked by their common occupation.

The community, or group, is another element that obviously emerges in discussion of authenticity. It appears in the IFMC definition of folk music in two ways that resonate with Sheehy's remark about mariachi: the group as a source of musical creativity and an agent for selection of what will endure. Joli Jensen and many other scholars have looked at it from the opposite perspective: music constructing community, and musical change disrupting community.

> When a new genre's authenticity is challenged it is an acknowledge-ment that culture constructs social groups. In displacing the honky-tonk sound as the dominant kind of country music, the Nashville Sound abandoned, even betrayed, those fans who loved the sound of steel and fiddle. Social groups—call them fans, audiences, markets, or communities—are constructed in and through cultural genre. Changes in the genre change the ways people in these groups can define themselves and their relationship to each other. (1998: 163)

Here, a musical genre is an "authentic" item, in that it is expected to adhere to a model on which there is consensus and bears meaning around which a group can form. This notion is familiar from discussion above of the process of community building in nation-states.

The roots of an idea called "authenticity," then, lie in the modern Western world and in cultural politics. Ideas about authenticity emerged in relation to folk culture, and even when they develop about something without that connection, they generally involve a link to tradition or at least to some idea about "the past." Notions of authenticity in music are generally held to be constructed: "Claims about authenticity . . . are involved in a power struggle over the ownership of value in which tra-dition and modernity are key terms" (Wade 2000: 25). Many of us, I would guess, would agree with Australian Tony Mitchell that "notions of musical purity and authenticity are an idealistic form of colonialist nostalgia" (1993: 335). But at the same time, we ethnomusicologists bal-ance a profound respect for traditional [indigenous knowledge], includ-ing dance and song, with an admiration for the creative projects of innovative contemporary artists" (Diamond 2008: 34). While the soci-ologist George Lipsitz suggests that "concepts of cultural practice that privilege autonomous, 'authentic,' and non-commercial culture as the only path to emancipation do not reflect adequately the complexities of culture and commerce in the contemporary world" (1994:16), we still find notions of authenticity proclaimed, as people make music mean-ingful and useful in their lives. As Tim Rice put it, if authenticity is to retain any meaning at all, it has to mean that music is authentic when it responds in some meaningful way to the culture and society around it, as it virtually always does (2004: 101).

ACTIVITY 6.5 *Can you identify some musical genre you think about in terms of "authenticity"? If so, articulate your ideas about what makes an item in that genre "authentic" or not. Then consider the points above, relative to your ideas.*

TRANSCENDING BOUNDARIES

Ethnomusicologists are now vitally interested in the transcendence of boundaries by both people and music. This was greatly spurred by the burgeoning attention to popular music from the 1980s—musics that have been circulated and are circulating across just about every imaginable boundary. Indeed, music can be useful where people desire or need for boundaries to be transcended. In East Africa, for instance, where a number of ethnic groups with different value systems reside together, musical contexts provide important opportunities for negotiating differences. Negotiation takes the form of friendly competition, as popular entertainment events include musical performances such as song duels, choir competitions, drumming, and dance contests (see Barz's volume on East Africa in this series).

Gender boundaries in instrumental performance are being transcended by some individual musicians. Stella Chiweshe of Zimbabwe is the first woman to achieve acceptance and fame as an *mbira* performer, and in Bulgaria Maria Stoyanova has established a fine reputation on a male-gendered bagpipe, the **gaida**. In Mexican and Mexican American culture, shifting gender relations are inviting women to take a more active role in mariachi performance (CD track 1-7); whereas women were typically excluded from public performance except as singers, many are now taking up the instrumental genre.

"Trans" is the operative prefix in "transcending boundaries". "Trans" is attached to terms for process, for instance. "Transculturation" has been espoused by the ethnomusicologist Margaret Kartomi to replace the term "acculturation" (1981: 234). Kartomi defines "transculturation" as "a process of cultural transformation marked by the influx of new culture elements and the loss or alteration of existing ones." Originally proposed by the Cuban anthropologist Fernando Ortiz, the term "transculturation" was intended to avoid the connotation of political hegemony implied by the older term, but it does more than that. It causes us to reconsider the matter of cultural encounter in the process of musical change. The term "transculturation" neither specifies nor even implies a physical location where the cultural transformation occurs. No people are specified, as in the "groups of individuals" in the definition of "acculturation" above. No circumstance of transmission is specified, as in "sustained first-hand contact." What is more or less specified is a sense of time, suggested by that contested word "culture." "Culture" usually implies some kind of history, some kind of continuity, some kind of "tradition." With the exception of that last factor, the term "transculturation" would seem appropriate to cover the circumstances of the circulation of musics worldwide.

> **ACTIVITY 6.6** *Since place, people, and circumstances of "influx" are not specified, you may find the idea of "transculturation" applicable to music that has been created within a diasporic group. Taking a music you are familiar with—salsa, gospel, Asian, American jazz, country-style polka, for instance—as a case study, write a brief essay arguing for or against the utility of the term "transculturation" as defined by Kartomi to guide your thinking about that music.*

"Trans" is the operative prefix again in terms that describe the transcending of boundaries of place, as in "transnational" and "translocal." This takes us to the lively issue of globalization, to which I shall return below.

The Mass Media. Circulation of knowledge—and its corollary, access to knowledge—without the necessity of a personal encounter is the hallmark of the mass media—print; radio, and television; phonograph, cassette, CD, DVD, and MP3 files; video and film—all of which are important means for transcending boundaries. This was first approached in chapter 1 in the section on transmission by aural/oral, tactile, and visual means. The use of mass media is usually an element mentioned as key in the process of modernization that I discussed earlier in this chapter. Now, of course, the mass media are a potent force in the lives of just about everyone on the planet.

Many scholars share the opinion that the mass media's effects on musical cultures are neither positive nor negative in themselves; the effects depend on the uses to which they are put and the responses they engender. In a thought-provoking introduction to *Ethnicity, Identity and Music*, Martin Stokes suggests that the control of media systems by states, through ownership of the technology and its ability to exclude rival systems through censorship, is a tool of social control that few authoritarian states have overlooked. But media are not a sure means of enacting social control. A consumer can turn off a radio or television set, or tune to some other station. However, the rapid changes in recording and sound reproduction technology in recent years have arguably democratized recording and listening, and consequently weakened the grip of state and music industry monopolies (Stokes 1994: 12).

The uses of the media are too numerous to write about here, so two examples must suffice. Media can certainly play a vital role in legitimizing a music. Mwesa Mapoma has reported that in contemporary Zambia change is expected within expressive culture, and the mass media foster both traditional music and new popular music that is being created, primarily by youth who are adapting Western instruments to traditional norms (1991). The recording industry especially has been an important and powerful agent in the process of defining ethnicities and classes. We need only think of "race records" in the early history of the commercial recording industry in the United States to remember that.

The mass media are, of course, technological developments and the effects of technological developments are indisputably complex. An anonymous reader of this second edition in draft raised an important perspective:

> Has technology cleansed us of the person in music? There are two guitars recordable from every performance—the guitar where every movement of the fingers across the frets can be heard, where we hear the work of the performer with every movement. Or, we hear the pure sound of the instrument—a purity of guitar sound without the guitarist as if heard from 25 feet away. Did this begin with the first recording?

For musicians and their audiences, issues of the effects of media have never been simple. Changes in technology have had tangible effect even on TMI—"the music itself." The revolutionary, if de facto, privileging of one fixed rendition of a song—mistakes and all—frozen on a 78 RPM disc, as "the" authoritative version, confronted musicians in India and elsewhere with one of the most profound conceptual changes in the history of music. When recording of early discs began in India, the leading male musicians who had been given their *guru*'s repertoire during a long and arduous period of musical apprenticeship took to it slowly and reluctantly. A strong reason for their reluctance either to record or to broadcast their intellectual property was an intuitive apprehension that these unknown new technologies could reduce their direct control over the reception and consumption of their art—who could listen to it, under what circumstances, and what listeners could do with that music. They would, in effect, transcend the boundaries of the artists' authority (Vishwanathan and Allen 2004: 88).

When scholars began to study music on a global basis and faced the tremendous power of the current Euro-America capitalist colonialism, the predictions of impending cultural "gray-out" forecast a dire future for music. However, new recording technologies no longer imply quite the same kind of dependence upon large companies, and local industries all over the world are fostering local musical productions. A reader of the draft of this second edition reminded me of the "longtail" effect of the Internet, whereby tiny niche markets can be catered to because it costs virtually nothing to store the music and make it available for download—the ubiquity of obscurity. The issues involved here are huge. This takes me to the topic of globalization.

Globalization.   Globalization is the quintessential path to and result of transcending boundaries. "Globalization" suggests increasing connectivity around the world with respect to many spheres of life and the taking up of values and practices in multiple locations simultaneously. An early term for it in music scholarship was a "trans" word: "transnationalization." "The notion of globalization understood as transnationalization—taken often as a synonym for universalization, meaning Americanization for some, Japanization for others, and neo-colonialization for yet others—takes for granted the erasure of geopolitical boundaries and the transcendence of space through mass-mediated communication . . . instantly shifting population groups and their reconstituting of space relations in tandem with the intense trafficking of ideas and goods and the networking of people" (Guilbault: 2005, Vol. 5 p. 149). The term "translocal" has been useful for the ethnomusicologist Tom Turino as he suggests an analytical possibility for narrowing the often unrestricted use of the term "global." He reserves the term "global" to describe phenomena such as the contemporary system of nation-states that "literally or very nearly encompass the totality of the earth" (2000: 6).

For us ethnomusicologists who are Asianists particularly, the circumstances of global connectivity with integrated global markets, exchange of technology, values, and practices seem nothing recent. The limitation of the idea of "globalization" to the contemporary condition is short-sighted. We think of what is now called the Silk Road—which took goods and ideas in organized ways between the Mediterranean and the Pacific from the late second century BCE (until the late nineteenth century)—that was a significant factor in the flourishing of the great civilizations of China, Egypt, Mesopotamia, Persia, India, and Rome and helped to lay the foundations for the modern world. Religious beliefs of Christianity, Buddhism, and Islam, paper and silk manufacturing—and musical instruments—were carried back and forth across the landmass of the known world (as opposed to the whole world known now). One result was the dissemination of a type of plucked lute—the *oud* in West Asia, its successor *pipa* in China (CD track 2-35) and *biwa* in Japan (CD track 1-38), as well as its successor lutes of European musical practices.

Other great empires (little mentioned in Western tellings of history) have existed since, facilitating widespread connectivity with integrated markets over great geographic expanses. The Turkish Ottoman Empire (1299 to 1922 CE) is a case in point, as Rice discusses in his volume on Bulgaria and Marcus does in his volume on Egypt and the eastern Arab world. The Ottoman Empire caused cultural connections through the sharing of instruments, musical and poetic forms, concepts and practices. Colonial formations did the same in the nineteenth and twentieth centuries, causing the dissemination of European and Europe-derived instruments, musical and poetic forms, repertoire, concepts, and practices that are spoken to in the volumes on Trinidad, Egypt, First Nations, Java, China, Japan, and more. The Soviet bloc caused the same over enormous geographic expanses, including establishing models that would be followed by the communist government in China (see Lau 2008). The process of globalization is both historical and ongoing.

Worldwide integration through technology and market exchange is the hallmark of globalization, and we are beginning to understand that many, if not most, musics have emerged from processes of hybridization or fusion. In his *Subcultural Sounds: Micromusics of the West*, the ethnomusicologist Mark Slobin has commented on fusion while noting the diversity of styles in the music of the *klezmer* musician Andy Statman. A leading mandolinist in bluegrass/newgrass music in the 1970s, Statman helped to found a fledgling *klezmer* movement, "a drive by younger Jewish-American musicians of differing pasts and persuasions to forge a new 'ethnic' style based on their neglected 'Jewish' roots." In the next fifteen years Statman's music branched out past the older *klezmer* sound to include not only his old favorite, bluegrass, but beyond. He explained to a reporter from the *New York Times* that "the orchestra plays traditional Jewish European music, but we also flow freely into bits and pieces of what we like. . . . It's our own form of improvisation, and folk music and the bluegrass influence is right there"; Statman calls the result "Moroccan African Mongolian klezmer music" (12 April 1992). Slobin rejoins: "In figuring out this stance, remember that the 'traditional Jewish European music' itself was a blend of styles including Moldavian, Ukrainian, and shades of Balkan, all transformed in New York in the 1920s and 30s" (1993: x).

In addition to fusion, then, a preference for eclecticism can result from "intense trafficking of goods and ideas." For another example, the folklorist's definition of "folk song" is an artificial construction of no particular importance to traditional Irish singers themselves. These folksingers' repertoire includes music hall song, locally composed songs, country music, rock, rhythm and blues, rap, fusion styles, and others (Scott and Hast, 2004). Needless to say, this challenges notions of authenticity.

In addition to hybridity/fusion and eclecticism, the widespread "intense trafficking of goods and ideas" sometimes gives rise to a weakening or even loss of their original association with a sense of place. Scholars speak of a process of indigenization by which new cultural ideas or expressive objects may be adopted but made or used as something that functions within the existing structures, institutions, or values of a society. The Japanese genre of imperial court music (*gagaku*, CD track 1-38) is a case in point. Brought to Japan between the fifth and eighth centuries of the Common Era, when influences were strong from China and other Asian musics, a process of indigenization of the ensemble and its music from the ninth century was so effective that its foreignness has faded in the minds of most Japanese (Wade 2005). Indigenized in a much shorter period were social dances performed in square formation, first brought to Ireland by French dancing masters in the mid- to late nineteenth century; they were quickly indigenized in Ireland by the composition of new choreography and the use of Irish dance tunes for the accompanying music (Scott and Hast 2004: 5). In Ireland, too, the bouzouki has become a favorite instrument, so popular that an indigenized Irish variant is in regular production and general use. Christian choral music is another case in point, as discussed by Barz in the volume on East Africa (CD track 2-40). Finally, is not American jazz a quintessential product of a process of indigenization!

In addition, the intense trafficking of intellectual property challenges concepts of the ownership of "culture" (the right to intellectual property). Questions with far-reaching implications are being raised. Should you or should you not be able to download music from the Internet without worrying about who owns it? Should the composer of the national anthem of a new nation-state be paid royalties on the song, as one individual recently asserted to his government? Should DJs be able to sample copyrighted materials without permission? Should poorer, economically dependent nations be forced by the United States and other powerhouses in the entertainment industry to change their local copyright conventions to conform to international copyright conventions that clearly work to the advantage of the powerhouses (a process seen by scholars of popular music such as Jocelyne Guilbault as a new form of colonialism)?

ACTIVITY 6.7 *To think about the issues of intellectual property rights, write a quick summary of your own practices for acquiring the music you want to hear. Then use the Internet to find at least three commentaries by musicians on access to their music and at least three on the part of "the industry" or the legal profession to glimpse what it sees as the issues. Finally, analyze where your practices and concerns lie within those opinions.*

As transnational corporations these days create integrated global markets and change the nature of our cultural encounters, the importance of the nation-state and ethnic groupings as sources of identity and identification recedes somewhat. Individuals grow more cognizant of their multiple, shifting identities (multiple subjectivities) as they think in terms of their nationality as well as their ethnicity, their affiliation with others in a transnational diasporic "community" (Clifford 1994), or gender or religious affiliation or something else that supersedes localized boundaries. For ethnomusicologists, this has meant looking at the ways people are making music meaningful and useful as they situate themselves in a globally oriented world—transcending old boundaries with a sense of freedom or erecting new ones to gain some sense of control, as they explore multiple musical practices made available and visible through the media and make aesthetic choices for themselves.

The Local. Yet "the local" endures, in several senses of the word. For some transnational music, the original place associations of the music remain intact, however widely the musical style circulates and is played with creatively. Tango is Argentinian no matter where it is found; Irish music is Irish, no matter where it is made or who makes it; mariachi played in Los Angeles is recognized by everyone to be Mexican. The cultural space each occupies is linked to, but no longer dependent on, place.

The ways in which "the local" intersect with "the global" are myriad. Historians and other scholars see, for instance, a particularly urban cultural formation—a sense of shared "cosmopolitan" habits of belief, thought, technology use, practices, and the like—that can be found among particular groups of people across borders of different countries around the world. Ethnomusicologist Tom Turino has found a valuable analytic with which to look at Andean (particularly Peruvian) musical traditions and practices; see his book in the Global Music Series. He uses the term "cosmopolitan" to refer to objects, ideas, and cultural positions that are widely diffused throughout the world. Through the lens of music of Zimbabwe, in East Africa, he sees cosmopolitanism as always localized and always shaped by and somewhat distinct in each locale. "Cosmopolitan cultural formations are therefore always simultaneously local and translocal, i.e., situated in many sites which are not necessarily in geographical proximity; rather, they are connected by different forms of media, contact, and interchanges"—what he calls "cosmopolitan loops" (2000: 7–8).

Whether global or cosmopolitan, global-local or local-translocal, musicians at the present time negotiate complex sets of relationships. The example of a Haitian group, Boukman Eksperyans, is given by the sociologist George Lipsitz in his important book *Dangerous Crossroads*:

> Ever since their recording debut in 1989, the members of Boukman Eksperyans have been making music rendering them both dangerous and endangered. . . . Their 1990 carnival song, "Ke'-m Pa Sote" ("My Heart Doesn't Leap, You don't Scare me") played a part in the popular revitalization of voudou, helping to spark [an insurgent movement]. By connecting the dance hall with the voudou temple, "Ke'-m Pa Sote" also united town dwellers and rural peasants in opposition to the corruption that permeates Haitian politics. . . . Through its music, Boukman Esksperyans inverted, subverted, and reappropriated for revolutionary ends the rituals and symbols long employed by the [Haitian paramilitary forces] to preserve tyrannical rule. By the same

token, they attempted to use the commodity culture brought to Haiti over centuries by foreign investment and foreign invasion as a focal point of resistance to the exploitation and oppression perpetrated on the people by outside powers and the country's own comprador elite. . . . The same circuits of investment and commerce that bring low-wage jobs to Haiti's factories and fields carry the music of Boukman Eksperyans to a wider world audience. The same connections between U.S. multinationals and Haitian poverty that insures a perpetual presence on the island by the American security state also makes the visibility of Boukman Eksperyans in the U.S.A. a strategic resource for the group as they try to criticize their government and still stay alive. (1994: 8–10)

Boukman Eksperyans make music meaningful and useful not only in their lives, but in the lives of many others for whom they sing.

ACTIVITY 6.8 *Explore just how "global" your "local" musical choices are by making a systematic inventory. Visit the largest recording store in your location and make a catalog of the types of music available for purchase. Tune in to every radio station you can receive. Investigate all the explicitly artistic channels available through your TV. (Leave aside the Internet for this one.) Then situate yourself with regard to those choices, thinking about the perspectives discussed in this chapter.*

I have focused here on only a few of the lively issues that unify the case studies in this Global Music Series. My approach has been to contextualize them, to put them in the broader perspective of the intellectual work of the field of ethnomusicology. I now direct you to those case studies, where you can see the issues addressed in a "local" context.

CHAPTER 7

Thinking about Fieldwork

∞

Study through fieldwork is a particular hallmark of ethnomusicology, and this chapter guides you in experiencing that for yourself. Basically, doing fieldwork is the process of learning about something primarily directly from people. Fieldwork is a window through which to learn how people experience music and express culture.

Where is the field and what is the work? Historically, "the field" meant any place other than a library (where materials recorded in some form are the primary source). And because most ethnomusicologists worked someplace other than in their own culture, "the field" meant somewhere distant. In reality, however, "the field" encompasses the library and the Internet as well, because the best way to start is to find what has already been reported on the subject. In the broadest and most pragmatic terms, the "field" is anywhere we can learn about a topic, including with our own family and friends. Our home communities offer abundant field locations.

The "work" in fieldwork has always meant any kind of activity that contributes to learning about music. Take the process of locating sources, for instance: early recordings of calypso that were important for Shannon Dudley's book on carnival music in Trinidad (2004) were none too easy to find, but necessary for his tracking of the sociocultural meanings of steelband (chapter 1: p. 7). Collecting of tunes has been hugely important to most everyone who has worked on Irish music (CD tracks 1-4, 1-8, 1-26). Meeting musicians and audience members is another kind of locating of sources, as Ruth Stone did in order to learn what Liberian musicians and audiences valued in performance (chapter 3: p. 97). Beverley Diamond was fortunate to locate Inuit and First Nations peoples who would welcome her into their communities for fieldwork, including the indoor spaces where she could observe the juggling game (CD track 2-43).

Doing a lot of observing is another aspect of the work in fieldwork. (Remember visual learning that was discussed in chapter 1.) Attending numerous concerts provided Scott Marcus a window into the dynamics of the performer-audience relationship in Egyptian music (Chapter 5: p. 152). Tom Turino visited town plazas on market days to learn about the meaning and use of the *charango* (chapter 2: p. 50).

A third example of activity in fieldwork—and one that most ethnomusicologists treasure—is making music; you can learn a great deal by being a participant observer. Perhaps more importantly, when we put ourselves in the position of being a student of music along with other music makers, our experience is one of sharing rather than staring, and our relationships become less distant.

Even casual conversation about music turns into "work" whenever we begin to think about it systematically rather than in random fashion and to keep a record of what we have learned. Another term for hanging out at that point is "field research." You read of Rajna LeDoux's experience with her vocal teacher in Turkey (Chapter 4: p. 122), and you tried experiencing Korean rhythm as Donna Kwon did in her study of the percussion ensemble practice that is pictured in Figure 3.3. If George Ruckert and Matthew Allen had not studied North Indian and South Indian musics as practitioners, they could not have become so comfortable with those formidable (to me) rhythmic practices (CD tracks 2-14, 2-16, 2-43, and 2-44). Lisa Gold could explain the challenge of coordinating sudden stops of *angsel* because she has years of experience as a participant observer playing Balinese gamelan (Chapter 5, CD track 2-42).

Learning from people can be fruitful and fun if three guiding principles are followed:

1. Keep focusing on the purpose of your project.

2. Remember that you are seeking to learn from others, not seeking to prove something you have already decided is the case.

3. Imagine yourself in the position of any person with whom you are consulting. What kinds of questions would you enjoy (or not enjoy) being asked, for instance? Here the "golden rule" really applies: treat others as you want them to treat you! This is a matter of the ethics of field work.

PICKING A PROJECT

WORD OF ADVICE: *For your project choose something you can easily manage to do. It does not need to be a complicated topic; it should be a straightforward starting point. A broad topic should be narrowed. That is, your project should be small scale and short term.*

Anticipating that you may wonder what I mean by "a complicated project," I picked just one from this book as an illustration. In Chapter 1 (pp. 18-19), I cited Tim Rice's reading of the politics of wedding music in communist-period Bulgaria. For Rice to have gained that understanding took considerable field research, i.e., it was a very complicated project. He had to have investigated the history of Bulgarian Muslim communities and their musical repertoires. He had to learn about government policies, how they were enforced, and what the effects were. He also had to gain knowledge of the nonminority Bulgarians who were the clients of the Roma musicians in order to sense the hopes for freedom they harbored and explore why music other than their own "folk music" served better to express them. All that took years.

The project you pick can be almost anything, as long as you keep it small scale and short term. A project could be derived, for example, from any number of points made in this book that particularly interest you. Activity 2.5 (p. 56) is intended to point you in that direction. For another example, relating to the section on dissemination of musical knowledge, if you take or have taken instruction on an instrument or voice, you might shape a project around your teacher's pedagogy. How were or are you taught? What materials does your teacher use, and why were they chosen? Does your teacher teach other students the way she or he teaches you? What has been your teacher's learning experience, and what is its relation to the present teaching methods? To do this project, you would draw on your own participant observation, interview your teacher and other students, and perhaps observe lessons of other students (with permission of both the teacher and the students, of course).

Thinking from the people point of view, a good place to start might be doing a life history, to learn about someone's musical experience and the meaning of music in his or her life. Activities 1.1 and 1.7 could be the basis for such a project, for instance.

- Is there a member of your family who loves music, with whom you have never talked about it? This might be a good way to get to know a grandparent or aunt or uncle better.
- What is the musical experience of someone you know from another culture?
- Is music meaningful and useful to them, and if so, in what ways?

Thinking from the topical point of view, identify something having to do with music that you are really interested in and build a project around it. For example:

- If you play in a band or sing in a chorus, explore the history of the group: When and why was it founded? What sort of people have belonged to it, and why? Who has supported it financially? Where has it performed? How does it fit into the general music scene in the area?

- Consider the same sort of project, but with a group on campus that you do not participate in. This presents a greater challenge with regard to locating sources.

- If there is a kind of music you really love, learn if there is a local group that performs it and find out about "living that music" from the music makers' perspectives. One of my students studied the reasons why other students play in pickup bands. She looked into points raised in this book—choice of music to play, ideas about skill level, their motivation for making the music, their intended audience and what relationship they envisage with that audience in their musicking, and the like.

- If you like instruments, look for an instrument maker or repairer in your vicinity and learn about them from that perspective. One of my students found a local luthier to interview and observe at work. First, however, he studied about the construction of lutes in printed sources, so he could build on a body of information and therefore ask better questions. He followed up on such questions as what could affect the sound of the instrument, how the pitch was set, the specifications an intended buyer (if any) might have made, the economics of instrument production, and other questions.

- If you are interested in another field of study, try a topic that combines it with music. One of my students investigated the correlation of abilities in math and music.

- Propose a hypothesis to test. One of my students hypothesized that studying to music helps improve concentration.

- If you have become interested in any music unfamiliar to you before studying with this book, design a project that will take you into it more deeply. This is a good opportunity to learn more about a culture other than your own, for example.

WORD OF ADVICE: *Dedicate a notebook or computer file or some other repository to this project right from this early stage. I prefer something easily portable because I find that I need to use it at unexpected as well as anticipated times—when an idea suddenly occurs to me or someone makes a good suggestion that I might pursue, for instance.*

WORD OF ADVICE: *Make a list in your journal of several possible projects. Many things can happen, so you need a backup idea.*

WORD OF ADVICE: *Keep a record in your journal of all ideas and activities, with entries dated. Note even things you try that do not work, such as effort to connect with a consultant.*

PLANNING THE PROJECT

Once you have an idea for a project, you should plan how to carry it out. Asking yourself some questions is a good way to test the viability of your project—whether or not you can manage to do it. If it becomes clear that one project is not easily doable, repeat this questioning process for other projects on your list until you find the right one for your interests and circumstances.

What: What sorts of activities will I need to carry out to do this project? Will it be sufficient to interview persons, or will I need to attend performances as well, or just hang out?

Who: Who will I need to speak to—one person or several? If one, is that person likely to welcome my questions and have time for me? If several, how many and why? Do I want to ask the same questions of each one, or do I want to learn about something different from each one?

When: Will it be easy to arrange a time to see the people I need to see? Where is the flexibility in my schedule? Can I adjust to their schedule, since they are doing me a favor? If they can meet only at night, for instance, can I manage that? If hanging out or volunteering to help with something in return is important, how much time can I allow for that?

Where: Where will I need to go to carry out this project? If it is at some distance, how will I get there? How much time will it take to get there and back? How far is too far?

Cost: Is this going to cost something monetarily? Do I need to make toll calls to speak with people? Do I have to pay mass transit fares or buy gas or cross a toll bridge to get somewhere? Do I need to purchase a hosting gift if I visit someone's home? Pay for tickets for a performance or two? Have equipment such as recorders and cameras and supplies for them?

DOING THE PROJECT

WORD OF ADVICE: *In your journal, make a tentative schedule for doing the project—by when you need to have done what. It's a good idea to work backward from whatever deadline you may have.*

One caveat: If you have any plan to publish a written report or research essay (see "Finishing the Project"), it may be required on your campus to get the approval of the Committee for Protection of Human Subjects before you do the project. You, as the principal investigator, and your teacher, as the faculty adviser, must acknowledge responsibility for the conduct of the study and the protection of the rights and welfare of the human subjects who are directly or indirectly involved in the project. The requirement to get approval and the nature of the application clearly relate mostly to scientific research, but the concerns raised are appropriate for some ethnomusicological research as well. Our consultants are, after all, "human subjects." If approval of your project is required, you need to allot time in your tentative schedule for the approval process.

Sometimes the most time-consuming part of a project is establishing the contact with the person or persons you need to speak with. Figure out before you call just how you are going to introduce yourself. Be ready to say who you are and why you are calling (see guiding principle 1 on p. 196). Do not forget to keep a record of each call you make or message you write—even if you do not reach the person or get a response. Be persistent: after waiting a reasonable length of time (being considerate of your consultant and having decided how much time you can afford to wait, given your schedule), call again; try several times within two weeks. If you try several times within two weeks and never connect, then you know you had probably better not count on meeting that person. If you do connect, and the person really does not seem to want to meet with you, follow guiding principle 3 and graciously say, "Thank you for your time anyway." Move on to Plan B.

WORD OF ADVICE: *Call or write or—even better—go to the research location now! Do not put it off. Begin making contacts even before you have taken some of the steps suggested below.*

Here is where "the field" is located in the library. (I hope you resist the temptation to completely replace the library with the Internet.) Search for studies already published that might guide you in your project. If, for instance, you are going to do a life history, find some published life histories that are based on interviews to get the flavor of such research; jazz history offers many such accounts, for instance. If you are going to learn about a musical organization, find a published history of a musical organization and analyze what questions were asked in order to write that history. If you are going to interview someone from another culture, do some basic reading about that culture and listening to its music. You will learn much more if you build on something. Keep notes on it all in your journal with clear citations of where you found the information and full information on the sources. For assistance with the format for bibliographic information, use as a guide the entries in my References section for this book.

Creating a survey questionnaire is one way to conduct research; conducting an interview is another. Before you meet with anyone, make a tentative list of questions you will work into the conversation. Formulate questions so that you are not leading the respondent to an answer.

Practice interview or survey questions on a friend. You may discover that they are too general, too detailed, too personal, unclear, or drawing answers that are not the sort you were looking for. Keep honing the questions as you do the research; you need good questions to get good answers.

Think ahead about how you are going to capture what you hear in a conversation. Will you want to ask the person if you can record the conversation? Ethics dictate that you must not assume that it is OK and, besides, if your consultant is nervous about it, that could affect the quality of the conversation. If you or the person you are meeting prefers it, be satisfied with your notetaking; jot down as much as you can manage. Have the machine and any supplies ready, however, in case you prefer and are permitted to record. Do not depend on plugging anything in; also, insert batteries and test the machine before you need to use it. (Take extra ones, too!) You'll find it useful to jot quick notes even while recording, to cue your follow-up questions.

The same ethics pertain for making a visual record of some sort. Get permission first. I find that most consultants do not mind having their photograph taken, at least as a kind of documentation, and appreciate receiving a copy as a follow-up thank you. Before you end your meeting, show your consultant what you have written and get signed permission to use it in your final project.

For further guidance, a list is the best help.

- Make a checklist of everything you need to take when you go to meet with someone. It is very useful if you have a sudden opportunity.
- When you are interviewing someone, listen carefully. Follow up on things they say, as well as asking your planned questions.
- In all your relationships with people, imagine yourself in their places. Show sensitivity in your interactions. Act with others as you want them to act with you!
- Label and date your recordings. Be sure to get people's names right. Keep a list of them in your notebook.
- Keep a list of the photographs you take.
- As soon as possible after meeting with someone, add to the notes you took during the interview anything you forgot or did not have time to record. Also, summarize in your journal the most important things you learned. Then write up your impressions of that

person as an informant—were they knowledgeable, vague, helpful, reluctant, and so on—as a guide for using the information they gave you. Discerning whether a person is a relative "insider" or "outsider" can be helpful (but you must define what you mean by those two statuses). If you try to do your project on the Internet, you will not be able to do the same sort of evaluating of your source that you can do in person.

In the case study volumes of this Global Music Series, you will find the authors situating themselves with regard to their insider-outsider status. Sometimes that status is utterly clear on everyone's part, as in "We, Dora Hast and Stan Scott, are outsiders here, American musicians with a long-standing passion for Irish traditional music. Jerry's invitation [to the session] on this night in early June, 1997 is a pleasant surprise" (2004: 1). Sometimes it is less clear: "At a village dance I attended in the Pirin region in 1973, I noticed a man staring at me. . . . He demanded gruffly, "Who are you?" I explained that I was an American student spending the year in Bulgaria researching traditional music. He thought about this a minute before exclaiming, "You lie! . . . You speak Bulgarian and you dance Bulgarian dances. Therefore you are a Bulgarian" (Rice 2004: 44). The question of who is an insider, who an outsider, is sometimes related to the issue of authenticity, as in Activity 6.4. It can be quite political and a matter of some sensitivity to which you need to be attuned.

- Figure out some way to double-check information you receive—by asking a second person the same question or checking a newspaper article perhaps.
- Reread this chapter periodically to keep you on track.
- Enjoy yourself.

FINISHING THE PROJECT

To finish your project, plan some kind of oral or written presentation. Your journal, summaries and further notes, tapes, photos, questionnaires, and double checks are your resources for this. Do not forget to articulate some sense of your experience, as well as the results of your study.

- Organize an oral presentation.
- Create some kind of art: a long poem or series of poems, a song, a visual essay, a painting or a video, a theater piece.
- Write a report on your project or essay on the research project. Sending a write-up to the people with whom you worked is a good and ethical thing to do.
- However you decide to do it, be sure to follow up with your consultants to thank them.

In addition to having learned about something that interests you, by carrying out your fieldwork project you will have learned more about how people make music meaningful and useful in their lives. In addition, you have put yourself in a better position to evaluate the results of ethnomusicologists' field research. There is a world of it out there to explore.

Glossary of Musical Terms

∾

Acceleration Speeding up the pace of the basic beats.

Acculturation A theory of change in the process of cultural encounters.

Ādi tāla South Indian meter of 8 counts subdivided 4 + 2 + 2.

Aerophone Instrument whose primary sound-producing medium is vibrating air.

Aesthetics Artistic values.

Accompanist Person performing a supporting musical part.

Ālāp-joṛ-jhālā-gat North Indian instrumental form.

Alto Lower female voice; instrumental range below soprano.

Angsel In Balinese music, a cue, sign, or articulation of a dance movement and music marked by a sudden rhythmic break or accent.

Arpeggio Pitches of a chord sounded sequentially.

Assymetrical meter Rhythmic grouping with subgroups of irregular numbers of counts.

Aural transmission Learning by hearing.

Badhat In North Indian music, "growth, development."

Ballad In folk music terminology, a narrative song.

Bar In Western meter and notation, one metric group of beats (also called MEASURE).

Bass Lowest vocal or instrumental range.

Ba yin Ancient Chinese classification system for instruments.

Beat In rhythm, equal-length durations or long or short subgroup in some systems of rhythmic grouping; in pitch, periodic variations in loudness when two sound waves with different frequencies overlap.

Berimbau   Brazilian musical bow used in *capoeira*.

Binary form   Musical form of two different sections (AB).

Bridge   On a chordophone, a component that holds the string up from the main body of the instrument.

Bunraku   Traditional Japanese puppet theater.

Cadence   Musical term for an ending.

Call and response   Generally, the juxtaposition of solo with group; more specifically, a musical repartee between parts.

Canon   Strict imitative polyphony, with the identical melody appearing in each voice but at staggered intervals (*see* ROUND).

Capoeira   Brazilian dance/martial art/game with musical accompaniment.

Changdan   Rhythm patterns drummed or otherwise articulated in Korean music.

Chang-gu   A Korean drum.

Charango   Small Peruvian chordophone in guitar family.

Chungmori changdan   A Korean rhythmic pattern.

Chord   In tonal music, three or more pitches sounding together in a functional way; intervals stacked vertically.

Chordophone   Instrument whose primary sound-producing medium is a vibrating string.

Chord progression   A sequence of chords that structure the music.

Chorus   In musical structure, long refrain added to song verse; main section of a popular song.

Chromatic scale   Scale using all twelve Western pitches within an octave.

Classification   A category with clear criteria.

Clave   In Caribbean and Latin American music, a rhythmic pattern repeated without change as a rhythmic foundation for a musical selection.

Colotomic meter   Articulation of the metric grouping by one or more instruments in a Southeast Asian ensemble.

Composing   Creating music, whether in the mind or in writing, whether to be repeated in the same form or subject to variation.

Compound meter   Meter in which each beat consists of a subgroup of three counts/pulses.

Concertina   A free-reed type of aerophone popular in Irish music

Concertmaster   Female or male leader of the violin section of a European orchestra who functions as assistant to the conductor.

Consonance   From medieval European thought, intervals or chords that sound relatively stable and free of tension; generally, an aesthetically pleasing interval or chord.

Corpophone   One's body used as a musical instrument.

Corrido   Mexican and Mexican American narrative song genre.

Culture (musical)   Ways in which people make music meaningful and useful in their lives.

Dalang   In Indonesian theater, a puppet master.

Dapu   In Chinese music, the process of a musician realizing a prescriptive notation in sound.

Deceleration   Slowing down the pace of the basic beats.

Descriptive notation   Detailed notation of what a performer is to play or sing.

Diatonic scale   Scale comprising some arrangement of half and whole steps.

Didjeridu   Australian aborigine aerophone.

Dissonance   From medieval European thought, intervals or chords that sound relatively tense and unstable; generally, a discordant interval or chord.

Di-tze   Chinese flute-type aerophone.

Dominant   In tonal music, the fifth pitch up from a tonic; root of a dominant chord (V).

Downbeat   In Western meter, count 1.

Drone   One or more pitches sounding persistently.

Dumm   In Arab music, a mnemonic syllable for the deepest or lowest sound a drum can produce.

Dynamics   The volume of sound.

Electronophone   Instrument whose primary sound-producing medium is electricity.

Enharmonic pitches   In tonal music, two names for the same pitch.

Ensemble   Musical group.

Filulu   A Tanzanian flute-type aerophone.

Flat In notation, a sign indicating that the note to which it is attached is to be played or sung a half step lower.

Form The design of a musical selection.

Forró Northeast Brazilian dance genre.

Frequency (pitch) In acoustics, rate of vibration (cycles per second) in a string, column of air, or other sound-producing body.

Fret On a cordophone, a component under a string but not touching it that indicates pitch placement.

Functional harmony Chords as used in the Western tonal system.

Gagaku Japanese court instrumental ensemble and repertoire.

Gaida Bulgarian bagpipe.

Gamelan In Indonesian music, "ensemble".

Gender Cultural constructions of maleness and femaleness.

Genre A type of music.

Gong ageng Largest gong in Indonesian *gamelan*.

Groove The way ensemble musicians interact during performance.

Guitarrón Mexican bass-sized chordophone in guitar family.

Half step Interval of a MINOR SECOND.

Harmony Pitches heard together; in tonal music, system of functional chords.

Heptatonic Systematic set of seven pitches.

Heterogeneous ensemble sound Combining instruments with different timbres.

Heterophony "Different voices"; musical texture of one melody performed almost simultaneously and somewhat differently by multiple musicians.

Hijāz A particular tetrachord used in Egyptian melody.

Hocket *See* INTERLOCKING PARTS.

Homogeneous ensemble sound Combining instruments with similar timbres.

Homophony "Same voice"; musical texture of block chords, or melody with chords.

Idiomaticity Musical material resulting partially from an instrument's capability.

Idiophone Instrument whose primary sound-producing medium is the body of the instrument itself.

Imitative polyphony Musical texture of one instrument or voice "imitating" the material of another part.

Improvisation Result of a musician exercising relatively great flexibility with given material.

Instrumentation Instruments (including voice) used in a musical selection.

Interlocking parts Texture of one musical part subdivided among several musicians; in a polyrhythmic texture, coordination among multiple musical parts.

Interval Distance spanned between two pitches.

Intonation Sense of pitch placement.

Īqā (*usul* in Turkish) Arabic term for "rhythmic mode."

Jiangnan sizhu Chinese ensemble music from the area south of the Yangtze River around the city of Shanghai.

Jig Irish dance genre in compound meter.

Kabuki Popularist type of traditional Japanese theater.

Kalimba South African Nsenga idiophone, commonly called "thumb piano."

Kempul Hanging gong in Central Javanese *gamelan*.

Kenong Large kettle gong in Central Javanese *gamelan*.

Ketawang A colotomic form in Central Javanese music.

Kethuk Small, relatively low-pitched gong in Central Javanese *gamelan*.

Key In tonal music, a tonality named after the main pitch.

Kompak Balinese ensemble music aesthetic.

Komungo Korean zither-type chordophone.

Kotekan In Balinese music, term for interlocking parts.

Koto Japanese zither-type chordophone.

Kutkori changdan A korean rythmic group of twelve counts.

Leading tone In tonal music, the pitch a half step above or below the tonic.

Major scale Western scale with whole steps and half steps arranged W W H W W W H within an octave.

Major second Western whole step; interval spanning two half steps.

Makam See *Maqam*.

Makedonsko horo Bulgarian dance genre in assymetrical meter.

Maqam (Turkish, *makam*) Term for melodic mode in the Arabic language.

Maqam Rast A melodic mode of Egypt and the eastern Arab world.

Maqsum An Egyptian rhythmic mode.

Mariachi Mexican and Mexican American ensemble.

Measure In Western meter and notation, one metric group of beats (also called BAR).

Melodic mode Generally, pitch material for melody bearing particular expressive qualities; in Western music, one of several species of the diatonic scale.

Melody Any selection of pitches in succession. "A melody" is a particular succession of pitches, see motive, tune.

Membranophone Instrument whose primary sound-producing medium is a vibrating skin.

Metallophone Xylophone-type idiophone with metal keys.

Meter Regular grouping of beats.

Metric cycle Repeating articulation of a grouping of beats.

Microtone Term for an interval smaller than the Western half step.

Minor second Smallest interval in Western music; also called *half step*.

Mnemonic Formula (in music, usually syllable) to aid in memorizing.

Modulation In a piece of tonal music, shifting from one tonal center to another.

Monophony "One voice"; musical texture of a single melodic line and nothing else.

Motive Melodic or rhythmic fragment used to construct a larger musical entity; THEME.

Mṛdaṅgam In South Indian music, a barrel-shaped drum.

Muqaddima Term for the introduction in Arab ensemble music.

Musician   A person who experiences music as a practice.

Musiqa   Term in Arabic language for secular music.

Nahāwand   A particular tetrachord used in Egyptian melody.

Netori   Term for a prelude in Japanese *gagaku* music.

Ney   In Arab music, a flute-type aerophone.

Nonmetrical rhythm   Not organized in regular rhythmic groupings.

Octave   In Western music, interval spanning eight pitches, the highest duplicating the pitch name of the lowest; generally, the distance between two pitches in which the frequency of the second pitch is twice that of the first.

Oral transmission   Teaching by speaking, singing, or playing.

Orientalism   System of European discourse about the Middle East (West Asia) and India (South Asia) (Edward Said).

"Oriental" scale   Nondiatonic scale with major, minor, and augmented seconds arranged in the pattern m A m M m A m.

Ostinato   Constantly recurring melodic, rhythmic, or harmonic motive.

Overtone series   Like "harmonic series," referring to the constituent frequencies of sounds but numbered differently, the first overtone being the second harmonic.

Parlando rubato   Nonmetrical rhythm.

Part-counterpart   Form in which one part is responded to by one or more supporting parts.

Pentatonic   Systematic set of five pitches.

Perfect pitch   Exceptional aural memory for pitch intonation.

Pesindhén   Female singer in Javanese music.

Phrase   Usually, melodic unit; a musical thought.

Pipa   Chinese lute-type chordophone.

Pî phât   Thai instrumental ensemble.

Pitch   The quality of "highness" or "lowness" of sound; a sound produced at a certain number of cycles per second.

Pitch area   Acceptable range of intonation for a pitch.

Pitch hierarchy   Some pitch(es) in a pitch set given more importance.

Pitch register   An area in a pitch range.

Polyphony   "Multiple voices"; musical texture of two or more melodic parts performed together.

Polyrhythm   Musical texture of multiple rhythmic patterns performed simultaneously.

Prescriptive notation   Minimalist notation that gives instruction on how to sound out the music (see also tablature).

Program music   Instrumental selection associated with a story or other extramusical idea.

Pulse   Equal-length durations.

Qānūn   In Middle Eastern music, a struck box-zither type of chordophone.

Qawwālīyā   North Indian or Pakistani singer of Muslim Sufi music.

Quarter tone   Term used loosely to refer to pitches at an interval smaller or larger than those in the Western scale in Arab music, half-flat.

Qur'ān   Sacred text revealed to the Prophet Muhammad.

Rāga   Term for melodic mode in India's music.

Range   A total span; the distance from the highest to the lowest pitch.

Rast   A particular tetrachord used in Egyptian melody.

Recitative   Singing that imitates and emphasizes in both pitch and rhythm the natural flow of speech.

Reel   Irish dance genre in duple meter.

Refrain   Repeating text and melody added to a verse.

Repertoire   Group of pieces that are linked in some way.

Rest   A momentary silence in music; in notation, a sign indicating momentary silence.

Rhythm   Any succession of durations. "A rhythm" is a particular succession of durations.

Rhythmic mode   Rhythmic grouping bearing particular expressive qualities.

Riqq   In Middle Eastern music, a frame-drum (tambourine) type of membranophone.

Ritardando (or *ritard*, Italian)   Gradual slowing of the pace of the basic beats.

Roma   Peoples formerly referred to as gypsies.

Round   Tune designed to be performed as a CANON.

Rubato   Ebb and flow in the pace of the basic beat.

Salsa   Popular Caribbean dance music genre.

Samba   Brazilian popular music genre.

Saṅgīta   In India, term for "music" encompassing music and dance.

Sanjo   A Korean solo instrumental form.

Saron   Indonesian metallophone-type idiophone.

Scale   Pitch set (and therefore intervals) presented in straight ascending or descending order.

Scat syllables   Vocables used by jazz singers.

Selection   A piece or performance.

Sharp   In musical notation, a sign indicating that the note it precedes is to be played a half step higher.

Shō   A Japanese free-reed type aerophone

Siku   Peruvian panpipe (flute-type) aerophone.

Sikuri   Peruvian ensemble of three sizes of *siku*.

Sitār   North Indian lute-type chordophone

Sizhu   Chnese ensemble of stringed and wind instruments.

Solfège   Syllables used to name pitches; sometimes, mnemonic drum syllables.

Solo   Performance by one person; a musical part meant to stand out.

Sonata form   A tripartite musical form of Viennese origin.

Soprano   Highest vocal or instrumental pitch range.

Speed   The rate of the basic beats.

Staff notation   Western system of notating music on a five-line staff.

Steelband   Trinidadian ensemble featuring tuned metal pans.

Strophic form   Form consisting of an entire melody repeated.

Style   The combination of qualities that create distinctiveness.

Subdominant   In tonal music, the fourth pitch up from a tonic; root of a subdominant chord (IV).

Syakuhati (*shakuhachi*) Japanese flute-type aerophone.

Syamisen (*shamisen*) Japanese lute-type chordophone.

Syncopation In terms of beat, stress between the beats, offbeat; in terms of meter, accenting a beat where stress is not expected.

Tablā In North Indian music, a drum

Tablature Type of notation that gives technical performing instructions.

Tactile transmission Teaching by touch.

Takk In Arab music, the mnemonic syllable for the high-pitched sound produced when striking a drum where the head meets the rim of the instrument.

Tāla Term for India's system for organizing measured musical time.

Tambura A Bulgarian lute-type chordophone.

Tānpūra A hybrid lute-zither-type chordophone used to produce a drone in India's music.

Tarab In Arab music, the aesthetic goal of an ecstatic state.

Tempo *See* SPEED.

Tenor Higher pitch range of a male singer or instrumental pitch range below alto.

Tetrachord Four-note scalar segment with first and fourth pitches separated by the interval of a fourth.

Texture Musical relationships among ensemble parts.

Theka A one-cycle-long stroking pattern by which drummers articulate a North Indian metric grouping.

Theme The basic subject matter of a piece of music.

Through-composed Form in which musical content changes from beginning to end of a selection.

Tihāī A North Indian cadential practice.

Timbre Particular quality of sound; tone color.

Tīntāl A North Indian meter of sixteen counts.

Tonal center Some pitch in a pitch set given most importance in melody; key note, fundamental, primary pitch, tonic.

Tonal music The system organized around having a functional tonic.

Tone *See* PITCH.

Tone cluster A vertical set of pitches, without the functional implications of chords in the tonal system.

Tonic A tonal center; in Western music, the fundamental pitch of a scale or key; root of a tonic chord (I).

Topeng A Balinese dance form.

Toque A rhythm pattern played on *berimbau* in Brazilian *capoeira*.

Triad In tonal music, a simultaneous sounding of pitches a third and a fifth above the root of a chord; generally, a simultaneous sound of three pitches.

Transculturation Term for a process of change in cultural encounters.

Tune A relatively singable, fairly short, complete melody.

Tuning Pitch(es) to which an instrument is set.

Tuta kasha Peruvian courting tune.

Unison All performing the same part.

Vihuela Mexican lute-type chordophone used in *mariachi* for rhythm.

Vocables Song text syllables that are not linguistically meaningful.

Visual transmission Teaching and learning by visual means including music notation, graphical, film, and the like.

Waltz Dance in triple meter.

Whole step Interval of a MAJOR SECOND.

References

Anderson, Benedict. 1991. *Imagined Communities: Reflections on the Origin and Spread of Nationalism*. Rev. ed. London: Verso.

Baily, John. 1985. "Music Structure and Human Movement." In *Musical Structure and Cognition*, 237–58. London: Academic Press.

Baines, Anthony, and Klaus Wachsmann, trans. 1961. "Erich M. Von Hornbostel and Curt Sachs Classification of Musical Instruments." *Galpin Society Journal* 14(3):3–29.

Barth, Frederick, ed. 1969. *Ethnic Groups and Boundaries: The Social Organisation of Culture Difference*. London: Allen and Unwin.

Barz, Gregoory. 2004. *Music in East Africa: Experiencing Music, Expressing Culture*. New York: Oxford University Press.

Begay, Shirley M. 1983. *Kinaaldá: A Navajo Puberty Ceremony*. Rough Rock, Ariz.: Navajo Curriculum Center, Rough Rock Demonstration School.

Berliner, Paul. 1978. *The Soul of Mbira*. Berkeley and Los Angeles: University of California Press.

———. 1994. *Thinking in Jazz: The Infinite Art of Improvisation*. Chicago: University of Chicago Press.

Berrios-Miranda, Marisol. 1999. "The Significance of *Salsa* Music to National and Pan-Latino Identity." Ph.D. diss. University of California, Berkeley.

Blacking, John. 1955. "Eight Flute Tunes from Butembo, East Belgian Congo." *African Music* 1(2):24–52.

———. 1961. "Patterns of Nsenga *kalimba* music." *African Music* 2(4):3–20.

———. 1997. *How Musical is Man?* Seattle: University of Washington Press.

Bordieu, Pierre. 1977. *Outline of a Theory of Practice*. Cambridge: Cambridge University Press.

Brinner, Benjamin. 1995. *Knowing Music, Making Music*. Chicago: University of Chicago Press.

———. 2008. *Music in Central Java: Experiencing Music, Expressing Culture*. New York: Oxford University Press.

Buia, Carole. 2001. "Best of Both Worlds." *Time*, special issue, *Music Goes Global*, 158(14)(fall):10–12.

Certeau, M. de. 1984. *The Practice of Everyday Life*. Berkeley and Los Angeles: University of California Press.

Chopyak, James D. 1987. "The Role of Music in Mass Media, Public Education and the Formation of a Malaysian National Culture." *Ethnomusicology* 31(3)(fall):431–54.

Clifford, James. 1988. *Predicament of Culture: Twentieth Century Ethnography, Literature and Art*. Cambridge, Mass.: Harvard University Press.

———. 1994. "Diasporas." *Cultural Anthropology* 9(3):302–38.

Coplan, David. 1990. "Ethnomusicology and the Meaning of Tradition." In *Ethnomusicology and Modern Music History*, edited by Stephen Blum et al. 35–48. Urbana: University of Illinois Press.

"Criteria for Acculturation." 1961. In *Report of the Eighth Congress of the International Musicological Society*, 139–49. Kassel: Bärenreiter.

Danielson, Virginia. 1997. *The Voice of Egypt: Umm Kulthûm, Arabic Song, and Egyptian Society in the Twentieth Century*. Chicago: University of Chicago Press.

Diamond, Beverley. 2008. *Native American Music in Eastern North America: Experiencing Music, Expressing Culture*. New York: Oxford University Press.

Dudley, Shannon. 2004. *Carnival Music in Trinidad: Experiencing Music, Expressing Culture*. New York: Oxford University Press.

Farley, Christopher John. 2001. "Music Goes Global." *Time*, special issue, *Music Goes Global*, 158(14)(fall):4–7.

Frisbie, Charlotte J. 1967. *Kinaaldá: A Study of the Navajo Girl's Puberty Ceremony*. Middletown, Conn.: Wesleyan University Press.

Gold, Lisa. 2005. *Music in Bali: Experiencing Music, Expressing Culture*. New York: Oxford University Press.

Guilbault, Jocelyne. 2005. "Globalization and Localism" in *Enciclopedia della Musica*, Vol. 5. Torino: Einaudi. pp. 138–156

Handler, Richard. 1986. "Authenticity." In *Anthropology Today* 2(1) (February):2–4.

Hast, Dorothea E. and Stanley Scott. 2004. *Music in Ireland: Experiencing Music, Expressing Culture*. New York: Oxford University Press.

Herrera-Sobek, Maria. 1993. *Northward Bound: The Mexican Immigrant Experience in Ballad and Song*. Bloomington: Indiana University Press.

Hesselink, Nathan. 2006. *P'ungmul: South Korean Drumming and Dance*. Chicago: University of Chicago Press.

Hobsbawm, Eric, and Terence Ranger, eds. 1983. *The Invention of Tradition*. Cambridge: Cambridge University Press.

Hornbostel, E. M. von. 1928. "African Negro Music." *Africa* 1:30–61.

Jameson, Fredric. 1991. *Postmodernism, or The Cultural Logic of Late Capitalism*. Durham, N.C.: Duke University Press.

Jensen, Joli. 1998. *Nashville Sound: Authenticity, Commercialization, and Country Music*. Nashville: Country Music Foundation Press and Vanderbilt University Press.

Johnson, Charlotte I. 1964. "Navajo Corn Grinding Songs." *Ethnomusicology* 8(2):101–20.

Karpeles, Maude. 1951. "Some Reflections on Authenticity in Folk Music." *Journal of the International Folk Music Council* 3:10–16.

———. 1968. "The Distinction between Folk and Popular Music." *Journal of the International Folk Music Council* 20:9–12.

Kartomi, Margaret J. 1981. "The Processes and Results of Musical Culture Contact: A Discussion of Terminology and Concepts." *Ethnomusicology* 25(2)(May):227–49.

———. 1990. *On Concepts and Classifications of Musical Instruments*. Chicago: University of Chicago Press.

Kingsbury, Henry. 1988. *Music, Talent, and Performance: A Conservatory Cultural System*. Philadelphia: Temple University Press.

Klaser, Rajna. 2001. "From an Imagined Paradise to an Imagined Nation: Interpreting *Sarki* as a Cultural Play." Ph.D. diss. University of California, Berkeley.

Koskoff, Ellen. 2001. *Music in Lubavitcher Life*. Urbana: University of Illinois Press.

Kubik, Gerhard. 1979. "Pattern Perception and Recognition in African Music." In *The Performing Arts*, edited by John Blacking and J. W. Kealiinohomoku, 221–49. The Hague: Mouton.

Lau, Frederick. 2008. *Music in China: Experiencing Music, Expressing Culture*. New York: Oxford University Press.

Lerdahl, Fred, and Ray Jackendoff. 1983. *A Generative Theory of Tonal Music*. Cambridge, Mass.: MIT Press.

Lewis, J. Lowell. 1992. *Ring of Liberation: Deceptive Discourse in Brazilian Capoeira*. Chicago: University of Chicago Press.

Lipsitz, George. 1994. *Dangerous Crossroads. Popular Music, Postmodernism and the Poetics of Place*. London: Verso.

Lui, Tsun-yuen. 1968. "A Short Guide to Ch'in." *Selected Reports* (UCLA) 1(2):179–204.

Mapoma, Mwesa Isaiah. 1991. "Traditional Music in Contemporary Zambia." *Tradition and Its Future in Music. Report of SIMS 1990 Osaka*, edited by Yosihiko Tokumaru et al., 347–50. Tokyo: Mita Press.

Marcus, Scott L. 2007. *Music in Egypt: Experiencing Music, Expressing Culture*. New York: Oxford University Press.

Middleton, Richard. 1990. *Studying popular music*. Milton Keynes, U.K.: Open University Press.

Mitchell, Tony. 1993. "World Music and the Popular Music Industry: An Australian View," *Ethnomusicology* 37: 309–38.

Monson, Ingrid. 1999. "Riffs, Repetition, and the Theories of Globalization." *Ethnomusicology* 43(1)(winter):31–65.

Murphy, John P. 2006. *Music in Brazil: Experiencing Music, Expressing Culture.* New York: Oxford University Press.

Nettl, Bruno. 1954. *North American Indian Musical Styles.* Philadelphia: American Folklore Society.

———. 1975. "The Western Impact on World Music: Africa and the American Indians." In *Contemporary Music and Music Cultures,* edited by Charles Hamm et al., 101–24. Englewood Cliffs, N.J.: Prentice Hall.

———. 1995. *Heartland Excursions: Ethnomusicological Reflections on Schools of Music.* Urbana: University of Illinois Press.

Nijenhuis, Emmie te. 1974. *Indian Music: History and Structure.* Leiden: E. J. Brill.

Nzewi, Meki. 1991. *Musical Practice and Creativity: An African Traditional Perspective.* Bayreuth: IWALEWA-Haus, University of Bayreuth.

Qureshi, Regula. 1987. "*Qawwali*: Making the Music Happen in the Sufi Assembly." *Asian Music* 18(2)(spring/summer):118–57.

"Resolution on the Definition of Folk Music." 1953. *Journal of the International Folk Music Council* 5:23.

Reyes, Adelaida. 2005. *Music in America: Experiencing Music, Expressing Culture.* New York: Oxford University Press.

Rice, Timothy. 2001. "Reflections on Music and Meaning: Metaphor, Signification, and Control in the Bulgarian Case." *British Journal of Ethnomusicology* 10(1):19–38.

———. 2004. *Music In Bulgaria: Experiencing Music, Expressing Culture.* New York: Oxford University Press.

Ruckert, George E. 2004. *Music in North India: Experiencing Music, Expressing Culture.* New York: Oxford University Press.

Russet, J. C., and David Wessel. 1999 "Exploration of Timbre by Analysis Synthesis." In *The Psychology of Music,* edited by Diana Deutsch, pp. 113–69. San Diego: Academic Press.

Said, Edward. 1978. *Orientalism.* Harmondsworth, U.K.: Penguin.

Santosa. 2001. "Constructing Images in Gamelan Performances: Communicative Aspects among Musicians and Audiences in Village Communities." Ph. D. diss. University of California, Berkeley.

Sheehy, Daniel. 2006. *Mariachi Music in America: Experiencing Music, Expressing Culture.* New York: Oxford University Press.

Slobin, Mark. 1993. *Subcultural Sounds: Micromusics of the West.* Hanover, N.H.: Wesleyan University Press and University Press of New England.

Small, Christopher. 1998. *Musicking: The Meanings of Performing and Listening.* Hanover, H.H.: Wesleyan University Press.

Stokes, Martin, ed. 1994. *Ethnicity, Identity and Music: The Musical Construction of Place.* Oxford: Berg.

Stone, Ruth M. 2005. *Music in West Africa: Experiencing Music, Expressing Culture*. New York: Oxford University Press.

Sugarman, Jane. 1997. *Engendering Song: Singing and Subjectivity at Prespa Albanian Weddings*. Chicago: University of Chicago Press.

Taruskin, Richard. 1995. *Text and Act: Essays on Music and Performance*. New York: Oxford University Press.

———. 2001. "Nationalism." In *The New Grove Dictionary of Music and Musicians*, 2d ed., edited by Stanley Sadie, 17:689–706. London: Macmillan.

Taylor, Tim. 1997. *Global Pop*. New York: Routledge.

Théberge, Paul. 1997. *Any Sound You Can Imagine: Making Music/Consuming Technology*. Hanover, N.H.: Wesleyan University Press.

Turino, Thomas. 1993. *Moving Away from Silence: Music of the Peruvian Altiplano and the Experience of Urban Migration*. Chicago: University of Chicago Press.

———. 2000. *Nationalists, Cosmopolitans, and Popular Music in Zimbabwe*. Chicago: University of Chicago Press.

——— . 2008. *Music in the Andes: Experiencing Music, Expressing Culture*. New York: Oxford University Press.

Vander, Judith. 1988. *Songprints: The Musical Experience of Five Shoshone Women*. Urbana: University of Illinois Press.

Vishwanathan, T., and Matthew Harp Allen. 2004. *Music in South India: Experiencing Music, Expressing Culture*. New York: Oxford University Press.

Wade, Bonnie C. 2005. *Music in Japan: Experiencing Music, Expressing Culture*. New York: Oxford University Press.

Wade, Peter. 2000. *Music, Race, and Nation: Música Tropical in Colombia*. Chicago: University of Chicago Press.

Wessel, David, and Matthew Wright. 2002 "Problems and Prospects for Intimate Musical Control of Computers." *Computer Music Journal* 26(3):11–22.

Williams, Raymond. 1977. *Marxism and Literature*. Oxford, U.K.: Oxford University Press.

Wilson, Olly. 1992. "The Heterogenous Sound Ideal in African-American Music." In *New Perspectives on Music: Essays in Honor of Eileen Southern*, edited by J. Wright, 327–38. Warren, Mich.: Harmonie Park.

Resources

Fieldwork Guide
Fargion, Janet Toppi, ed. A Manual for Documentation, Fieldwork and Preservation for Ethnomusicologists. 2nd ed. 2001. Society for Ethnomusicology.

Reference Works
The Garland Encyclopedia of World Music. 1998–. Routledge.
The New Grove Dictionary of Music and Musicians. 2001. Macmillan.

Journals: General
Cultural Anthropology. 1986–. American Anthropological Association.
Dance Research Journal. 1968–. Committee on Research in Dance.
Ethnomusicology. 1953–. Society for Ethnomusicology. See "Current Publications: Bibliography, Discography, Films and Videos" section in every issue through vol. 44 (2000), thereafter at ⟨http://www.ethnomusicology.org⟩.
Ethnomusicology Forum. 1992–. Formerly the *British Journal of Ethnomusicology.*
The Journal of American Folklore. 1888–. American Folklore Society.
Journal of the American Musicological Society. 1948–.
The World of Music. 1957–. Bärenreiter.
Yearbook of Traditional Music. 1968–. International Council for Traditional Music.

Journals: Particular Musics
African Music. 1954–. African Music Society, South Africa.
American Music. 1983–. Society for American Music.
Asian Music. 1969–. Society for Asian Music.
Black Music Research Journal. 1980–. Fisk University.
Black Perspective in Music. 1973–90. Foundation for Research in the Afro-American Creative Arts.
Center for Black Music Research Digest. 1988–. Columbia College.

Latin American Music Review. 1980–. University of Texas Press.
Popular Music. 1981–. Cambridge University Press.
Popular Music and Society. 1971–. Bowling Green State University.
Journal of Popular Music Studies. 1993–. U.S. Branch of the International Association for the Study of Popular Music.

Audio and Visual Materials
For listing and reviews of sound recordings, videos, and films, see *Ethnomusicology*. Here only prominent series and archives are listed.
American Folklife Center, Library of Congress.
Alexander Street Press Music Online.
Archives of Traditional Music, Indiana University.
Insight Media. New York, N.Y.
JVC Smithsonian Folkways Video Anthologys of World Music and Dance. 30 vols. 1990–.
Smithsonian Center for Folklite and Cultural Heritage Washington.
Smithsonian Global Sound.
The Survey of Korean Music: Video Program Set. Seoul, Korea: National Center for Korean Traditional Performing Arts.
UCLA Ethnomusicology Archives.
You tube.
University of Washington Ethnomusicology Archives.

Recording Companies
Arhoolie Foundation.
Archives Internationale de Musique Populaire.
Bärenreiter Musicaphon.
Canyon Records.
Le Chant du Monde.
Nonesuch Records.
EMI-Odeon.
Lyrichord.com.
Music of the World.
Ocora/Radio France.
Shanachi Records.
Silver Wave Records.
Smithsonian Folkways.

Index

∞

Folk music, 136, 174, 181–182, 183, 184, 191, 197. *See also individual entries*
Forró, 80
France, 99, 164, 169, 191
Frequency, 60, 104, 109, 110, 125
Fret, 55, 106–107, 108, 188
Function, 20–21, 68, 167; pitch, 120

Gaida, 2, 186
Gagaku, 66–67, 76, 129, 191
Gamelan, 105; Balinese, 56, 57, 72, 75, 109, 125, 196; Javanese, 15–16, 36, 47, 67–68, 71, 84–86, 102, 108, 109, 119, 1389–140, 162, 178
Gender, 1, 17, 35, 52–53, 56, 59, 61, 74, 95, 133, 153, 175–178, 186, 192
Germany, 59, 99, 119, 170
Ghana, 94, 96
Global, 22, 52, 164, 165, 166, 171, 187, 189–192, 193
Gong, 57–58, 63, 84–86, 94. *See also Gamelan*
Gospel, 17, 155, 187
Groove, 73, 95, 156
Grouping, 92, 94, 97, 161. *See also Changdan*; Polyrhythm
Guitar, 30, 48, 52, 108, 118, 125, 127, 188
Guitarrón, 36, 48, 69, 108

Haiti, 193–194
Harmonics. *See* Frequency
Harmony, 83, 103, 111, 124–129, 132, 145, 158, 163. *See also* Chord; Tonal center
Harp, 44, 46, 54
Harpsichord, 56
Hawaii, 31, 32, 33
Heterophony, 131–132, 136
Hocket, 130
Homophony, 132
Horn, 41, 45, 46, 97, 117
Hybridization, 190–191

Identity, 21, 109, 164, 167–180, 182, 192. *See also* Class; Cultural status; Ethnic; Gender; National; Religion
Idiophones, 39, 40, 42, 43, 45, 47, 61, 65, 66, 98. *See also individual instrument entries*
Igbo, 47
Improvisation, 19, 95, 103–104, 122, 134–137, 141, 143, 151, 158–159; instrumental, 71, 89, 141–144, 191; vocal, 62, 122, 177
India, 4, 6, 17, 24, 25, 37–38, 48, 75, 114, 118–119, 124, 152, 170, 171, 183, 188–189, 190. *See also* North Indian (Hindustani) music; South Indian (Karnatak) music
Indigenization, 191
Indonesia, 57–59, 135, 146, 178. *See also* Balinese music; *Gamelan*; Javanese music

Interlocking, 10, 63, 68, 130, 152
Interval, 103, 111–114, 124–126
Instrument, 19, 35–72, 83, 98, 134, 146–147, 163, 166, 169, 175, 179, 182, 184, 188, 197; Africa: 47–48; Classification, 36–48; China, 36–37, 39; Europe, 38–39; India, 37–38; Indonesia, 47; International (expanded Sachs-Hornbostel), 39–47, 61. *See also individual entries*
Intonation, 110
Iraq, 91
Iran, 35, 106
Ireland, 5, 9, 13–15, 59, 62, 103, 119, 129, 135, 136, 149, 156–157, 191, 193, 195, 203. *See also* Jig
Islam, 6–7, 118, 152, 190, 197. *See also* Sacred music

Jamaica, 21, 139
Japan, 30, 53, 119, 164, 169, 170, 171, 173, 176, 177, 183, 189, 190. *See also Gagaku*; *Koto*; *Shakuhachi/Syakuhachi*; *Shamisen/Syamisen*; Theater music
Javanese music, 26, 57–59, 65, 106, 119, 135, 190. *See also Gamelan*; Indonesia
Jazz, 21, 22, 49, 66, 70, 80, 103, 137, 138, 162–163, 176, 183, 187, 191, 201. *See also* "Take Five"; "West End Blues"
Jewish culture, 118, 119, 176. *See also* Klezmer; Sacred music
Jig, 80, 83, 156

Kalimba, 65
Kenya, 149
Key, 121, 123, 145
Keyboard, 26, 43, 44, 59, 63, 104, 110, 111–113, 115, 157. *See also* Computer; Piano
Klezmer, 190–191
Komungo, 55, 107, 111, 154
Korea, 37, 40, 55, 110–111, 153, 171, 196. *See also* Changdan; Chang-gu; Gong; *Komungo*; *Puk*
Koto, 53, 67, 107, 131, 138, 177
Kpelle, 10, 47, 53, 97, 151–152, 154, 195
"Kumbaya," 149

Lancaran, 84–86
Latin America, 36, 97, 98, 170, 180
Learning. *See* Transmission
Lebanon, 91
Liberia. *See* Kpelle
Listener, 3, 20, 67, 86, 153, 154, 165, 189; fan, 183, 185
Lute, 4, 41, 44, 46, 48, 54, 61, 68, 86, 107–108, 131, 132, 190, 198. *See also individual entries*
Lutoslawski, Witold, 68, 117, 126
Lyre, 44, 46